2nd EDITION

Entrepreneur
MAGAZINE'S

ULTIMATE

GUIDE TO

Google
AdWords

How To Access 100 Million People in 10 Minutes

PERRY MARSHALL AND BRYAN TODD

EP
Entrepreneur.
Press

Jere L. Calmes, Publisher
Cover design: Beth Hansen-Winter
Composition and production: Eliot House Productions

This publication is designed to provide accurate and authoritative information in regard to the subject matter covered. It is sold with the understanding that the publisher is not engaged in rendering legal, accounting, or other professional services. If legal advice or other expert assistance is required, the services of a competent professional person should be sought.

Library of Congress Cataloging-in-Publication Data
Marshall, Perry S.
    Ultimate guide to Google adwords advertising/by Perry Marshall and Bryan Todd.—2nd ed.
    p.   cm.
    Rev. ed. of: Entrepreneur Magazines's Ultimate guide to Google adwords. c2007.
    ISBN-10: 1-59918-360-9 (alk. paper)
    ISBN-13: 978-1-59918-360-2 (alk. paper)
    1. Internet advertising. 2. Google. 3. Web search engines. I. Todd, Bryan. II. Marshall, Perry S. Entrepreneur Magazines's Ultimate guide to Google AdWords. III. Entrepreneur (Santa Monica, Calif.) IV. Title.
    HF6146.I58M36 2009
    659.14′4—dc22   2009023392

Printed in USA

14 13 12 11   10 9 8 7 6 5 4 3

Contents

CHAPTER 4

How to Pay Less and Get More Clicks: Lay a Foundation of Properly Organized Campaigns 27

CHAPTER 5

Develop High-Quality Keyword Lists to Craft Killer Headlines 39

CHAPTER 24

No More Bitslinging: How to Literally Create Wealth with Your Customer List 225

CHAPTER 25

How to Get High Rankings in Google's Organic (Non-PPC) Search Results . 231

CHAPTER 26

That Last Winner-Take-All Edge: Google's Tools for Smarter AdWords Results 249

Wait! Before You Read This Book . . .

f you're brand new to Google AdWords and you're just getting started, you MUST read this short section first.

■ ■ ■

And:

If you've got years of AdWords experience under your belt or you already own the first edition of the *Ultimate Guide*, at the end of this introduction I'll give you shortcuts and page numbers for the advanced new material in the book.

If you're a rank beginner...

Then the first thing you need to do is get your $25.00 Google AdWords credit. Get it at www.perrymarshall.com/bookbonus—enter your contact information and inside the member's area you'll get a Google coupon code. (This code is valid for brand new advertisers only.)

Now that you've done that, let me tell you *how* to go about learning AdWords. Please follow me carefully here.

There's an old saying, "You can't learn to ride a bicycle at a seminar." This definitely applies to AdWords. Pay-per-click, and truly everything you ever do in direct marketing, is a hands-on thing. It's not theory, it's real-world, school-of-hard-knocks.

About the school-of-hard-knocks bit: When AdWords was brand new there were lots of inexpensive clicks and you could find your way by making lots of cheap mistakes.

Those days are over. Today that strategy will get you killed.

Nevertheless, when you open a Google AdWords account, go ahead and enter keywords, write some ads, and set some bid prices. It's okay if you don't really know what you're doing; the first couple of chapters of this book will show you exactly how it's done. You'll learn. But here's the most important thing of all:

Set a low daily budget, say $5.00 or $10.00 per day, to make absolutely sure that your first experience with AdWords is a GOOD one, not a painful one.

Because . . .

The worst thing you can do in your new career as a Google advertiser is accidentally run up $2500 of clicks with no way to pay for them. Yes, most advertisers have to go through some trial and error before things really come together. But you don't have to crash and burn in order to learn. There are many assumptions that even Google makes about the right way to set up an account which, if you follow them blindly, could result in some costly mistakes.

The best thing you can do is *enjoy the process of watching those clicks come in and see your handiwork produce results.*

And if you're hands-on from the word go, everything you read in this book will make ten times more sense.

So cash in your AdWords credits, roll up your sleeves, and jump in. As you go from one chapter to the next, make changes to your Google account. You'll literally be able to see the performance difference in a few hours.

Before you've even spent $10.00 on Google clicks, please make sure you're using this book as your guide. If you don't, you'll make a slew of common mistakes and blow through a load of cash that you could have used to grow your business.

Also, make sure you read the special reports and listen to the audio files in the Book Bonus member's area. They're at www.perrymarshall.com/bookbonus.

If You're a Veteran Pay-Per-Click Marketer . . .

This is the 2nd edition of the *Ultimate Guide to Google AdWords* and we've added a bevy of new sections for those who are already experienced Google advertisers. Here are some of our favorites:

- Compared to the old "banner ads" of the 1990's, Image Ads are an entirely new game on Google. Fewer than 10% of all Google advertisers use them. So if the content network is important to you, you can achieve a significant advantage. See Chapter 9.
- Quality Scores are your #1 friend or enemy, especially if you're in a competitive market. Quality Score will literally make or break your Google campaigns. See Chapter 11.
- I've added new, advanced material at www.perrymarshall.com/bookbonus for savvy advertisers, including new ways to find under-used keywords and superior methods for slicing the Content Network.
- We crafted a completely new chapter on Search Engine Optimization. Find out how to get *free* clicks from Google in Chapter 25.
- All-new strategies for the Content Network: Managed vs. Automatic Placements, in Chapter 8.
- In my personal opinion, the most fun and insightful chapter in the whole book is "17 Things Yo Momma Never Told You About Google." Every bit of it is high-level, actionable, from-the-trenches strategies for making your entire online business more savvy, more profitable, more fun. That's in Chapter 28.

One last thing:

I mince no words: Google is THE benchmark for advertisers and information providers worldwide. In fact from the standpoint of ordinary people getting things done every single day in the world, Google is the most trusted brand in business. If you're up to Google's standards, you're world class.

I'm not saying that's easy. But I do promise—it IS rewarding. Make no mistake about that.

Follow the guidelines in this book and you'll be a world-class promoter in your market, your niche, your chosen profession. I wish you the very, very best of success.

—Perry Marshall

CHAPTER 1

Force Prospects to Choose Your Site and Buy, Instead of from Your Competition

Google can bring thousands of visitors to your website 24 hours a day, 7 days a week, 365 days a year . . . whether you're taking a shower, eating breakfast, driving to work, picking up your kids at school, taking a phone call, sleeping, sitting on the pot, daydreaming, busting your butt to beat a deadline, chasing some customer, typing an e-mail message . . .

■ ■ ■

And it can all happen on autopilot. 100% predictable. Consistently, like clockwork.

Ten years ago, an impossible dream . . . today, a reality.

Just think of the lengths we entrepreneurs, business owners, and salespeople go to just to get a company off the ground, just to get a sale.

I could recount in agonizing detail the *years* of my life I spent dialing the phone, pounding the pavement, making cold calls, renting trade show booths, going to no-show appointments, booking meetings that were a total waste of time.

But not anymore. I no longer go to them; they come to me. It's been that way so long, I'm now very much used to it.

They'll come to you too.

Getting new customers is a real grind for a lot of people. It's the #1 obstacle to starting a new business. But all that can be a thing of the past. Instead of you chasing customers, they can now come to you, all day and all night.

History will show Google AdWords to be the most important development in advertising this decade. Never before has it been possible to spend five bucks, open an account, and have brand new, precisely targeted customers coming to your website within minutes.

There are a lot of things you might want from Google. Maybe you're adding an online component to your retail operation, giving you steadier cash flow and deeper discounts from your suppliers. Maybe payroll is going to get easier. Maybe your consulting business will be positioned better.

Maybe you're already getting traffic but free listings are too unreliable. Maybe you've been successful selling on eBay and now you want to play with the big boys. Maybe you're a working mom and you'll finally be able to come home.

If you're privy to the secrets of online marketing, all those opportunities open up to you willingly. You have a fresh hot sales leads waiting for you in your e-mail box every morning when you sit down at your desk. You have customers buying from you, orders coming in 24/7/365.

Instead of you chasing them, they come to you. Instead of trying to *guess* whether your next product launch will work, you can *know*.

Why is this even possible? Because in the last five years the very direction of business itself has reversed.

In the old days (remember the 1990s?), entrepreneurs and salespeople chased customers with phone calls and letters and ads in the newspaper. Now customers chase businesses on the web.

Back then you had a list of prospects and you tried to get them to buy. Now the buyers—millions of them—are trolling the web every second of the day, looking for businesses that can scratch their itch.

Ever heard Woody Allen's saying, "90% of success is showing up"? The phrase takes on a whole new meaning in the 21st century. If you just *show up* on Google and its search partners, when people type in the right phrase, a starving crowd will bust your doors down to eat at your restaurant.

They'll fill every table and book the kitchen with orders. If they like the daily special and the dessert, they'll come back and eat again.

There's a big feast going on, *if* you show up.

Here you'll discover the secrets of showing up. Not just somewhere, but the right places and times. In front of the right people. And if you're already advertising on Google, you'll learn how to cut your bid prices 20%, 50%, maybe even 70% or more.

This book is for

- · Online Catalog and "Mail Order" marketers
- · Local retail stores and service businesses
- · Niche product marketers
- · Home businesses run from spare bedroom or basement office
- · Authors, speakers, consultants, and publishers
- · Business-to-business marketers collecting sales leads
- · Non-profits, churches, and charities
- · Resellers, repair services, parts suppliers
- · Online communities and membership sites

Google AdWords can help your business whether you're the little old lady selling quilts in Eastern Kentucky or the multi-national corporation. You don't have to be a geek to do this; many of the best online marketers are nontechnical people who succeed simply because they understand their customers.

A lot of these success stories are from "invisible entrepreneurs." By invisible, I mean that their next door neighbors have no idea what they do, and probably just assume they're unemployed or something. But they're running micro-empires from their spare bedroom. And they're in hundreds of industries, ranging from the mundane to the ridiculous to the outrageously specialized.

Some of these guys and gals are making *serious cash*. Tens, even hundreds of thousands of dollars a month. And they're not in "sleazy" businesses, either.

> **Google gets searched more than 235 million times every day.**[*]
>
> Every one of them is typed in by a person who has an itch they want to scratch.
>
> [*]Source: comScore (www.comScore.com), July 2008

In this book I'm going to show you exactly how they do it.

MAKING SURE SEARCHERS FIND (AND BUY FROM) YOU

Got a watch with a secondhand?

Tick. 5,000 people just searched Google for something and went to somebody's website.

Tick. 5,000 more.

Tick. 5,000 more.

180,000 people a minute. Every minute, all day long.

All night long.

Here they come. Every second. Every minute. Every hour.

Are they finding your website?

Are they buying from you?

Or are they finding someone *else's* website and buying from there instead?

They could be finding you. They *should* be finding you. They *can* find you and buy from you. Many of them will come to your site, buy from you, and come back again and again, *if* you follow the simple instructions in this book.

Google AdWords can be the traffic monster that feeds your autopilot marketing machine and churns out a profit for you every day and every night, hitting the entire world up for customers while you sleep. Not just tire kickers but highly-qualified buyers who are proactively looking for exactly what you sell right this very minute.

Buying from *you*. Not somebody else.

If the internet matters to your business, then no book you've ever bought has more potential to make or save you money than this one.

This book is written so you can blow through it, fast, and get going immediately on your course to make serious money with Google insider marketing tactics. That's the fun part: Quickly implementing killer tactics that will flood your business with prospects and profit.

But there's a serious side, too. I've held nothing back here. So not only will you know how to play the Google AdWords game, you'll discover how to craft powerful marketing messages and hooks, bond with your customers, and dominate your market.

In this book you'll discover:

· Tragic, costly mistakes that almost *all* Google advertisers and online entrepreneurs make—and how to easily avoid them (including techniques Google itself *should* teach you, but doesn't)

· How to disaster-proof business startups and product launches, and pound the risk out of new ventures (most times you've only got one or two shots to nail it—why would you want to leave anything to chance?)

- Profiles of successful online businesses: Having coached hundreds of online entrepreneurs to success, I've accumulated a list of vital characteristics that separate winners from the losers—many of which defy normal "business school wisdom"
- How to create ultra-persuasive Google ads and web pages that not only convert visitors to buyers, but automatically improve with time, making it impossible for your rivals to catch up to you
- The advanced (but simple) shortcut secrets of getting deep into your customer's head . . . so you know exactly where his hot buttons are, and how to punch them at will, creating customer loyalty that reaches fanatical levels, and a rabid customer base that eagerly buys almost everything you ask them to buy

And if you're already advertising on Google, you'll get 30% to 300% more visitors, for less money than you're paying right now.

While many hard-core "let's get after it" types will mark up and dog-ear this book, you can really start seeing results *while* you're reading it. There are shortcuts you can take tonight, and see results before you go to bed an hour later.

Your business can literally be better by tomorrow morning.

So strap on your crash helmet because you're in for a wild ride. *Onward!* Stick with me and my partner Bryan as we show you the secrets to online business success.

PERRY MARSHALL

Access the online supplement to this book with more than $85.00 worth of extended book chapters, audio interviews, information on specialized topics, and ongoing updates on Google's ever-changing rules at www.perrymarshall.com/book bonus.

Here are some cool success stories I've gotten from my customers:

"I was getting about 2830 clicks per month with Google AdWords at $1.06 per click. I've spent about 8 hours total reading your stuff and implementing it. Based on the results of my last few days I am on track to get 7815 clicks in the next month and spend the same $3,000 a month . . . a savings of $23,400 per year, or $2925 per hour for the 8 hours I have invested. This is without doubt one of the absolute best investments I've ever made and I haven't even started! And yes, I have done most of this while sitting at home in my underwear."

—KEITH LEE, TMS, KENT, WA

"I'm telling everyone that your book is "required reading" if they want to market online. I actually read your 'Definitive Guide' in one day, and that evening started my first AdWords campaign. I now have four of them running, and the average click-through rate for all campaigns is above 2%. I also get well over a 3% CTR (some as high as 15%) on my more targeted keywords. This has increased the traffic to my sites tenfold in some cases, and has made my monthly revenues much more consistent (which is always nice). Best of all, I've never had a keyword shut down by Google for low CTR, and I've only done one round of "peel and stick" with my ads. I give all the credit to my recent AdWords success to you and your book."

—RYAN DEISS, THE GREAT EZINE EXPERIMENT, AUSTIN, TX

"I finished my first ad campaign this past weekend and implemented it late Sunday evening using information primarily from you. The only other source I used was Google's FAQ. By Wednesday, all my keywords were strong or moderate with a 0.9% Click Thru Rate. My webpage logs counted 34 visitors to my site from Google's AdWords campaign and I had the first sale on my page for a 3% conversion rate. Not great, but not bad either for a "very first timer" without all the bumps and bruises! Brand new customers for mere cents!"

—REX A. HUDSON, WORLDWIDE INFORMATION SUPPLY ENTERPRISES LLC, CLOVER, SC

"Since your last coaching call, we made the keyword matching changes as you recommended, and have the following to show you. Our overall CTR is 4.4%—our best ad is 12.4% and the worst one is a very respectable 3.1%!"

—SIMON CHEN, THE EIGHTBLACK GROUP, MELBOURNE, AUSTRALIA

"In two months have cut my Google advertising in half with five times the results. I now realize that a lead is a lead and I do not have to spend 50 cents for the same lead that now costs me 7 cents! Thanks for all of your help."

—Bob Goldstein, Mr. Checkout Distributors Inc., Boca Raton, FL

"I took my click-thru rate from 0.9% to 5.7% after listening to your MP3 session. And our site just jumped from a Google Page Rank 2 to a Page Rank 6 yesterday, after the last Google dance."

—Tony Kara, Mendax Microsystems, Montreal, Quebec

"I was only about thirty pages in ... but you did write: "Now Just DO it! You can have this up in ten minutes ..." So I put up some new ads for my site. Within thirty minutes I got an order for $67.47. Since then I've built my list into the thousands of subscribers in less than three months!"

—Ken Alston, www.Japanese-Maple.com, Earlysville, VA

"It's simply amazing watching my Click Thru Rate go from 0.3% up to 48.0% in less than thirty minutes. The most important part is, I AM BEATING THE COMPETITION in cost and better yet finding areas of "no competition". Thanks for such awesome marketing advice, your material is by far the most valuable I have purchased. Your concepts are working for me, and I intend on running this as a service for a lot of my web hosting clientele."

—John Finney, HOST4NET Affordable Web Site Design and Hosting

"WOW! I got a 500% increase in response . . . with just a quick "Band-Aid" fix. Can't wait to see what happens when I follow all of your suggestions."

—Jenny Hamby, Copywriter & Seminar Marketing Consultant, SeminarMarketingPro.com, Plainfield, IL

CHAPTER 2

How to Build Your Own Autopilot Marketing Machine

We're not going to just teach you a handful of Google tricks. We're going to show you how to make the internet your slave. (Plus you'll find out why selling on the internet is way simpler than most people think, because . . . only a handful of things really matter anyway.)

■ ■ ■

If you're at a party and tell folks you're starting an online business, they won't spare a bit of advice. They'll give you an endless list of things they think you need—Flash animations, dedicated servers, shopping cart scripts, Meta tags, secure authentication, blogs, (are your eyes glazing over yet?), domain name registrars, Facebook, Cascading Style Sheets, Twitter . . . all kinds of stuff.

Some of the things on that list will certainly come into play for you at some point. But people way smarter than you or me have blown hundreds of thousands of dollars before the first visitor even showed up and bought anything.

Big mistake.

Techno-wizardry is, for the most part, a distraction, and a waste of time. So in this short chapter we're going to show you the moving parts you need and just how simple a thriving, profitable website can be.

IT ALL STARTS WHEN PEOPLE SEARCH FOR SOMETHING

Suzie types in "facial wrinkles" at her computer and here's what shows up on Google:

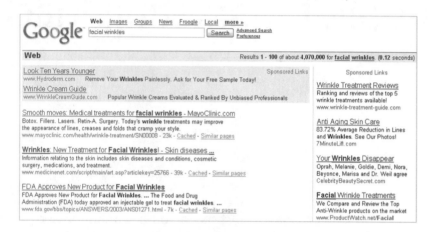

On the top and right are the AdWords ads, which are paid. Running down the left are the free "organic" search listings.

She clicks on the ad on the right that says

Your Wrinkles Disappear
Oprah, Melanie, Goldie, Demi, Nora,
Beyonce, Marisa and Dr. Weil agree
CelebrityBeautySecret.com

Or . . .

Suzy is trolling the web and she's at PriceGrabber.com reading reviews of the book *The Complete Idiot's Guide to Cosmetic Surgery*:

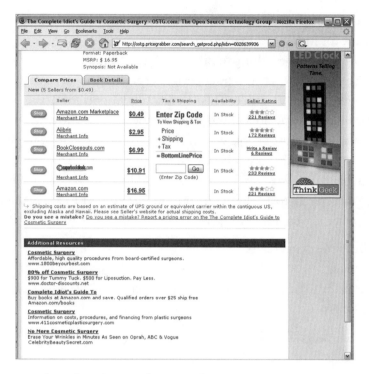

And she sees the ad at the very bottom that says

No More Cosmetic Surgery

Erase Your Wrinkles in Minutes As Seen on Oprah, ABC & Vogue

CelebrityBeautySecret.com

This ad is also served by Google through the *AdSense* program, to dozens, hundreds, possibly thousands of websites.

The ad sounds interesting. She clicks on the ad and she's taken to this page:

That's the first step. Now there are only three things that can happen: Suzy can buy, she can ask for more information, or she can leave.

For a lot of sites, the best thing to offer is information, instead of offering a product up front. The way Suzy gets it is by entering her address to get a gift, sample, download, white paper, report, or guide. This is especially important if the problem Suzy wants to solve is an ongoing area of interest, as opposed to a one-time impulse buy.

If this was a product for people with diabetes, for example, it would be very good idea to collect Suzy's e-mail address, because if Suzy is a diabetic, she's going to have diabetes next week and next year, not just today. Could be a valuable e-mail list! Plus this gives you a chance to talk to all the Suzies on your list and get to know them better.

So, again, when she comes to your site, there are only three things that can happen:

1. Suzy buys the skin cream.
2. Suzy leaves.
3. Suzy asks for information and can come back later—because you've got her e-mail address.

You do need to get her e-mail address, and invite her to come back and try another product.

That's the process. That's what this is all about. *Anything that gets this done is good. Anything that complicates it or gets in the way is bad.*

See, this is really simple. Futzing around with Flash presentations and nineteen different ways to build a web page, all that stuff is beside the point. The point is: *Scratch Suzy's itch and move the stuff from your shelf to hers, as quickly, easily, and simply as possible.*

YOUR MISSION, SHOULD YOU CHOOSE TO ACCEPT IT

Your mission is to buy clicks for $1.00 and make $2.00 while Suzy is on your website. Your mission is to make more money from your clicks than your competitors make from theirs.

That's it.

The rest of this book is all about how to do this.

Most people don't realize how powerful this is in the grand scheme of things—and why Google AdWords is usually the best place to make this happen.

IF YOU DO THIS RIGHT, IT CAN LITERALLY MAKE YOU RICH. HERE'S WHY . . .

My friend and legendary marketer Jonathan Mizel says, "Internet traffic goes where it's rewarded, respected and paid for." If you reward and respect your visitors—and if you're able to pay more for them than everyone else advertising in your category—*then you can have as much traffic as you want.* The traffic will literally *seek you out.*

This is not an exaggeration. It's completely true. But traffic will only seek you out when it's profitable.

So you develop your Google campaigns, send traffic to your site, collect information requests, make sales, follow up with your customers, and . . . do whatever you need to do to make the whole process flow like water running downhill.

Then (and only then) do you go to all of the *other* traffic sources available to you, like Yahoo, Bing, banner ads, e-mail lists, and affiliates.

As we'll discuss in other chapters, affiliates (people who send you traffic in exchange for commission on sales) can be a *huge* source of traffic. If your website doesn't pay, affiliates won't send you anything. But good affiliates will turn the tide in your favor, making you the dominant force in your market.

By following the steps in this book, you'll set yourself up to get massive amounts of traffic and your business will grow exponentially.

A FEW TOOLS THAT WILL HELP YOU IF YOU'RE JUST GETTING STARTED

Whether you're selling skin cream or e-books or computer games or imported wood carvings, you need a handful of things to be in business:

· A domain name
· A website with web pages
· An e-mail broadcast/autoresponder service
· A shopping cart service
· A product to sell
· A Google AdWords account

The online supplement to this book (www.perrymarshall.com/bookbonus) has links to dozens of resources for getting these things done, plus additional tutorials and MP3 files. But here's a quick rundown of the most important stuff:

· You can register a domain name at www.GoDaddy.com. You can also host your website there. You don't need a fancy website.
· You can create your web pages with Microsoft Front Page or Macromedia Dreamweaver.
· An excellent e-mail system is www.AweberSystem.com; you can queue up automatic messages that go out when people request information or buy; you can send e-mail newsletters and announcements to your customers and

prospects, and AweberSystem does a good job of getting your messages through the spam filters.

· If you're just getting started, *do not* futz around with installing software on your server, etc. Go to a third party like www.1ShoppingCartSystem.com—they have a great service that allows you to quickly set up order forms, take orders, process credit card transactions, follow up with e-mails, and manage your customer list.

· The product is up to you, but even if you don't have one yet you can be an affiliate for someone else's product and sell theirs. It's a great way to get your feet wet, because you're not committed to anything long term. You can use your Google ads and your website to learn about any market you want and decide if you want to stay in it. You can find thousands of affiliate products and programs at www.ClickBank.com and www.CJ.com. You can also use these sites to sell your own digital product. These sites process orders for you, handle refunds and basic customer service problems, and pay affiliates.

The next chapter shows you how to quickly set up a Google account.

THE NEW GOLDEN AGE OF ENTREPRENEURSHIP

Years ago if you wanted to start a direct marketing business, not only did you have to have a product and get set up to fulfill sales, you had to depend on a bunch of other people and complex procedures just to sell the very first unit. You had to rent mailing lists, hire printers to print letters, send out the letters, place ads in magazines . . . and then *wait*. Weeks or months usually, a few days at the absolute minimum.

The process was very cumbersome.

Now you can use third-party tools like the ones I described, stick up a website, open a Google account, and have traffic coming to your site in ten minutes. *Literally ten minutes.*

If the project fails, you scrap it and try a different one.

If the market stinks, you go find a new one.

If your project succeeds, it can grow faster than ever before in the history of the world.

Let's get this Google account started, shall we?

CHAPTER 3

How to Build a Google Campaign from Scratch— The *Right* Way

Ten minutes from right now you can have a Google campaign up and running, sending visitors to your website. The speed at which you can do new things and make changes in Google's system is stunning.

■ ■ ■

But speed can also be a trap. Sometimes people do rash things when they're in a hurry.

This is not a long chapter, but it contains some seriously important concepts. Take a little time and go through these steps and it'll save you a lot of money. And you'll still have your Google campaign up and running in an hour or two—and it'll be set up better than 95% of the other Google campaigns on the net.

THREE QUESTIONS THAT TELL YOU THE BEST WAY TO ENTER YOUR MARKET

What keywords are you going to use to go into your market? Answering that question the right way can spell the difference between success and failure. Ultimately you're out to hunt down the single keyword that will bring you the most paying customers, and tweak your entire sales process around it. At the start of this new decade, that's what the most successful AdWords advertisers we know are doing.

To find that bull's eye keyword, or "Keyword Center," we're going to use Google's Keyword Tool (Google.com/keywords) and Traffic Estimator (adwords.google.com /select/TrafficEstimatorSandbox). And we're going to ask three vital questions:

1. How Many of the People Who Type in This Keyword Are Already "Sold" on the Concept You're Promoting?

To answer this question, you need to know what concept you're promoting.

And that's where we recommend that you stop right now, pull out a piece of paper and physically write down a one-sentence description of your ideal money-in-hand-and-ready-to-buy paying customer. Usually that person already knows something, or has already made up his or her mind about how to solve the problem at hand, and has decided to go online looking for a solution. Your description may look like one of these, which we borrow from our friend Glenn Livingston, who teaches this Bull's Eye concept in powerful depth (PerrySentMe.com):

- "My best prospect is someone who already believes in non-pharmaceutical and natural remedies for migraines and is actively searching for the best one to purchase."
- "My best prospect is someone who has already made up his or her mind to buy pottery online."
- "My best prospect already knows pay-per-click management services exist and is proactively searching to hire one."

Have this physically written out and keep it there in front of you as you go through the keyword search process.

Now you're going to head over to Google's keyword tool and enter some phrases that you think reflect customers who are in that mind-set. Let's take the migraine example. A starter idea would be "natural migraine remedies," as that would seem to specify people who are looking for a *natural* solution, something for *migraines* as opposed to more general issues, and *remedies* as opposed to facts or data or information.

How would you like to generate keyword ideas?	Enter one keyword or phrase per line:
⦿ Descriptive words or phrases (e.g. green tea)	natural migraine remedies
○ Website content (e.g. www.example.com/product?id=74893)	☑ Use synonyms ▸ Filter my results [Get keyword ideas]

Choose columns to display: ⓘ
[Show/hide columns]

Keywords	Advertiser Competition ⓘ	Local Search Volume: August ⓘ	Global Monthly Search Volume ⓘ	Match Type: ⓘ [Broad]
Keywords related to term(s) entered - sorted by relevance ⓘ				
natural migraine remedies	▭	1,300	1,000	Add ⌄
natural migraine remedy	▭	1,000	880	Add ⌄
natural remedies migraines	▭	Not enough data	880	Add ⌄
natural remedies for migraine	▭	480	390	Add ⌄
natural remedies for migraines	▭	720	720	Add ⌄
natural remedies for migraine headaches	▭	Not enough data	170	Add ⌄
migraine headaches natural remedies	▭	Not enough data	210	Add ⌄
migraines natural remedy	▭	Not enough data	140	Add ⌄
natural remedy for migraine	▭	390	320	Add ⌄
				Add all 9 »
		Download all keywords: text, .csv (for excel), .csv		
Additional keywords to consider - sorted by relevance ⓘ				
migraine remedies	▭	8,100	8,100	Add ⌄
herbal migraine remedies	▭	Not enough data	480	Add ⌄

Google gives a decent-sized list here. We can now go through keyword by keyword and compare them to our written customer description, choose the keywords we feel are a fit, and ignore the ones that aren't.

Yes, this is a subjective judgment, which is fine; you can make an educated guess. One out of three? Fifty percent? Nine out of ten? If you feel it's less than one out of three, skip it as a keyword, for now.

You may collect a total list of no more than 1–2 dozen keywords. That is perfectly fine.

2. How Many People Are Searching on This Keyword?

We're aiming to find the ultimate Bull's Eye keyword here. We don't have to nail it down today, but this narrows the playing field and makes the job easier.

For your 1–2 dozen keywords you can go with what Google's keyword tool already told you. Or you can take each one and do a further keyword tool search on it and add in totals from other variations that you believe would *fully match your written customer description.*

Note how many searches some of the variations lower on the page get:

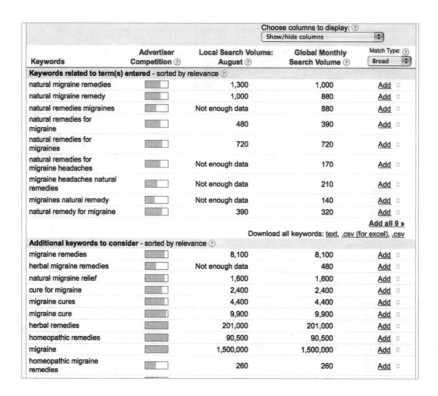

You'll want to factor that in when choosing your top keyword(s).

3. How Much Money Are People Making Off This Keyword?

We're looking for the keywords where the money is. The market has its own way of answering this. The maximum cost per click people are paying is pretty much always the upper limit of the amount of money available in that market.

Head over to Google's Traffic Estimator to find this out. Yes, this tool is wildly inaccurate when predicting positions you'll be in for bid prices. But on the question of average and maximum bids it's reliable.

When I ran the Traffic Estimator for "natural migraine remedies" and other variations (in the United States), I got this:

. . . which of course is just the beginning. I can collect as many relevant keywords like this as I want, and then make the educated comparison among them to find the best fit for my profile. You're off to the best start when you've got 6–12 *tightly-matched groups* of keywords.

And ultimately you're best off with that one single Bull's Eye keyword. Glenn Livingston goes through this in depth at PerrySentMe.com.

HOW TO SET UP YOUR CAMPAIGN

To start into your campaign, go to https://adwords.google.com, and find the "Start now" button:

Right off the bat there's one hidden setting you'd better tweak: Under "Networks, devices, and extensions" click the "Let me choose . . ." radio button. We strongly recommend that you uncheck the buttons next to both the content network and search partners:

1. Choose Your Location and Language

Next, decide how large or small a geographic area you want to target. You can choose whole countries, regions of countries, states or provinces, or cities. You can also choose custom-designated geographic areas, such as latitude-longitude coordinates or the radius of a set number of miles or kilometers around a specific address. You can choose the country you want to show in, followed by your state/province and even a city or group of cities. Choose from the list Google gives you automatically, or click on "Select one or more other locations":

2. Choose Your Currency and Set Your Daily Budget

If, for example, you can only afford $50 per day instead of $170, it's better to control your spending by cutting your bid prices, than by only cutting your daily budget. This is because the daily budget tool causes your ads to be served for only part of the day, rather than a full 24 hours.

Lower positions convert to sales better, generally, because they attract fewer click-happy people. So if you're on a limited budget it's better to just go to the last position on the page and be seen all the time than to be at the top, cut your daily budget, and be seen only a fourth of the time.

Note: Set your daily budget such that if you screw up big-time, your checking account won't be emptied out. You can always come back and bump it up, but it's always nice to have a safety net. That's how you should use the daily budget tool.

3. Create Your First Ad Group and Write Your First Ad

We'll enter the "CRM Software" ad that we've written:

Now let's explain what we just did, and why.

More people click on ads when the *headline* includes the keyword they're searching on. So use your keywords in your headline when you can. You're limited to twenty-five characters, so for some search terms you'll need to use abbreviations or shorter synonyms.

The *second and third lines* allow for 35 characters of text each. In most markets you'll be more successful if you describe a *benefit* on the second line, followed by a *feature* or *offer* on the third line. Later on you can test which order works.

The *fourth line* is your *display URL,* which is the web address that people will see in your ad. The URL you show has to resolve to an actual location on your site, though it doesn't necessarily have to be the specific landing page that you take people to.

The last line is your actual *destination URL,* or your landing page. You can use a tracking link for this, or a link that takes people to your chosen page.

HOW TO FRUSTRATE AN EAGER BUYER

If you want to irritate your customer, send him to your home page hoping he'll just look around. (Everyone loves to troll around somebody's site for ten minutes looking for something that should be obvious but isn't . . . right?) But if you actually want him to sign up or buy from you, take him to a specific page that's tailor-made for his specific search.

Want more clicks? You should always test a second ad against this one, and find a winner. Google will let you enter that ad after you've finished setting up your account.

4. Set Your Maximum Cost per Click

Set your maximum price per click now (called your "default bid"), but realize this: every keyword is theoretically a different market, which means that each major one will need a bid price of its own. Google will let you set individual bids for each keyword later.

Ad group default bids (Max. CPC)

Search ⑦ $ ▢

Content: managed placements $ ▢

Content: automatic placements $ ▢

Leave blank to use automated bids. ⑦

5. Insert Your Keywords

Paste your keywords. We'll start with just one set, and we'll put them in brackets [ ] and quotes " " to see precisely how many searches of each type we'll get.

Keywords

⊟ Select keywords

Enter one keyword per line.

```
[customer relationship management software]
[crm software]
```

Note: When you're getting started, it's *not* a good idea to dump hundreds or thousands of keywords in. Start with a tiny handful of important ones and work from there.

6. Review Everything

Double-check your ad, your keywords, your cost per click, your daily budget, to be sure you start your campaign off the right way.

7. Enter Your Billing Information

Your ads will start showing as soon as you confirm your payment information. Now you're set.

THINGS YOU CAN TWEAK NOW

You can almost always improve on the number of clicks you'll get from the ad you've just written. As you'll see later, it's almost impossible to guess what is going to make people click; you need to let the visitors vote. So write a second ad you think can beat it, and go back into your ad group to post it:

CRM Software
Manage 1000 to 10,000 Customers
30-Day Free Trial & 24/7 Support
www.CRM1to1.com/FreeTrial

Google will rotate this automatically against your first ad, and after a few days or weeks you can pick the winner and delete the loser. Results will come in faster if you test just two at a time.

You can also add more keywords to your list, adjust your cost per click or destination URL for individual keywords, create more ad groups and campaigns, and adjust your campaign settings to fit your style.

In Chapter 25 we'll look at the bells and whistles that Google gives you for managing and tweaking your campaigns, and we'll give you some cool tips for getting more clicks and sales from your ads through smarter traffic management.

When you follow these steps, a campaign will grow that is unique to you and your customers. The success is yours, and so is the profit. It's your business, unlike any other, with your fingerprints and personality all over it. Yours alone. Nobody can replicate that.

THE MAGIC IS IN THE PROCESS

The most important thing you could possibly know about a Google campaign is that it's not a single technique or something that you set up once and forget about.

Now we do have clients who've barely touched their Google campaigns in two years and they're pumping the visitors through every day. However, the real power in Google AdWords is the fact that by logging in every few days or once a week you can make constant refinements and 2X, 5X, 10X your traffic. The number of visitors grows even while your cost per click declines over time.

This doesn't take a lot of time—sometimes only a few *minutes* each month. But you earn compound interest on those efforts because your profit margins get fatter as the traffic grows.

HOW TO SET YOURSELF UP FOR SUCCESS

Now you know how to build a small, basic ad campaign. Now the foundation for future success is laid by organizing larger groups and campaigns properly. In the next chapter you'll learn how to do that.

Meet Uncle Claude

If You've Ever Sold Anything on the Internet, This Man Is Your Uncle

Every field of knowledge exists because a handful of luminaries made ground-breaking discoveries and showed others the way. And there's almost always one who stands head and shoulders above the others.

In management it's Peter Drucker. In engineering it's Thomas Edison. In physics, Albert Einstein. In Rock & Roll, it's the Beatles. For saxophone players it's John Coltrane.

In results-driven advertising, it's Claude Hopkins, who lived from 1866-1932. Whether you know it or not, if your website is generating a profit, it's because you've discovered something that Hopkins figured out, probably before the turn of the century.

Uncle Claude invented the coupon (did you know he created it so that advertisers could track their results?) and pioneered concepts like split testing, premiums, free samples, and mail-order marketing. In fact his book *Scientific Advertising* is so important we've included it in the online supplement to this book at www.perrymarshall.com/bookbonus.

In the rest of this book, we take Hopkins' ideas, which in the late 1800s took months to implement and test, and show you how to do the same thing, literally ten thousand times faster. We've included choice nuggets of wisdom from him in many of the upcoming chapters.

Thanks to Uncle Claude, it's never been easier—or more scientific—to make a fortune in marketing.

How to Pay Less and Get More Clicks

Lay a Foundation of Properly Organized Campaigns

We do a *lot* of Google AdWords consultations, both through our coaching programs and people who come to our site looking for help. We get on the phone with our customer and the two of us log into the Google account and see what can be improved. It's not unusual to improve performance by 50% or 100% in as little as 30 minutes.

■ ■ ■

We have found that the number-one mistake people make is:

Improperly organized campaigns.

Badly organized ads and keywords will cripple your Google campaigns and cost you a ton of money.

Properly organized campaigns get results from the beginning and are easy to adjust and optimize. Over time this makes a huge difference.

In a *perfect* world, you'd serve up a "perfect" ad for every single keyword someone types in. Since each keyword is different, each ad would be different too. If you had 2000 keywords then you'd have to write 2,000 ads too.

In the real world, that's kind of impractical. So you cluster similar keywords together with a single ad.

Ad groups are the smallest individual units that contain your keywords and your ads together. You can have multiple ad groups in a single campaign. A campaign is just a handy way to organize ad groups, usually according to broad topic.

In a single Google account you can have as many campaigns as you want. Some of the campaigns in your account may be on a completely different topic, selling completely different services, and sending traffic to a completely different website.

How you separate out your *campaigns* is up to you. How you separate *ad groups*, however, is one of those things where there's a right way and a wrong way.

THE WRONG WAY TO ORGANIZE AN ADWORDS CAMPAIGN

Most beginners set up their campaigns to look something like this:

Smith Telecommunications
Robust Solutions for
All Your Voice Mail Needs
www.smithtelecom.com

auto attendant
business telephone systems
call management systems
voice mail
voice mail equipment
voice mail service
voice mail systems

Then they send all the visitors to the home page, which has a bunch of different links to services, equipment, Q&A, About Us, Contact Us, etc.

So if we made a map of their AdWords campaign, it would look like this:

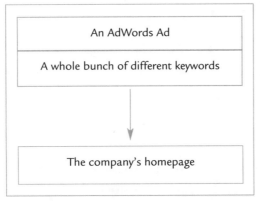

Here's why this method of setting up an AdWords campaign is destined to fail:

- There are too many different kinds of keywords in the same group. Every one of these keywords needs to be in its own group, *each with a list of very similar words and phrases.*
- The ad doesn't match the keywords, and it can't, because there are too many different kinds of keywords in the group.
- "Smith Telecommunications"—or the name of almost any business—is a *lousy* headline. The clickthrough rate (CTR) is going to be very low, and the bid prices will therefore be higher.
- The ad is about Smith Telecommunications, not what the customer really wants. Your ads need to be about your customer, not about yourself!
- A person who searches for "voice mail service" needs to be taken to a page about voice mail service; a person who searches for equipment needs to be taken to a *different* web page about voice mail equipment. These are two entirely different topics. If a person has to figure out where to go after they land on your web page, you're making them work too hard. You need to take show them exactly what they were searching for.

THE RIGHT WAY TO ORGANIZE AN ADWORDS CAMPAIGN

Now if you structure your campaigns properly from the beginning, it's a *lot* easier to make this work. Here's how you organize your ads and keywords:

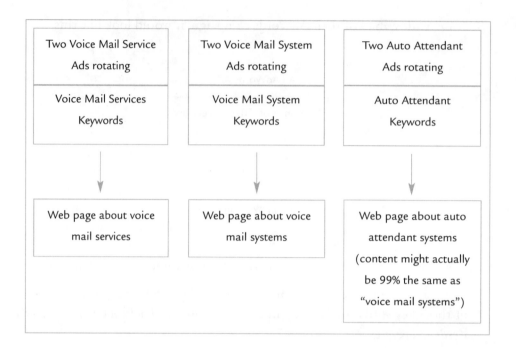

To do this, take all of your different keywords and use Wordtracker (http://free 1keywords.wordtracker.com; www.wordtracker.com) or to organize them into narrow "silos" of very tightly related terms. It will look like this:

Voice Mail Services	Voice Mail System	Auto Attendant
voice mail provider	voice mail systems	answering attendant auto system
voice mail service	voice mail systems for realtors	auto attendant voice mail services
voice mail service provider	telemarketing and voice mail systems	auto attendant
voice mail services	phone systems voice mail	auto attendant phone system
	home office voice mail systems	auto attendant software
	home office telephone voice mail systems	auto attendant system
		auto attendant voice mail
		phone auto attendant

Now there's another step we need to take before pasting this into a campaign: Consider negative keywords. Here's a list of keywords that come from "Voice Mail Software":

voice mail software
voice mail business software
voice mail software for panasonic
voice mail broadcasting software
voice mail business software
multiple voice mail software
mac voice mail software
multi line voice mail system software vru
norstar voice mail software
software to record voice mail
free voice mail software

You might not want visitors who want something for *free*. Your company also has nothing to do with voice *broadcasting* and you don't have anything for *Macintosh* computers. So turn those into negative keywords by putting a minus sign in front of them. The above list now looks like this:

voice mail software
voice mail business software
voice mail software for panasonic
voice mail business software
multiple voice mail software
multi line voice mail system software vru
norstar voice mail software
software to record voice mail
–free
–mac
–macintosh
–broadcast
–broadcasting

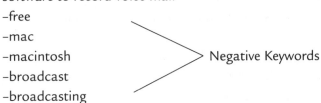 Negative Keywords

So when you set up your ad campaigns, each one of these keyword lists is going to go into a different group with its own set of ads.

SPLIT TEST YOUR ADS!

IMPORTANT TIP: The key to long-term success on AdWords—and keeping your bid prices down—is always split testing two ads at the same time, then deleting the inferior one, and trying to beat the best one. Always have two ads running at the same time.

The Ads: We'll write two. Google will rotate them simultaneously. One will have a better CTR than the other; we'll later delete the inferior one, write a new one, and try again. Little by little your CTR will go up, up, up.

Voice Mail Software Make Your Communication Easier With Custom, Expandable Systems www.SmithTelecom.com/VMsoftware	← Headline contains your keywords ← 2nd line contains a BENEFIT ← 3rd line contains a FEATURE or OFFER ← 4th line: Display URL has a keyword in the subdirectory /VMsoftware that will help the CTR
Voice Mail Software For Any Business & Any Phone System Same Day Installation & Easy Terms www.SmithTelecom.com/VMsoftware	Same formula for Ad #2, but we're testing a different message. Notice that we capitalize the important words.

So here's what we've done:

- We've generated a list of various keywords: Voice mail system, voice mail software, voice mail service, auto attendant, etc.
- We've used keyword research tools to drill down and generate many variations on these keywords
- Each family of keywords goes into its own group
- We rotate two ads at the same time, all the time, and constantly try to beat our best
- When visitors click on the ad, they are taken to the exact page on your site that has a specific solution to their exact problem—not the homepage. No guessing or clicking all over the place to find what they want.

Here's another example of how to cluster keywords into groups and campaigns, for a variety of martial arts related terms:

Organize Your Campaigns and Ad Groups					
	Campaign #1 Self Defense	Campaign #2 Martial Arts	Campaign #3 Fighting	Campaign #4 Security & Safety	Campaign #5 Protection
Ad Group #1	Women's Self Defense	Karate	Wrestling	Personal Safety	Self Protection
Ad Group #2	Defense Class	Tae Kwon Do	Grappling	Women's Safety	Women's Protection
Ad Group #3	Defense Video	Aikido	Hand-to-Hand Combat	Personal Security	Child Protection
Ad Group #4	Defense Tactic	Hapkido	Weapons Combat	Children's Security	Assault Protection

Do you want to make it easy to manage campaigns and match your keywords well to ads within each ad group? Organize your campaigns this way and it will be. More importantly, you'll get more clicks.

CUT OUT IRRELEVANT KEYWORDS AND IMPROVE YOUR CTR EVEN MORE

Sometimes in your keyword collecting you'll inadvertently be bidding on terms in your keyword list that don't belong at all. For example:

Most of the keywords here, in fact, are irrelevant to what we were going after. They got zero clicks. Of course, the "losing my religion lyrics" search term takes the cake. We'll delete that keyword and then stick in the term "lyrics" as a negative keyword, and we'll get a higher CTR, since now that big fat "0" is no longer bringing down the average.

THE PEEL & STICK STRATEGY: GET A HIGHER CTR JUST BY MOVING YOUR KEYWORDS AROUND

Look at this example of an ad group with keywords that are getting a great CTR. Notice how some of these keywords could be headlines of their own:

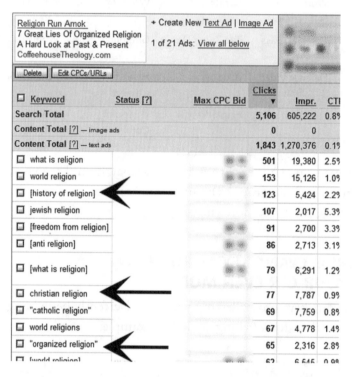

We noticed that. So we pulled those keywords out of that list and came up with several brand new ad groups. Here's one:

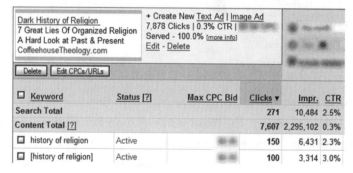

The CTR on [history of religion] jumped from 2.2% up to 3.0%. That's *an improvement of 36%,* with so little work!

But it gets better:

Keyword	Status [?]	Max CPC Bid	Clicks ▼	Impr.	CTR	Av
Search Total			189	3,753	5.0%	
Content Total [?]			0	2,094	0.0%	
"organized religion"	Active		145	2,885	5.0%	
[organized religion]	Active		29	542	5.3%	
organized religion	Active		15	326	4.6%	

That improved the clickthrough rate by 79%! Impressive. Plus, you'll notice that the keyword shows up not once but twice in the ad copy. That didn't hurt one bit.

Want a better CTR? Want higher positions on the page without paying any more per click? Want more profit in your pocket at the end of the month? This trick will work for you again and again. It's called *Peel & Stick*.

You take a high traffic keyword, *peel* it out of a group, and *stick* it in a new one, with its own ad. It only takes a few minutes.

WHY PEEL & STICK IS SO SIMPLE, SO POWERFUL

Sometimes after you turn on your traffic you'll discover that there are keywords in your ad groups that get a lot more hits than you were expecting. *And* their CTRs, you're convinced, could be a lot higher.

Delete any keyword you find like that and stick it into a new ad group with a clever ad that matches it perfectly.

That's Peel & Stick. As simple as that. This can do wonders for your CTRs.

Why does this work so well? Very simply, it's because people are more likely to click on your ad if they see your keyword in the headline.

Want to improve your CTR by as much as 80%? Organize your keywords differently.

MORE EASY-TO-FOLLOW EXAMPLES

Here are some ads that some of our associates ran for their businesses, with a sample of a few of the actual keywords they used. Best part is, they're far from perfect. They can be improved even more:

How to Sell Anything

Skills Your Competitors Don't Have
Powerful Secrets You Won't Believe
www.XYZ.com

how to sell
[how to sell]
"how to sell"
–marijuana
–devil
–soul

These negative keywords are kind of funny. You definitely don't want those searches!

Power Supplies to Order

Custom Design Requests Welcomed
Any OEM Application, ISO 9002
www.XYZ.com

power supply
power supplies
12 volt power supply
5v power supply
class 2 power supply
ac power supply

Try a separate ad group just for "AC power supply."

Dentures to Be Proud Of

Free In-Office Consultation & More
For a Smile that Wins New Friends
www.XYZ.com

dentures
affordable dentures
denture repair
same-day dentures
permanent dentures
partial denture

How many clicks is "denture repair" or "partial denture" getting? If there are a lot, each of them needs peel & stick.

A/C Transformers Qty 250+

For OEM Applications, ISO 9002
Custom 1-Day Quote, Fast Delivery
www.XYZ.com

transformers
power transformer
transformer accessories
power supply transformers
power transformer tube
–robots in disguise

Admittedly, the length of some of these search terms might make peel & stick a bit challenging, especially if you're trying to fit the keyword in the headline and be descriptive at the same time.

Toothache Relief, Finally!
Your Local Pain-Free Dentist
Improves Your Health & Much More
www.XYZ.com

> toothache
> toothaches
> toothache remedies
> toothache cure
> toothache relief
> toothache pain

If "toothache remedies" gets enough searches to make a difference, do peel & stick with it.

Day Trading Course
Develop Your Personal Schedule
Maximize Your Trading Potential
www.XYZ.com

> trading course
> [trading course]
> trading training
> [trading training]
> "trading books"
> commodities course
> futures course

If "trading training" is getting enough clicks already, pull it out and put it with a new ad. "Commodities course" and "futures course" belong in their own separate ad groups, no question.

If you organize your Google ad groups so that your keywords call out to searchers from your headline and ad text, you can get more visitors to your site, earn better positions on the page, and pay less money for your clicks.

Do you want to improve your clickthrough rate by 10%, 30%, 80%, or better, and not have to pay a penny more per click? It's all in how you organize things.

As simple as this is—so simple that most people miss it the first time—it's the single most effective secret that has helped our customers get more clicks without paying a penny more.

Uncle Claude Sez

You are presenting an ad to millions. Among them is a percentage, small or large, whom you hope to interest. Go after that percentage and try to strike the chord that responds . . . . They will decide by a glance—by your headline . . . . Address the people you seek and them only.

CHAPTER 5

Develop High-Quality Keyword Lists to Craft Killer Headlines

At my house we've got a wonderful children's book called *No, David!* David is a little boy whose mom is constantly telling him, "No, David!"

David is about to knock over a potted plant.

"No, David!"

David is chewing with his mouth open.

"No, David!"

David is playing baseball in the living room.

"No, David!"

David is about to push the aquarium off the table and spill the gold-fish out on the floor.

"No, David!"

■ ■ ■

From the first moment, my son Cuyler was *glued* to this book. For months it was his favorite book in the whole world.

Why?

You already know why.

It's because Cuyler's Mamma (and Daddy) were always shouting *"No, Cuyler!"* (Maybe it was because he was knocking over potted plants, chewing with his mouth open, playing baseball in the living room, and spilling the goldfish all over the floor.)

The only way to make it better would be to have a book called *No, Cuyler!* (Who knows? Maybe somebody will start selling personalized versions of the book.)

Cuyler had a favorite part of the story. Know what it was?

It was at the very end, when David's mom says, "Come here, David."

Mamma gives David a hug and says, "I love you, David."

Cuyler *loved* that page. Especially the hug he got every time we closed the book.

Cuyler loved *No, David!* because this book described a day—every day—in the life of Cuyler. *No David!* is like a page from his own diary.

Nothing endears you to your customer like reading him his own diary, showing that you know what it feels like to be *him*.

And *that's* what it means to enter the conversation inside your customer's head. When you step right into his thoughts and talk to him the way he talks to other people and himself, about things that are important to him, he'll listen to you. Just like Cuyler did.

> You'll capture the attention of your customer when you enter the conversation already taking place inside his head. With Google, you do this—and get more clicks as a result—by using your keywords skillfully in your ad. Bid on more keywords, and you can capture the attention of more people.

The keyword they type in *is* the conversation inside their head, at that very moment.

Your ad will capture peoples' interest when it repeats to them what they're thinking. So putting your keywords in your headline *and* in the body of your ad *and* in your URL are all part of a sound advertising strategy.

The more places in your ad that you have keywords showing up, the better your chances of getting the clicks. That means the headline. That means the body of the ad. It even means the display URL. If someone types in "German" or "Learn German," notice how many times they'll see their keyword in this ad:

> **Want to Learn German?**
> 5 Crucial Principles You Must Know
> To Master German, and Fast
> www.MasterGermanFaster.com

If effective marketing means speaking directly to what people are searching on, and repeating it back at them, how do you go about finding out what people are searching on in the first place? Where do you go to get the good keywords, especially the keywords that are worth the most money?

GETTING MORE TOOLS FOR YOUR TOOLBOX

Review Chapter 1 again on how to implement Glenn Livingston's Bull's Eye Method for finding the single most valuable keyword to your business. It used to be that the operating assumption was that the more keywords you could possibly find, the better. Not so anymore. The most recession-proof AdWords advertisers have carefully chosen the one hill in their market worth dying on, and build their business around it.

But when you want to expand on what you have, or want to enter entirely new markets, this chapter will point you in the right direction.

The quickest place to start is with Google's free keyword tool, available via the green "Tools" or "Opportunities" tab at the top of your account page, and at google.com/keywords. It gives you an immediate sense of how valuable each of your keywords will be relative to the others.

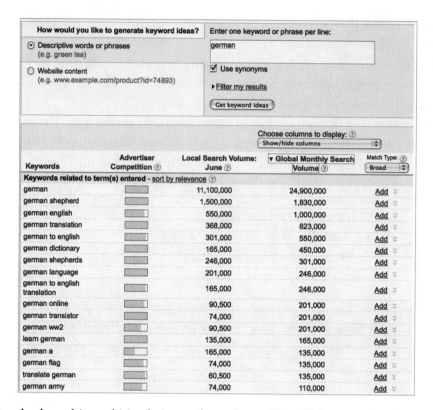

One look at this and it's obvious where the traffic will be. It's also obvious that you've got keywords here that don't belong.

GET RID OF VISITORS YOU DON'T WANT

You haven't spent a penny yet and you can already guess what your major *negative keywords* are going to be. These are words you include in your list where you specifically do not want your ad to show when people type them in. You can manually enter terms into your keyword list with negatives in front of them:

> –dog
> –puppy
> –shepherd
> –pointer
> –dictionary
> –translator
> –translation
> –flag

–girls

(etc.)

Or from Google's keyword tool you can select match type "Negative" from the dropdown menu on the upper right, and click to add keywords in individually:

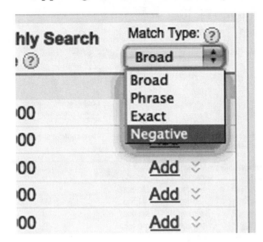

Now your ads won't show any time people include these words in their search.

SEARCH SMARTER WITH GOOGLE'S KEYWORD TOOL

With Google's tool you have another choice: If you've already got a full website up and you don't want to start completely from scratch in guessing at all the keywords that are there, click on the "Website content" tab and simply enter the web address for one or several pages on your site. Google will search the site and come up with your keyword list for you.

However, if you want to reach people with keywords that you know aren't obviously found on your website, click the "Keyword Variations" tab and enter one of your core keywords.

Google doesn't just give you variations of that keyword. Check the tiny box underneath marked "Use synonyms" and it also gives you a host of related suggested themes. This is no hack job, either. Google's results here are just the results you'd expect from a world-class search engine.

Google gives you plenty more still. You can see monthly and seasonal traffic trends for your keywords. Just click on the "Choose columns to display" drop-down menu and select "Show search volume trends," a month-by-month graphic of the average searches your term gets. We ran this feature for the term "Christmas" and it shows the dramatic increase in searches for November and December, and it suggests additional related keywords:

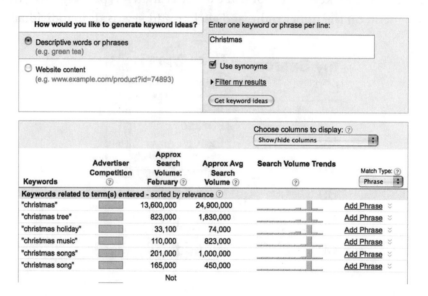

Very clever. And very helpful. You get information about your competition that you can't get from any other free service.

WORDTRACKER: MORE PAYING "MARKETS" STILL

You can use Google's free tool. There's also Wordtracker, whose free tool is at freekeywords.wordtracker.info. Whichever tool you use to find all of the searched-on variations of "learn German," every result listed will have those two words in it:

> learn to speak german
> learn german free
> learn german online free
> learn to speak german for free
> learn to speak german online
> german language learn online
> learn swiss german
> learn german software
> learn german cd

But aren't there people who want to learn German who don't use that exact phrase?

Sure are. There's also "study German" and even "study in Germany," not to mention the occasional guy who on a lark types in "learn Deutsch" or even "sprechen sie Deutsch."

But how do you know what other possible keywords there are? Answer: Google's keyword tool gives you a broad list further down its results page:

				Add all 150 »	
			Download all keywords: text, .csv (for excel), .csv		
Additional keywords to consider - sorted by relevance ⑦					
korean		7,480,000	11,100,000		Add ⌄
japanese		20,400,000	37,200,000		Add ⌄
history		30,400,000	37,200,000		Add ⌄
italian		13,600,000	16,600,000		Add ⌄
arabic		3,350,000	11,100,000		Add ⌄
travel		185,000,000	185,000,000		Add ⌄
polish		4,090,000	6,120,000		Add ⌄
portuguese		1,220,000	2,740,000		Add ⌄
russian		16,600,000	20,400,000		Add ⌄
languages		1,220,000	1,830,000		Add ⌄
spanish		20,400,000	24,900,000		Add ⌄
learning		13,600,000	16,600,000		Add ⌄
english		37,200,000	55,600,000		Add ⌄
learn		11,100,000	11,100,000		Add ⌄
language		13,600,000	16,600,000		Add ⌄
dutch		3,350,000	5,000,000		Add ⌄
french		24,900,000	30,400,000		Add ⌄
translate		4,090,000	13,600,000		Add ⌄
translations		823,000	1,500,000		Add ⌄
translators		368,000	550,000		Add ⌄
online translator		201,000	673,000		Add ⌄
online translation		450,000	1,220,000		Add ⌄
translator		4,090,000	11,100,000		Add ⌄
translation		11,100,000	24,900,000		Add ⌄
language translation		368,000	823,000		Add ⌄

It's an extremely broad list, as you can see. And we recommend using Wordtracker's wide search feature as well.

Let's say now that you're bidding on keywords for cell phones. Wordtracker's wide search will give you these additional suggested variations:

mobile phone
nokia
cellphone
cellular phone
ringtones
wireless
sony ericsson
samsung
sanyo
motorola
bluetooth
accessories

COULD YOU MAKE MORE MONEY TAKING A DIFFERENT ROUTE WITH YOUR KEYWORDS?

Let your imagination wander a bit, and you'll realize that these keywords that Google and Wordtracker have given you could take you into new markets you never would have considered.

More than a few people have figured out after looking over keywords and traffic that they'd make more money selling *accessories* for Nokia phones than being a reseller of the phones themselves.

There are countless examples of this kind of surprise discovery. That's why you do this research in the first place. Keep an open mind!

Wordtracker is not designed to give you click costs or profitability estimates. It's made to alert you to all of the possible directions you can take with your keywords. It does this by

1. showing you all the variations people have typed in over the last 60 days, and
2. telling you the number of searches each one has had through Dogpile and Metacrawler.

That's what you get when you do a deep search. Here are the results for "cellphone":

Searching...300 row(s) returned
Taken from all Dogpile & Metacrawler queries over the last 90 days.

Click here to add all keywords to your basket

Keyword (?)	Count (?)	Predict (?)	Dig (?)
cellphones	1219	1575	✎
cellphone	649	839	✎
unlocked cellphones	350	452	✎
cellphone rental	229	296	✎
cellphone accessories	213	275	✎
cellphone wallpaper	209	270	✎
cellphone wallpapers	201	260	✎
prepaid cellphones	179	231	✎
free cellphones	155	200	✎
cellphone reviews	144	186	✎

And here are Google's results for "cell phones":

Additional keywords to consider - sort by relevance ⑦				
cell		45,500,000	37,200,000	Add ⌄
phones		20,400,000	37,200,000	Add ⌄
mobile phones		2,240,000	20,400,000	Add ⌄
cell phone wireless		3,350,000	3,350,000	Add ⌄
samsung phones		450,000	1,830,000	Add ⌄
lg phones		550,000	1,220,000	Add ⌄
unlocked phones		1,220,000	1,220,000	Add ⌄
free phones		673,000	673,000	Add ⌄
prepaid cell		1,000,000	550,000	Add ⌄
prepaid phones		823,000	550,000	Add ⌄
cellphones		368,000	450,000	Add ⌄
cheap phones		450,000	450,000	Add ⌄
wireless phones		673,000	450,000	Add ⌄
cell service		550,000	368,000	Add ⌄
cell plans		450,000	301,000	Add ⌄
pda phones		90,500	246,000	Add ⌄
cell phone new		201,000	201,000	Add ⌄
t mobile cell		246,000	201,000	Add ⌄
tmobile phones		301,000	201,000	Add ⌄
bluetooth phones		165,000	165,000	Add ⌄
gsm phones		201,000	165,000	Add ⌄
new mobile phones		49,500	165,000	Add ⌄
camera phones		110,000	135,000	Add ⌄
nextel phones		201,000	135,000	Add ⌄
flip phones		90,500	110,000	Add ⌄
t mobile cell phone		135,000	90,500	Add ⌄
razr phones		40,500	60,500	Add ⌄
prepaid wireless phones		60,500	49,500	Add ⌄
cheap cellular phones		40,500	33,100	Add ⌄

The more keywords you have access to, the merrier.

HOW TO USE KEYWORDS TO OUTSMART YOUR COMPETITORS

Now if in fact every keyword is a market of its own, that means that a number of things are true:

1. Each keyword gets its own unique number of searches
2. Each keyword converts differently to sales
3. Each keyword has its own level of competition
4. Each keyword represents something slightly different that folks are thinking when they type it in.

Stephen Juth has put together a tool called AdWord Accelerator (www.Adword Accelerator.com) that helps you pick apart your competition. Pick any keyword and run a search on it with Stephen's tool, and you'll instantly see how the clicks, the cost, and the competitors are all different:

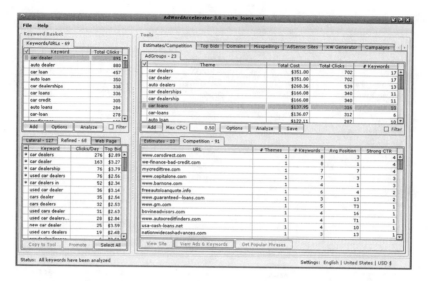

More about the significance of those quotes and brackets in a minute. But it's already clear just from this set of keywords which ones are going to be more valuable to you.

Notice that the exact-match version—the one in brackets—has four times as many advertisers competing for space, that it's lower on the page, gives you *one-fourth* as many clicks per day as the phrase match, but costs you 12% more on average to be there.

Your competitors don't know this!

Without tools like this in your toolbox, you'd likely miss this fact completely.

SOMETHING ELSE YOUR COMPETITORS DON'T KNOW

Now for a marketing insight from a different language: Mandarin Chinese.

I sell a book in Taiwan and Mainland China that teaches you how to learn Mandarin Chinese through your environment. It's a whole-life *Zen* approach that my customers insist is actually a tremendous resource for folks learning any language anywhere. Here are some of the search terms people use to find it:

> learn chinese
>
> speak chinese
>
> mandarin
>
> learn mandarin
>
> mandarin chinese
>
> learn mandarin chinese

Just the thought process alone behind each of these search terms is different. The person who types in "learn Mandarin Chinese" is already being more clear and specific than the person who types in "learn Chinese."

How so?

The former is someone who knows that he does *not* want to learn Cantonese, the dialect spoken down south in Guangdong Province and Hong Kong. You've already got a more self-aware thinker on your hands, and someone with a different set of questions and challenges in mind than the person who's thinking more generically about "picking up a little Chinese."

Never mind the different mind-set for the person who types in "study Chinese" instead of "learn Chinese." Think about it.

Your market is the same way. Every keyword represents a different mind-set, a different set of needs, a different personality. So how do you know who is who?

You can poll the folks searching on the different keywords. At SurveyMonkey.com you can set up surveys and questionnaires where you ask people specific questions about what they want or need, and then trace their varying answers back through the different keywords they found you on. More on this in a second.

NOBODY TYPES IN JUST ONE KEYWORD

This is a strategy taught by our associate Glenn Livingston, who has a comprehensive method for researching a market before you actually dive into it (Glenn-Livingston .com). Glenn points out a key fact about different keywords and how they represent different kinds of thinking:

People don't usually just type in one keyword, find what they're looking for immediately, and quit. They type in a series of keywords. So, for example, a person might type in "learn Chinese" at first, and then go back and type in "learn Mandarin" to get more information and see more options. Or it might be the other way around.

So if you can capture the full attention of a person typing in the *first* in a series of searches, you've intercepted him and saved yourself from being pitted against other competitors on his next search.

KEEP YOUR GUINEA PIG FROM SMELLING

Glenn explains this principle well. He's become known around the internet as "the Guinea Pig Guy" for his website www.GuineaPigSecrets.com. After doing careful surveys and ask campaigns he discovered that the number one question bugging the folks who typed in that particular keyword was, "How do I keep my guinea pig and his cage from smelling?"

Knowing that, Glenn incorporated a lead-in to that very issue in the headline of his landing page—just for people who came to his website via that keyword—and increased his sales significantly.

You'll win with Google's editors when you hit on that *explicit conversation*. You'll win with your customers—as Glenn did—when you hit on that *implicit conversation*.

This is true of online marketing, because it was first true of *offline* marketing. It's a principle of human nature that dates back to the days of bows and arrows, flint and fire. Whether you're selling goods and services by using a web page or by direct mail, or if you're simply trying to persuade another person to see your point of view, you speak directly to what he or she is thinking, both explicitly and implicitly.

When a guy tells you he wants to lose fifty pounds, he's probably not lying to you. But there's something even he doesn't realize: He really wants to lose 50 pounds *and* still be able to stop at Krispy Kreme every morning, get Burger King every day for lunch, and sit on the couch watching TV every night with a beer and a bag of Ruffles.

Sorry if this sounds cynical, but it's the advertisers that speak to *both* wishes who sell the diet pills and weight loss shakes and appetite suppressants, over and over again, year in and year out.

So you're aiming to hit people on *two levels*.

There's the "explicit conversation" in their minds, which is the exact keyword they typed in. It's what you want in your ad and, if at all possible, on your landing page. Google will even reward you for doing this with your ad by offering you a lower minimum bid and giving you better positioning on the page by convincing Google's computers that your ad copy is more relevant.

Then there's the second level—the "implicit conversation" in their minds, which is unique to each keyword, the secrets of which you may not discover until you've talked to your customers and done the research.

Glenn did that with his guinea pig site, and he's now impervious to competition.

It's when you hit that second level that your clicks turn into more sales. It's at that second level that you become impervious to ignorant competitors who don't understand your customer the way you do.

MORE MARKETS, MORE CASH: HOW TO GET BEYOND THE "OBVIOUS" KEYWORDS

You know about Wordtracker, and we've already talked about AdWord Accelerator as a great tool for sorting out the real competition among keywords and bid prices and singling out the best-performing ads. There are others as well that give you a different emphasis and have features of their own that make them unique and very much worth having.

In your toolbox out in the garage you need a Philips and a flathead screwdriver, not just one or the other. The same is true of these major keyword tools. Each one has its use, and owning more is like having a bigger toolbox.

And there's more to learn still.

The first list of keywords you come up with, even if it's a long one, will be incomplete. AltaVista once reported that 20% of all its searches were totally unique in the history of AltaVista. You never know what people are going to hunt for.

So here are some fresh ideas:

1. You'll want lots of *synonyms* and related subjects in your stockpile of keyword candidates, so that you can be sure you're reaching people who are looking for what you've got.

2. You can try bidding on *brand names*, though you'll have to work through the copyright issues yourself. Google has had a score of its own legal headaches as a result of allowing AdWords users to bid on trademarked names. Nevertheless, names of companies, magazines, associations, famous people and places may all relate to your product. For example, for "billiards" you might bid on the name of famous pool player Jeremy Jones. For drums you might bid on "Buddy Rich."

3. *Misspellings* are a big opportunity, because so many advertisers don't bid on them, and the click-through rate is often higher. For my *Lord of the Rings* promotion, "Tolkein" (misspelled) got twice the CTR of "Tolkien" (spelled correctly).

4. LexFN.com is a website that I find extremely useful and interesting—it's an elaborate thesaurus that uses web technology to find a scores of synonyms and related concepts.

For example, here are LexFN's results when searching on the term "billiards." You'll note the long list they give you. This can be a very fun site to play with!

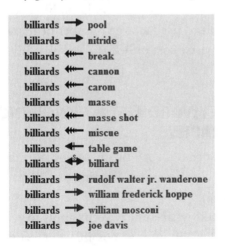

TRY THESE KEYWORD VARIATIONS

Keyword Variations

Variations on Nouns:	*Variations in Hyphenation:*	*Adjectives:*
Shoe	Email	Mini
Shoes	e-mail	Large
	e mail	Red
Variations on Verbs:	*Variations on Compound Nouns:*	*Adjective variations*
Drive	firetruck	Blue
Drove	fire truck	Green
Driven	fire-truck	Cheap
Driven		Premium
Driving	*Variations on Names:*	Budget
Steer	Tolkien	2006
Steering	Tolkein	Used
Steered	J.R.R. Tolkien	New
	JRR Tolkien	
Wrong Apostrophes:	John Ronald Reuel Tolkien	
Driver's	John Ronald Tolkien	
Tire's	John Reuel Tolkien	
	John Tolkien	

5. *Glossaries and indexes.* We recently built an AdWords campaign for a client where we went out and got a book on his subject. We went through the glossary and the index and used a large number of these terms in the glossary as keywords. Most of these cost only $0.05 a click, and they get a serious amount of traffic.

MULTIPLY YOUR KEYWORD LIST BY KNOWING THE LOCAL GEOGRAPHY

Sometimes places are associated with businesses—for example, if you had a casino you might get additional cheaper traffic bidding on "Niagara Falls" than merely bidding on "Casino."

For *local* businesses, take whatever keywords apply to your business and then add your state and as many close-by cities as possible. For example, a Cincinnati IT firm might use this list, which includes suburb names and deliberate misspellings of "Cincinnati":

> Ohio computer consultant
> Cincinnati computer consultant
> Cincinati computer consultant
> Cincinatti computer consultant
> Tri-state computer consultant
> Tri state computer consultant
> Eaton computer consultant
> Jamestown computer consultant
> Miamisburg computer consultant
> Sidney computer consultant
> Troy computer consultant
> Milford computer consultant
> Loveland computer consultant

Go to a map site and paste in a list of cities, then use an Excel spreadsheet to mix and match those terms. Use "computer consultant," "IT company," "IT consultant," etc.

HOW TO USE QUOTES AND BRACKETS TO UNCOVER CHEAPER, LESS COMPETITIVE KEYWORD NICHES

There's a way you can multiply your keyword list threefold, and at the same time bid on terms that your competitors are overlooking.

Quotes and brackets. They hide more surprises than you'd realize. Stephen Juth's tool AdWord Accelerator (AdWordAccelerator.com) helps you identify which of these variations will cost you less money and where there's less competition to fight through.

Now as you're sludging through the sometimes-tedious job of trying to come up with an exhaustive list of keywords, you may overlook a singular here or a plural there, and may forget a synonym or two that's closely related to one of your niche phrases.

Google has already foreseen this problem, and provides an extra feature, Expanded Phrase Matching, which adds singulars and plurals, similar phrases, and relevant synonyms to your keyword list for you.

You'll need to be careful here, however: this service will work for broad-matched keywords in your list, but it won't work for phrase matches or exact matches.

BROAD-MATCHED KEYWORDS

When you insert keywords at the time you're setting up your campaigns, these are the keywords that don't have any delimiters around them. For example:

> used cars
> japanese used cars
> used cars for sale

You need to be cautious, because if you don't provide negative keywords, that keyword phrase used cars will show your ad for all of the following searches:

> used cars
> german used cars
> used cars cleveland
> used police cars

and it may even show your ad for this wonky search:

> cars used in filming dukes of hazzard

PHRASE MATCHES

These keywords are placed with quotes " " around them. For example:

> "used cars"
> "japanese used cars"
> "used cars for sale"

These will make your ad show in searches that include these terms in this order, without extra words inserted. Such as the following:

> used cars
> old japanese used cars
> used cars for sale chicago

Your ad won't show for this search, however:

> used police cars

EXACT MATCHES

These keywords are placed with square brackets [ ] around them. For example:

> [used cars]

[japanese used cars]
[used cars for sale]

With these keywords, only people who typed in these exact phrases, in this order, will see your ad. None of the following keyword searches will show your ad:

used cars chicago
german used cars
old japanese used cars
used cars for sale chicago
used police cars

THE MATH OF NEGATIVE KEYWORDS: ONLY GOOD NEWS FOR YOUR CTR

Remember that if you include negative keywords in your lists, you'll pull down the number of impressions that your ads get because they'll show for fewer searches. Which means that your CTR will automatically go up. But notice the math of this: If you could pull down your number of impressions by 20%, your CTR would improve not by 20%, but by 25%. Likewise,

- If you cut unwanted impressions by 30%, your CTR will increase by 42%
- If you cut unwanted impressions by 40%, your CTR will improve by 67%
- If you cut unwanted impressions by 50%, your CTR will double.

Negative keywords won't affect the CTR of exact-matched keywords, but they will help your CTR on phrase—and broad-matched—terms. If you manage them the right way there's no way they *can't* help.

Imagine getting the same number of clicks as before, but because your CTR is double what it previously was, Google gives you your clicks at half price!

THE KILLER SECRETS

You've learned some invaluable principles here:

- Literally every keyword in your list is a market of its own.
- Every keyword represents a mind-set that people have when they type it.
- Behind everything explicit that your customers type in when they're searching, there's some want, need, question, or assumption that they have (but may be completely unaware of).
- Some keyword markets are bigger than others.

- Some keyword markets are more competitive than others.
- Some keyword markets produce more dividends for the winners than others.
- There are always keywords that are overloaded with competition, where bid prices are jacked up far beyond their real market value.
- At the same time there are always other keywords that are overlooked but which represent better, more responsive markets—which you can find if you use the right tools.
- You sell when you match that "implicit conversation" that your customers have with themselves.
- A roundup of keyword research tools, with reviews of their pros and cons, is available at www.perrymarshall.com/bookbonus.

HEADLINES AND KILLER COPY FROM *COSMOPOLITAN* MAGAZINE: HOW TO GET PAID TO LEARN FROM ANYBODY

I can't say I actually *like Cosmopolitan* magazine; after all, under the guise of supposedly liberating the modern woman, they've degraded her, turning her into a manipulative, greed-driven, appearance-obsessed, fashion-diet sex slave.

But every now and then when I'm at the grocery store I still buy a copy. Why on earth? Because these are the best headlines and writing formulas in the publishing business. The fastest route to writing a good headline is to simply steal one from *Cosmo*.

Last month I met with a client and spent most of the day developing a direct mail piece. They sell boring industrial hardware. It would put most folks to sleep, literally. But I brought copies of *Cosmo* and *Redbook* with me to assist. And it was an amazing process. The guys in the room thought we were crazy . . . until we started to actually apply the formulas. They were amazed at how well it works.

Here's what *Cosmo* did for us:

Cosmo Headline	*Our Headline*
The New Panties He'll Flip For	**The New Fuel Additive That Top Mechanics Flip For**
Brittany Murphy She's So Different Than You Think	**Linux** It's So Different than MCSE's Think
Be a Sex Kitten This Summer Hair, Makeup & Body Tricks to Make You Look Hot as Hell	**Be a Speed Demon This Summer** Project, Budget & Staffing Tricks to Make Your Operations Scream

"A Little to the Left"
How to Say What You Want in
Bed Without Bruising His Ego

**Did the Man of Her Dreams
Murder Her?**
Cosmo Investigates

"Budget Cuts Again?"
How to Challenge the CEO
Without Losing Your Job

**Did Bad Polymers Cause the
Firestone Fiasco?**
ACME Company Investigates

All of these speak directly to issues that engineers—or *Cosmo* readers—think about on a daily basis, sometimes an hourly basis. We just echoed those issues right back at them.

It's a method that works for you time and time again.

Oh—and if you'd like to use this approach without forking over five bucks for a *Cosmo* every month, just visit www.Magazines.com and click on the magazine covers to get a full-size view.

Uncle Claude Sez

The purpose of a headline is to pick out people you can interest. You wish to talk to someone in a crowd. So the first thing you say is, "Hey there, Bill Jones" to get the right person's attention.

So it is in an advertisement. What you have will interest certain people only, and for certain reasons. You care only for those people. Then create a headline which will hail those people only.

We pick out what we wish to read by headlines, and we don't want those headlines misleading. The writing of headlines is one of the greatest journalistic arts. They either conceal or reveal an interest.

CHAPTER 6

Writing Google Ads That Attract Eyeballs, Get Clicks, and Earn You Money

Your Google ads are an army of 100,000 tiny salesmen traversing the entire planet for you. And you only have to pay their salaries when the customers crack their doors open to listen to them.

■   ■   ■

Advertising is *selling in print*. That means the words you should use in your Google ads are the same words you use when you're on the phone or sitting across the table from a prospect, convincing him to buy something.

Before you try to write advertising copy, you should try to explain what you're selling to someone who might buy. When they raise their eyebrows and lean forward, pay attention to what you just said.

My friend and mentor John Carlton, one of the highest paid advertising copywriters in the world, spends weeks researching his clients' product or service, going from person to person or business to business, gauging their reactions and questions. John learns what buyers really want, and the certain turns of phrase that make or break the sale.

My own website sports a perfect example of this. I offer a CD called "Guerilla Marketing for Hi-Tech Sales People" (www.perrymarshall.com/gm) and the title of this CD came about exactly this way. I was walking a trade show floor wearing a "speaker" badge a couple of years ago and people would ask me what I was speaking on.

I tried a few different titles: "21 Secrets of High-Impact Low-Cost Marketing" . . . "The Cold Call Curse" . . . "Advertising Strategies for Technical Sales" . . . but the one that provoked positive reactions was "Guerilla Marketing for Hi-Tech Sales People." And that's what it's been ever since.

Those tiny Google ads will succeed for exactly the same reasons. The only challenge is your limited space. The headline is 25 characters or less, and each line of the body is 35 characters. The website URL displayed in the ad can also be up to 35 characters long.

So those are your limits. And that's okay, because your goal is not complex: just be *clear, simple,* and *relevant.* Claude Hopkins understood this well:

> *Literary qualifications have no more to do with it than oratory has with salesmanship. One must be able to express himself briefly, clearly, and convincingly, just as a salesman must. But fine writing is a distinct disadvantage. So is unique literary style. They take attention from the subject . . . . Fine talkers are rarely good salesmen . . . . Successful salesmen are rarely good speechmakers . . . . They are plain and sincere men who know their customers . . . . So it is in ad writing.*

English majors and Ph.D.s (and even MBAs) generally suffer from severe marketing debilitations. In advertising, an academic education is more of a liability than an asset! You don't need to be a literary genius.

Google ads are the language of the street, not the ivory tower. Speak to your customer in the language she responds to in everyday conversation, and she'll click.

RIVETING TO YOUR CUSTOMER, DEAD BORING TO ANYONE ELSE

Just like in print advertising and on web pages, your headline swings the biggest difference in response. It's in that split second of reading your headline copy that your customer first makes up his mind whether or not you're really relevant.

Start with that keyword your customer just typed in and fit it into your headline. That will be the first signal to him that you're truly relevant. This means that you'll want to create enough different ad groups that each of your major keywords can have an ad of its own.

Let's say that you sell customized power supplies. There's certainly more than one way a potential customer of yours might come looking for what you sell. She might search for "adaptors." She might search for "power supplies." She might search for "transformers."

So you'll go to your major keyword tool, such as Wordtracker or your special keyword generating software, and you'll come up with all of the possible major variations and related terms for your market niche. Then you'll separate them out into smaller groups that you can match to specific ads. For example:

Custom Power Adaptors
Record-Speed Custom Production Time
Get a Full Quote in 1 Business Day
XYZAdaptors.com

> adaptor
> adaptors
> ac adaptor
> power adaptor
> custom adaptors

Custom Transformers, Fast
Inventory Cost, Lead Time Advantage
Get a Quote in One Day or Less
XYZAdaptors.com

> transformer
> transformers
> power transformers
> electrical transformers
> voltage transformers

Power Supplies to Order
Inventory Cost, Lead Time Advantage
Get a Quote in One Day or Less
XYZAdaptors.com

> power supply
> power supplies
> switching power supply
> dc power supplies
> ac power supply

These ads aren't very flashy, are they? They're not loaded with over-the-top language; in fact, to folks like you and me they're, frankly, boring. But that's OK. They aren't meant for the average guy on the street.

This particular company caters to engineers. They speak the language that engineers would understand, relate to, and appreciate. They match their audience just fine. And they get a good clickthrough rate. (Too good, in fact.)

Using your major keywords in your headline, and creating as many different ad groups as you need to do this with all of your biggest keywords, is what makes the formula work.

WHEN YOUR INNER SALESMAN COMES ALIVE

After your headline, you've still got a second chance to convince your customer even further that you've got what he wants, and to get more clicks. This is where your inner salesman comes alive.

There's a second secret that makes this work. Check out the difference between these two ads:

Popular Ethernet Terms	**Popular Ethernet Terms**
3 Page Guide—Free PDF Download	Complex Words—Simple Definitions
Complex Words—Simple Definitions	3 Page Guide—Free PDF Download
www.xyz.com	www.xyz.com
0.1% CTR	**3.6% CTR**

The second ad got *36 times* the number of clicks as the first! What happened? What was the secret?

Look closely at the two ads. They both have the exact same wording. There's only one difference between them. What is it?

The first ad listed features and offers first, benefits second. The second ad listed benefits first.

This secret is just as true in long-copy print advertising as in those little thumbnail Google ads.

Features and offers are what your product has or what you're going to do. They describe it, what it includes, and how big or small or robust or thorough it is. Benefits, on the other hand, are the emotional payoffs your customer gets from using your product.

So the list of *features* for an e-book you sell may include these items:

· 12 timeless principles
· 24 chapters, 222 pages of rock-solid content
· 64 full-color photos

- Helpful, easy-to-read charts and graphs
- Step-by-step tips and instructions
- Fascinating stories, anecdotes, and personal experiences
- Introduction by Bill Gates
- Etc.

But your list of *benefits* will tell your customer how she'll actually be helped by what you've written. Sometimes there's a little bit of crossover between these and the features:

- Achieve a 46% improvement in less than 30 minutes
- Reach your goals in one-fourth the time using the 80/20 principle described in chapter five
- You can apply any one these 12 techniques immediately, and see instant results
- Catapult Energy Levels, Convert Fat into Muscle, Develop Strength, Endurance, and Flexibility all at the same time
- Discover how making *more* mistakes along the way becomes a strategy in itself that will grow your skill level even faster
- Get compliments from your friends as they ask you again and again (jealously), "What has *happened* to you?"

There's no way to pack all of this kind of content into a Google ad, granted. But the principle of dividing benefits from features is universal. Your Google ad is about benefits (emotional payoffs) more than anything else. And when you describe benefits *and* features both, it virtually always serves you to put benefits *first*.

The second ad did exactly that. Switching the order gave us a 3,600% improvement! We know this because we tested it. Will it work this way in your market? That's for you to find out.

You don't have to be a poet or a master copywriter to convince your customer that he or she will get something of value. State your case simply and clearly, and test to see if putting the benefits up front and the features second will boost your response.

TEST YOUR URL AND GROW YOUR AD'S EFFECTIVENESS

The display URL is the second most visible element in your ad. While Google has made it well nigh impossible to split test different domain names directly, if you do own separate sites with separate standalone content, you can "alias" those sites with additional new names and see how they perform in Google, using separate ad groups

for separate domains. (An old article describes how we do this, at PerryMarshall
.com/adwords/domains.)

If you're lucky enough to have a domain name that uses the exact keyword
phrase people are searching on, you're virtually guaranteed a high CTR. If you can
buy just such a domain and indirectly test it like I described, you could potentially
double your CTR.

Regardless, with your existing URLs we recommend you test other variations like
these in your display URL, including capitalization, use of the "www." and subdirec-
tories, which are always followed by the "/" slash:

- www.HealYourMarriage.com
- HealYourMarriage.com
- www.healyourmarriage.com
- www.HealYourMarriage.com/Forgiving

THE "GOLDILOCKS THEORY": WHY THE BEST ADWORDS ADS ARE NEVER OVER-THE-TOP

We thought we'd get ultra-creative one day, and we wrote up an in-your-face ad that
would shock Google users into clicking. We were just sure it would work. After all,
the number-one worst thing you can do is bore the hell out of people, right?

You can see what happened by the difference in CTR between the first "plain" ad
and the second "creative" ad:

D.I.Y. Sales Leads
Don't hire telemarketers
Make prospects chase you instead
www.perrymarshall.com
42 Clicks | 1.0% CTR

Escape Voicemail Jail
Get Customers to Chase You Instead
with Savvy Guerilla Marketing
www.perrymarshall.com
20 Clicks | 0.3% CTR

Deleted

We thought it was great. Our customers didn't. This happened again and again,
and we learned a valuable lesson:

Google users do not generally respond to hype. Nor do they respond to messages that are too plain. What works is something in the middle—intriguing, yet not pushy.

Andrew Goodman, the author of *Winning Results with Google AdWords*, calls it the "Goldilocks" principle. Not too hot; not too cold—you want the temperature to be *just right*.

A DIFFERENT KIND OF OVER-THE-TOP

Here's an ad that was very bold, *and* performed well at first . . .

Prospecting Sucks
Make B2B clients call you first
with smart guerilla marketing
www.perrymarshall.com
1.1% CTR

Disapproved

. . . until Google's editor saw it and *disapproved* it. Google doesn't let you use inflammatory words like "Sucks" or "Hate." It did let us get away with the word "stinks," however:

Prospecting Stinks
Telemarketing Annoys People
Guerrilla Marketing is King
www.PerryMarshall.com
1.3% CTR

SOME ALL-TIME MOST SUCCESSFUL GOOGLE ADS (THESE WILL SURPRISE YOU)

The ads that bring in record-high numbers of clicks are never the most flashy, the most outlandish, the most brilliantly composed copy you'll find. Never. They're simply a function of saying the right thing at the right time to the right people.

Here are some real-life examples of ads that our coaching clients wrote—ads that brought in record-high clickthroughs. You'll notice how unspectacular their language is, how they're specific rather than general, they never completely follow all of the "rules," and they're sometimes not even the best English!

But these have been tested *rigorously*. We worked and worked with our clients to help them create a message that perfectly matched what their customers were looking for, and their high CTRs show it:

Light Folding Tables So Strong and Durable you get an Unconditional Money-Back Guarantee www.mobiliteuk.com 24.5% CTR *—David Morgan* *Oxford, UK*	**Kona Condos for Sale** Big Island MLS and Agents Search Property Listings www.MarylRealty.com 18.2% CTR *—Claudia Hafner* *Waikoloa, HI*
The Lupus Recovery Diet New Book! Learn how I overcame Lupus without drugs or supplements. www.LupusRecoveryDiet.com 9.5% CTR *—Jill Harrington* *Mill Valley, CA*	**Mens Hair Growth Solution** 25 Facts You Don't Know About Your Hair Growth Problem. But Should! HowToStopHairLoss.com 25.1% CTR *—Ed Keay-Smith* *South Perth, WA, Australia*

Our friend Richard Stokes and his team over at AdGooroo.com share some examples of affiliate ads that perform stellarly on Google and therefore get solid positions and low bid prices and which get served well above 95% of the time on searches. Here are a couple:

Keyword "FTD fruit baskets":

Fruit Gift Baskets, FRESH
Always Fresh! Register & Save 5% on
Every Order. Nationwide Delivery.
CapalbosOnline.com/Since-1906

Keyword "fashion sneakers":

Fashion Sneakers & Shoes
Upgrade To Free Overnight Shipping
By Ordering One Item of Clothing!
www.Zappos.com/Fashion-Sneakers/

Why do these work?

- Both include the keyword phrase in the ad's headline.
- Both make careful use of exclamation points.

- The second has an implicit call to action ("Upgrade to . . .").
- Each word is capitalized, and the first ad makes use of all caps.
- The second ad makes careful use of the word "Free."
- Specific, concrete numbers are put to use wherever possible.

WHAT TO DO WHEN A HIGH CTR IS *NOT* YOUR GOAL

Your Google ads are an army of hardworking salespeople whose job it is to bring as many of the best prospects possible to your website. But you don't want just anybody. You don't want tire kickers; you don't want the looky-loos. You want genuinely interested people.

After all, you have to pay every time they click.

Sometimes you find yourself in a very crowded marketplace attempting to single out only a small percentage of people who you know are a real fit for what you offer.

That was the case with the adaptors example we showed you earlier. The business we were promoting provides custom-built electrical adaptors, converters, and transformers for high-tech original equipment manufacturers, and only deals in large-quantity orders.

You can imagine how many different types of people go looking on the internet for adaptors or converters or transformers in any given day. Even after we've used negative keywords (which we talked about in Chapter 3) to filter out the searches that we don't want—such as Transformer toy robots or online dollar-to-yen currency converters—we've still got people searching for the same terms we're bidding on who aren't looking for what we offer.

The guy who's just looking for a replacement power adaptor for his personal IBM laptop, for example—he's not our man.

So it's up to our Google ad to filter out the rest of that traffic, and to get as many *good* clicks as possible, but as few of every other kind. The more is not the merrier.

The key is being clear and specific. We're going to write an ad that addresses precisely the type of customer we're after:

AC/DC Converters for OEMs
Qty 250+, Rapid Custom Production
1-Day Quote & Overnight Delivery
XYZAdaptors.com

This ad won't win any awards for high CTR or stunning copy, but it knocks out three criteria: 1) it's for people wanting *custom* design, not off-the-shelf, 2) it's for OEMs (original equipment manufacturers) only, and 3) it's for orders of 250 units or more.

A lot of people are going to see this ad and pass it up. And that's okay. All we want are clicks from people who match these criteria. The ad will do its job.

Again, there's no black magic. Just tell your story. Be clear, straightforward, interesting, customer-centered, and, most importantly, relevant. Sell on the computer screen just like you'd sell in person. And people will see that you're for real, and they'll click and buy.

IF THE GUYS AT THE BAR WILL BUY IT, YOU'VE GOT A WINNING AD

Dan Kennedy tells the story of the highly paid, highly sought-after copywriter who writes sales letters aimed at blue-collar men. Before he delivers a project, he takes the draft down to the neighborhood bar, buys a round of drinks for all the guys, and then reads them the letter. Then he gets their comments.

They chime in and tell him to tweak this, fix that, change the wording here or there. But he knows he doesn't have a winner yet until one specific thing happens:

One of the guys in the group asks where they can get what the letter is offering.

That's when he knows he has a sales letter that's working. That's when it's ready for press. He's moved them from being critics to being buyers and they don't even realize it.

Take your copy—your Google ads, your sales page, your direct mail pieces, your e-mail blasts—and test them in other environments, other venues, with friends, or out on the street. When people are salivating over what you offer, then you've got a winner.

Uncle Claude Sez

The uninformed would be staggered to know the amount of work involved in a single ad. Weeks of work sometimes. The ad seems so simple—and it must be simple to appeal to simple people. But back of that ad may lie reams of data, volumes of information, months of research. So this is no lazy man's field.

Like Uncle Claude says, Google advertising isn't for lazy people. However, high performance ads can run with zero maintenance for months, even years. (Yes, even on the internet!) There are few assets more valuable than a system of effective ads that deposit money in your bank account 24/7/365.

CHAPTER 7

Triple Your CTR (and Cut Your Bid Prices by Two Thirds)—No Genius Required

AdWords rocket scientist Howie Jacobson kicked off a new campaign a couple of years ago, driving sales people to his site where he teaches them how to turn cold calling around into a profitable sales process. He started out with a simple Google ad:

> **Stop cold calling forever**
> Small business marketing system.
> Free report and 2 chapter download.
> www.leadsintogold.com
> 33 Clicks | 0.8% CTR

■ ■ ■

Today he's making traffic scream with killer ad copy that has more than *tripled* his clickthrough rate:

Cold calling not working?
Discover a powerful alternative.
Free report and 2 chapter download.
www.LeadsIntoGold.com
368 Clicks | 2.7% CTR

What's Howie's secret?

He's just brilliant, right? A copywriting genius, a Merlin, a sorcerer of the printed word, yes?

Howie will tell you no. (We think he's brilliant, as does every one of our customers who consults with him on their Google campaigns. But for this example he would argue otherwise.)

Seriously—what was his secret?

Answer: Howie just tested ad copy. That's all he did. You've seen the first and the last of his ads, but you haven't seen the score of other tests that he ran, that inch by inch grew his CTR by tiny percentage points over a two-year period. Here are just a few samples of the ads he put up for testing:

Stop cold prospecting.
Small business marketing system.
Free report and 2 chapter download.
www.leadsintogold.com
42 Clicks | 1.0% CTR

End cold calling forever
Small business marketing system.
Free report and 2 chapter download.
www.leadsintogold.com
430 Clicks | 1.7% CTR

End cold calling forever
Attract customers automatically.
Free report and 2 chapter download.
www.LeadsIntoGold.com
145 Clicks | 2.0% CTR

End cold calling forever
Lead generation system explained.
Free report and 2 chapter download.
www.LeadsIntoGold.com
338 Clicks | 2.2% CTR

Howie's full collection is available at www.LeadsIntoGold.com/genius. When you look over these ads, you see nothing spectacular. No shocking content, no in-your-face power words that jump off the page, no mind-blowing sales hooks.

Even more importantly, if you looked over all these ads by themselves and tried to *guess* which one would get the most clicks, I'll bet you couldn't. Not among these ads. *Only the market could tell you which one would be the winner!*

Howie knows his customers quite well, but he never had any brilliant flashes of insight, and he never consulted on these ads with any of the geniuses of the copywriting world.

Frankly, they couldn't have helped him anyway.

Instead, he did what all successful Google advertisers do: He ran two ads at a time. He compared their results. He deleted the loser and wrote another ad to try to beat the winner. He followed his nose, people clicked on what resonated with them, and the market told him what worked.

As the saying goes, "It is a fool who looks for logic in the chambers of the human heart."

The magic of AdWords is that nobody sensible sits and ponders an ad before clicking on it. A person sees your message, his brain runs an instant gut-reaction 0.1-second process, and the decision is made. He clicks, or he doesn't.

It won't do you any good to pontificate long hours over ad copy. Calling in focus groups to sit and discuss their feelings and reactions is a waste of your time, and theirs. In the Google world, people's decisions are instantaneous, and you can never predict with 100% accuracy what the market is going to react to. Your good common sense will tell you what should work. And then the market will tell you what actually *does* work.

HOW TO SET UP A SPLIT TEST: IT'S A NO-BRAINER

Google lets you do this with ease. When you've got an ad written, you can write a second one as well, just by clicking on the "Create new Text Ad" link next to the ad that you're currently running. Google will rotate this with your other ad, and you can compare the clickthroughs and eventually delete the loser and try to beat your best again:

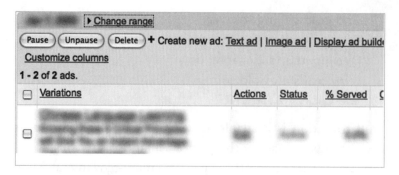

STATISTICAL SIGNIFICANCE: SOUNDS BORING, BUT IT'S *REALLY* IMPORTANT

(So important, one coaching student put himself out of business by ignoring this!)

During our personal AdWords coaching program last summer, I got a very frustrated e-mail from a member whose sales had gone South, not North, since the program started.

Not exactly what he was hoping for when he signed up, right? (Especially since we make outrageous performance guarantees to students who are accepted.)

This gentleman was getting a few sales a day and was re-writing his sales page also on a daily basis. He'd get two sales on Tuesday and assume the changes were bad, he'd change something, then he'd get five sales on Wednesday and assume the changes were good.

But little by little his sales started going down the toilet, heading toward zero.

By the time he sounded an alarm he was in dire financial straits. Furthermore, he hadn't saved the early versions of the sales page when it *was* working so it wasn't even possible to go back to what was working.

About a month later he let go of his employee and shut the business down.

As they say in Spanish, *¡Qué lástima!*

Again, by the time we found out about this it was too far gone to save. Here's what he failed to do:

1. He didn't use our SplitTester.com tool to figure out if his winning sales page was really a winner

2. He didn't keep a detailed record of his modifications and copies of all the versions along the way.

This problem applies to *anything* you test—not just Google ads, but opt-in pages, sales pages, etc.

When you do split test, how do you know when you've got enough results to be sure that your winning ad didn't just "get lucky," or the loser didn't just have a bad day or a bad week? How many trials do you need to run?

THE SPLIT TESTER TOOL AND HOW TO USE IT

With the help of our friend Brian Teasley (www.Teasley.net) we created a split-testing tool on the web, at www.SplitTester.com. With this tool, you can find out how likely it is that it was luck. Here's how this works:

Let's say we've got two ads. One gets a 1.2% clickthrough rate with two clicks total, and the other gets a 2% clickthrough rate with five clicks total. Was the better one really better, or was it luck? Let's see:

Enter Your Numbers Here:			
Number of Clicks (First Ad)	2	Number of Clicks (Second Ad)	5
CTR (First Ad, in %) *	1.2	CTR (Second Ad, in %) *	2.0
* Your CTR must be entered as a simple percentage. For example, enter 3.1% as "3.1", and not "0.031"; Enter 0.7% as "0.7"			
	Calculate	Reset	

When we click "Calculate" it says:

You are **not very confident** that the ads will have different long-term response rates.

But now let's say we've got 20 clicks for one and 35 for the other, not just 2 and 5: We click "Calculate" and it tells us:

Enter Your Numbers Here:			
Number of Clicks (First Ad)	20	Number of Clicks (Second Ad)	35
CTR (First Ad, in %) *	1.2	CTR (Second Ad, in %) *	2.0
* Your CTR must be entered as a simple percentage. For example, enter 3.1% as "3.1", and not "0.031"; Enter 0.7% as "0.7"			
	Calculate	Reset	

You are **approximately 95% confident** that the ads will have different long-term response rates.

Ninety-five percent confidence means that if we ran this test 100 times and got these results, the results would lead us in the right direction 95 times. That's pretty good—I'm willing to bet on those kinds of odds.

Here's a real simple rule of thumb: When your response percentages are fairly close between two competing ads, you need 30 or more responses to each one before you can declare a winner. And maybe even 50. But if one is already doing considerably better than the other, then it doesn't take as long—after 10 to 15 actions have been taken you can be fairly sure. Use www.splittester.com to find out.

When you do proper split testing, when you test two things side by side and make sure you're 90%, 95%, or 99% sure of your results before you go on, you're dealing with hard numbers and good, high levels of certainty. Your progress isn't squishy and uncertain; it's measurable and reliable.

Not only does that make for very effective marketing, it makes for a healthy company, good morale among the troops, and a happy bank account.

Uncle Claude Sez

Now we let the thousands decide what the millions will do. We make a small test, and watch cost and result. When we learn what a thousand customers cost, we know almost exactly what a million will cost. When we learn what they buy, we know what a million will buy.

We establish averages on a small scale, and those averages always hold. We know our cost, we know our sale, and we know our profit and loss. We know how soon our cost comes back. Before we spread ourselves thin, we prove our undertaking absolutely safe. So there are today no advertising disasters piloted by men who know.

CHAPTER 8

Triple Your Traffic with Placement Targeting and Google Image Ads

've always been leery of traffic from Google's content network. When I start a new campaign I almost always turn it off. (You should too, as it throws off your split tests. You get an uneven mix of Google and syndicated traffic in your ads, and you can't compare the CTRs.) Furthermore it frequently brings lower quality visitors who are less inclined to buy.

■ ■ ■

But not always!

Sometimes content-targeted clicks bring *better* traffic.

A couple of years ago I had a project that was running on Google traffic alone. I'd tested and tweaked the ads and I thought it was doing fine.

Then one day, almost by accident, I turned the content network on.

It produced a sudden *avalanche* of traffic. Good traffic, too. The number of visitors to that website grew by a factor of 5X!

> There's even more traffic waiting for you on Google's content network and through image ads and on targeted sites. Test it and find out if you can make it profitable. You could potentially double or triple the number of quality visitors to your site through these new venues of advertising.

Many of our customers have been able to double, triple, quadruple their traffic just by turning on content-targeted sites in addition to the regular Google and search network traffic. But what is the content network?

Google shows your ads on Google. It also shows your ads other places, unless you tell it not to. One possible place is the *search partners network*—the partner search engines that display Google's results, such as AOL, Ask.com, Earthlink, etc.

But this chapter isn't about that. It's about the *content network*—any and every website across the entire internet that displays AdSense, those "ads by Google." And that can mean a ton of traffic for you. Here's a shot from CNN.com with Google ads served on the lower right:

HOW IS THIS DIFFERENT FROM REGULAR GOOGLE SEARCHES?

A person who searches on Google is looking for a specific solution to his problem and is often in a spending frame of mind. The content network, on the other hand, shows ads on sites where visitors are reading articles, watching videos, commenting on forums and blogs, and not necessarily thinking about a particular solution to a particular problem. A person in this case is less likely to be in a buying frame of mind.

Success on the content network is more about distracting people, catching them unexpectedly, and guiding their interest to your product, service, or cause.

A major success strategy for ads on the content network is to tickle the reader's curiosity. Use words and language and imagery that are unusual, interesting, curious, compelling, even mysterious. The best content network advertisers do this to great effect.

HOW TO TURN IT ON AND OFF

Google turns on the content network by default. To change this, go into the campaign you want to adjust, click on the "settings" tab, and click "Edit" next to "Networks and devices." An additional box of options will open up:

You can then uncheck the box next to "Content." This setting will affect all of the ad groups in the campaign.

Google lets you bid different amounts for content network traffic. This way you don't overspend. (Get it wrong and you could rack up thousands of dollars in click costs in a matter of days!)

Setting the content bid for a specific ad group is easy. Just click on the dollar amount bid of the ad group you want to adjust (in this case, the maximum CPC for automatic placements in the second ad group, below):

A small window pops up that lets you enter the maximum bid you want.

Three Things Could Happen, None of Them Necessarily Bad.

When you turn on content traffic, you could find that:

1. You get ten times as many clicks here as on Google search.
2. You get low CTRs of 0.1% or 0.01% or worse (but which won't negatively affect your account).
3. One or two keywords or ad groups could convert superbly while the rest fall flat.

GOOGLE'S WONDER WHEEL: ROLLING OUT A SUCCESSFUL CONTENT NETWORK CAMPAIGN

First off, this tip will save you confusion and heartache:

Content network traffic should be managed in a new and separate campaign from your Google Search traffic.

And we *do not* recommend duplicating your Google search ad groups into a new content-only campaign and turning on the traffic. There's more nuance than that.

A clever tool called the *Wonder Wheel* makes it simple and intuitive. To see it, search on "red wagons" and on the results page click "Show options" on the upper left:

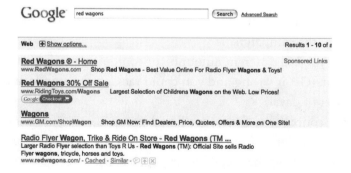

The Wonder Wheel option then shows up on the lower left. Click it and you get a wagon wheel visual of closely related keyword topics:

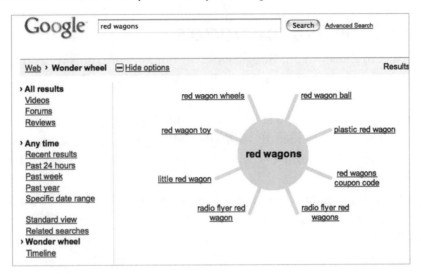

So here's how you turn this information into a content-targeted campaign:

Take the hub and each "spoke" of the wheel and create a separate ad group with that phrase as its sole broad-matched keyword. Write an ad for each one and turn on the traffic. An ad can use the exact keyword phrase in the headline but, unlike ad groups on Google search, it doesn't absolutely have to in order to get good CTRs.

The above "red wagon" Wonder Wheel example could give you as many as nine separate ad groups, one keyword phrase per group.

Once you've got that, click on any one of the spokes to expand it further.

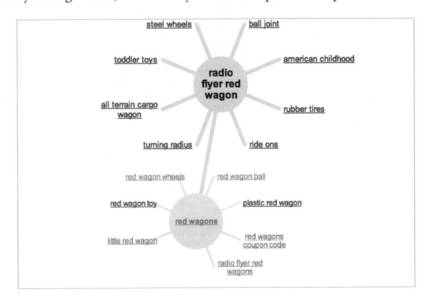

The resulting wheel gives you another set of terms from which you could create several more single-keyword ad groups. Just make sure your ads are still about red wagons.

GOOGLE IS LOOKING FOR "THEMES"

To find pages to show you on, Google looks at your keyword, plus your ad, plus your landing page, and infers a "theme" that they're about. Then it finds pages across the internet that match it.

That's one reason why you start with just one keyword per ad group: It's easier for Google's computers to identify *the theme,* and they have more latitude for finding pages that echo it. Cast your net wide early on, and Google will reward you with more placements.

The next thing you do is remove the bad placements. See the next chapter for an explanation of how to do that. When you're done, 2–3% of the sites Google showed you on will actually be productive. Keep those, and you're good to go.

Don't try to tweak this merely by adjusting your bids. That will shorten your reach. Keep your bids where they are and eliminate sites where you don't convert. You'll end up with 6–12 ad groups that are performing genuinely well.

And that's a long-term strategy that works.

AUTOMATIC OR MANAGED PLACEMENTS?

What we've been talking up till now are automatic placements. Google chooses the sites, but you have veto power.

Managed placements are different. They're sites you specifically tell Google to show you on. You control both automatic and managed placements from the "Networks" tab in the middle of your interface:

Settings	Ads	Keywords	**Networks**				
Your keywords determine which automatic placements are good matches for your ads.							
			Max. CPC	Clicks	Impr.	CTR ⑦	Avg. CPC (
Search - off			--	9	315	2.86%	$0.2
Google search - off				9	315	2.86%	$0.2
Search partners - off ⑦				0	0	0.00%	$0.0
Content				100	23,077	0.43%	$0.1
Managed placements ⑦hide details				0	0	0.00%	$0.0
Automatic placements ⑦hide details			auto	100	23,077	0.43%	$0.1
Total - All networks				**109**	**23,392**	**0.47%**	**$0.1**

■ **Content: managed placements**

To display ads on the content network, add managed placements. You have opted to only run ads on content pla

What if I have keywords in my ad group?
Keywords help refine the targeting for your ads, so they can help no matter where your ads run. Learn More.

HOW DO I FIND OUT WHERE GOOGLE IS SHOWING MY ADS?

Just click the "show details" link next to "Automatic placements" and what unfolds is a list of sites where your ads have shown:

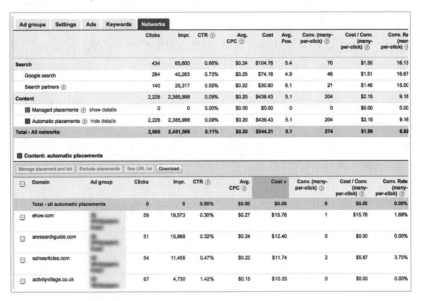

Don't want to show up in all those places? Just select the sites you don't want and click "Exclude placements":

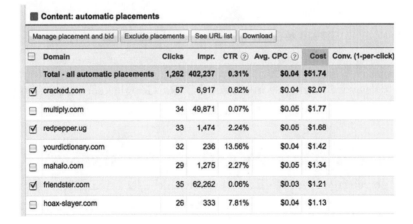

HOW DOES GOOGLE DECIDE WHERE TO SHOW MY ADS?

We talked about this in the previous chapter: For any single ad group, Google's system identifies a "theme" based on the keyword(s) you've chosen and your ad copy (and website) and then picks sites that fit.

But there's a growing, expanding process to this. Google is constantly looking for new and more relevant sites to show your ads on. That way you get more clicks, AdSense publishers get more commissions, and Google gets more revenue.

The Wonder Wheel illustrates this. If you bid on "red wagons" then of course Google shows you on red wagon sites. But it's going to expand on this, in two directions. One direction is to dig down and start testing your "red wagons" ads on the various "spokes" of the wheel: Radio Flyer red wagons, red wagon toys, red wagon wheels, plastic red wagons, etc.

Sites built around any of the spokes on any of these wheels may get your ads shown. If they get clicks, Google keeps trying.

The other direction is to go wider. Instead of just "red wagons" Google aims for sites about wagons of all kinds:

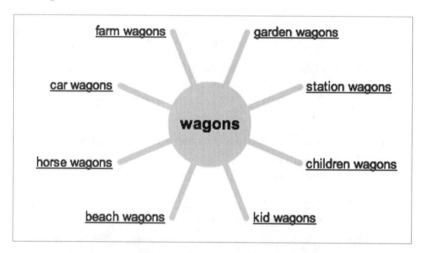

If in new keyword markets you get good CTRs, Google keeps expanding until the good CTRs stop . . . or until you hit the Jet Stream.

A WILD PHENOMENON WE CALL THE "JET STREAM"

Only a tiny percentage of AdWords ads ever reach the Jet Stream. It's the point where an ad gets served nearly everywhere across the entire content network, because it gets clicks no matter where Google shows it.

If an ad of yours hits the Jet Stream, you could get hundreds, thousands, even tens of thousands of clicks a day from around the internet.

But remember that you've got veto power over any site, or category of site, that you're showing up on. Use the "Exclude placements" feature as often as you need to in order to stay off sites that waste your money.

Ads that hit the Jet Stream typically have universal appeal, or stroke some sort of universal desire or curiosity. Obviously some markets are more jet-friendly than others; dating or weight loss or nutrition or social causes are more likely to write ads for that get clicks everywhere, than if you're operating in a very narrow-interest niche market. But regardless, curiosity is power, and the ability to stimulate it means more clicks from more places.

We provide to new members of our Renaissance Club a full report on Google's Jet Stream, available at PerryMarshall.com/renaissance.

WHAT ARE MANAGED PLACEMENTS?

Managed placements (formerly called "site targeting" or "placement targeting") are where you choose the sites, instead of Google. And you can do it without keywords. (You can also choose to bid on impressions rather than clicks.)

Any site on the internet that's set up to run Google ads is available for you to advertise on. Plus you can run image ads as well as text ads.

To set up managed placements, choose the campaign you want to start with. It will need to have the content network enabled. From there, you set up placements by ad group.

You've got a choice: You can either create a new ad group (which we strongly recommend), or add managed placements into an existing one.

To create a new ad group with managed placements, click on "New ad group":

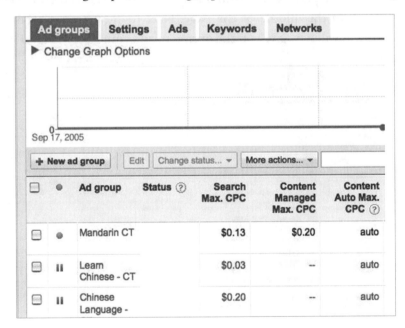

On the next page, scroll down to "Placements":

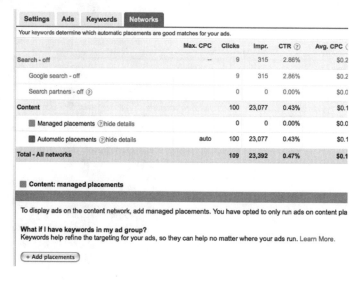

You can enter the sites you want to show ads on. And you can set separate bids.

To add managed placements to an existing keyword-based ad group, click on the "Networks" tab in the middle of the page. Next to "Managed placements," click "Show details." It will now give you the option to add your own managed placements to the ad group:

From here on, this "Networks" tab is where you'll go to see impressions, clicks, and other performance statistics for your existing managed placements. It will look surprisingly similar to the statistics page for your keyword performance:

KEYS TO MAKING MANAGED PLACEMENTS WORK

Just as with Google ads, the key to success is always constant, patient split testing. Peel & stick works here too, but instead of keywords we're now peeling and sticking *domains and URLs*.

Targeting individual pages can allow you to write laser-honed ads that are tailor-made just for the visitors to that page. And again, using language and imagery that's unusual, interesting, and compelling, which plays on the reader's curiosity, is one of the first things you'll want to test.

You'll find one of the most valuable metrics in your interface to be your *cost per conversion*. How much does it cost you to get a real customer, from each of the different sites and URLs you're serving? That determines what you keep, and what you throw out.

Uncle Claude Sez

"Human nature is perpetual. In most respects it is the same today as in the time of Caesar. So the principles of psychology are fixed and enduring. You will never need to unlearn what you learn about them.

"We learn, for instance, that curiosity is one of the strongest of human incentives. We employ it whenever we can."

CHAPTER 9

Google Image Ads: Banner Advertising Is Here to Stay

B ack in the internet Bubble Days of 1999, banner ads were one of few routes a small startup could take in order to get paid traffic online. Everyone and his chalupa-eating chihuahua was buying and selling banner space online, and if you wanted visitors to your site, banner ads were the only medium that promised any significant volume.

■ ■ ■

Then up jumped Google, and with Google, AdWords.

The internet has since come full-circle. Banner ads are far from being the only way to buy traffic now. But with Google they're one of the best bargains you'll find.

Rarely do our coaching clients ask us about banner ads. Which is a pity, because we've seen Google's image ads bring in hundreds of clicks per day for, in some cases, as little as $0.03 a click.

Rare, yes, but not at all unheard of. All provided courtesy of Google's content network, which by design finds and grows traffic and impressions and clicks for you automatically until you tell it to stop.

ARE IMAGE ADS ON GOOGLE A HUGE DEAL? YUP.

We estimate that 20 to 30% of Google's AdSense advertisers are willing to allow image ads—so there are *tons* of places where your ads can show. Clicks in some markets are still available for pennies apiece. And bizarrely, we also estimate that only 2 to 5% of all Google advertisers ever use banner ads at all.

Text ads don't catch the eye like image ads do. Text ads limit you to 130 characters; image ads don't. The only limitations in image ads are the size you happen to be working on at the moment, and what sorts of things users will and will not click on.

Image ads give you an infinite range of variables to test. And they bring you 3–10x times better CTRs than regular content-targeted text ads. This is because 1) visuals are more compelling than mere words, and 2) you could be the only Google ad that shows on a page.

It's quite simple: the same principles of good ad copy apply to image ads as well. Take a text ad, tweak a couple of phrases to make them complete sentences, decide what graphics will go in it, and you're done.

The point is still to enter the conversation inside your customer's head.

Be relevant, compelling, and credible. Use language that attracts. See if including numbers and statistics works. Put in a brief testimonial. Add a visual that supports your copy. Test and see what pulls best. Some elements you can try:

· Color and black-and-white images
· Images from nature
· Pictures of people (including famous people)
· All of the copy variations you'd test in text ads
· Photos of your product
· Graphs
· Computer screenshots

We've tested numbers of ads in both for-profit markets and non-profit markets. Here's how different image ads performed in one of those markets:

Ad	Clicks	Impressions	CTR	Cost	Conversion Rate
SCIENCE ASTRONOMY & GOD (SUPER INTELLECT OR NATURAL SCIENCE) Where did the universe come from? SCIENCE.COSMICFINGERPRINTS.COM	3,538	848,398	0.42%	$114.90	17.35%
MARS, THE STARS, & PLANETS	879	317,343	0.28%	$22.07	11.04%
THE HUBBLE TELESCOPE Did the Universe Come From... GOD??? INTERPRETING THE LATEST RESULTS www.cosmicfingerprints.com	1,283	144,719	0.89%	$49.49	14.65%

Note the different conversion rates. And note that the average cost per click in all of these cases came to less than $0.04. Not bad.

HOW TO SET IT UP

Choose the sizes that matter. The 80/20 rule applies here: start with the 250 x 300 rectangle. That's where you'll get shown the most, followed by the 728 x 90 leaderboard. YouTube can be a huge source of impressions for the 250 x 300 ads:

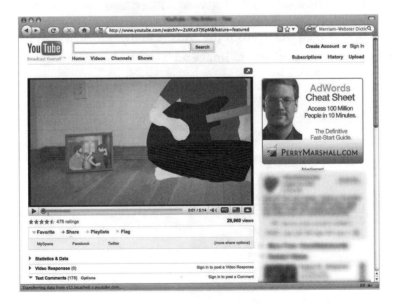

Create ads that catch the eye. There are nine sizes available. You can create ads in as many of them as you like. However, when you're split testing, only compare CTRs among ads of the same size, otherwise you might delete an ad that "lost" only because it's a different shape.

Building image ads is as easy as you want it to be. Hire a graphic artist, use PhotoShop, or check out Google's Display Ad Builder. Laura Husmann designs our own banner ads and she turns out excellent work. Her website is www.BannerAd Queen.com and has examples of her work.

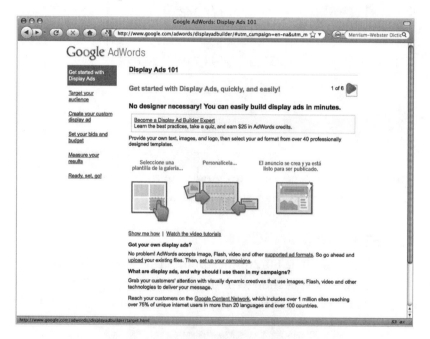

Add them in to your ad group. From the "Ads" tab in your AdWords interface, click on the "New ad" button and select "Image ad":

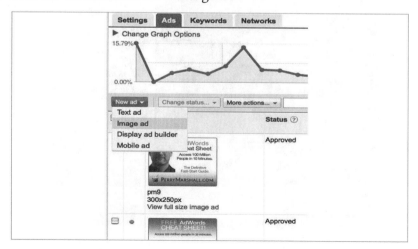

Upload your ad and wait. An editor will have to approve it.

YOU CAN CHOOSE WHERE TO SHOW YOUR IMAGE ADS

We've already told you about managed versus automatic placements on the content network (see Chapter 8).

Just note that Google's interface gives you special leverage with managed placements when image ads are involved. You set custom prices:

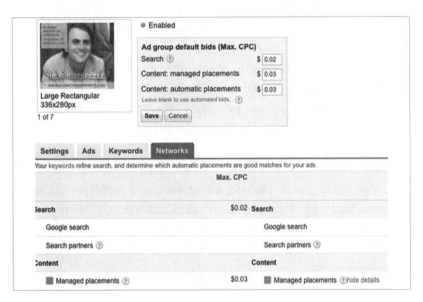

And of course you choose where to show:

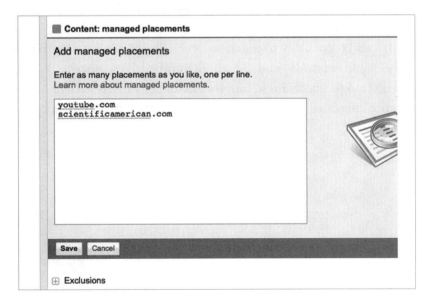

When you're running automatic placements, how does Google decide where to show your ads?

It's a process, not an event. Take a look at Chapter 8 and the Wonder Wheel concept, to see how Google does it.

A RARE FIND: A NEWBIE ADWORDS ADVERTISER READY TO DO IMAGE ADS

As I write this, I just finished an AdWords consultation earlier today with Paul, a sharp young advertiser who was eager to start from scratch with new campaigns promoting his self-help products on Google.

Every month that goes by we do scores of 1-on-1 phone consultations with AdWords users in every market imaginable. And one odd thing they all seem to share in common is that they virtually *never* ask us about image advertising on Google, despite the fact that this has been readily available to AdWords users for a good five years or more.

Paul was different. He hadn't turned on any traffic yet, but had three text ads already up and ready to go on Google, along with two handsome banner ads that promoted his landing page offer. He hadn't purchased a single Google click yet but knew he wanted to do content network advertising primarily, and to get as much traffic as possible from banner ads. He figured he could get banner ad clicks for less than he'd pay on text ads.

Good for him. He's right.

What I told Paul, I'm also telling you now: in so many established, competitive markets these days you're likely to find it *easier,* not harder, to cut out a patch of ground for yourself on the content network, than on Google search.

And Paul is also more likely to get clicks on his image ads for a tenth of the price as clicks on his regular text ads—and arguably a hundredth the price he'd pay for clicks on those ads on Google search. I told him that I look forward to seeing how this works for him, because I'm convinced he's going to be more than pleasantly surprised.

Uncle Claude Sez

Pictures in advertising are very expensive . . . . Anything expensive must be effective . . . .

Pictures should not be used merely because they are interesting, or to attract attention, or to decorate an ad. Ads are not written to interest, please, or amuse. You are writing on a serious subject—the subject of money spending.

Use pictures only to attract those who may profit you. Use them only when they form a better selling argument than the same amount of space set in type.

CHAPTER **10**

Local Advertising on Google: Mostly Virgin Territory

How Retailers, Restaurants, and Service Businesses Can Beat the Yellow Pages

Accoring to the Kelsey group, 60% of all internet searches are local. Some estimates run as high as 75%. But even if it was only 20%, that's still a *lot* of searches. Tens of millions a day, at least.

■ ■ ■

Whatever the number is, local search is undoubtedly the most untapped opportunity in Pay-per-click marketing. You want to sell weight loss plans, MP3 downloads, high definition TV's, or mortgages nationwide on Google? You can do it, but you'd better strap on your gladiator helmet and prepare for a fight.

But if you're an accountant, plumber, painter, repair shop, or podiatrist, it's an easy victory. In most local markets, your internet competitors have no idea what they're doing. Rarely will they read a book like this.

For example, my friend Bill is a minister who does weddings; he gets more business than he can handle bidding $0.50 on simple terms like "wedding officiant." His wedding officiant brethren aren't exactly the green berets of the marketing world.

This is also a great place to consult, setting up campaigns for neighboring businesses, because it's so underserved. Think about it:

- Hundreds of local businesses in your city spend upwards of $1,000 a month just on Yellow Pages ads—so these people are already spending money!
- The Yellow Pages reps are also selling internet Yellow Page listings, creating more awareness of online marketing. But they're not selling pay per click.
- Companies like Google are so busy dealing with existing opportunities, putting reps on the street to sell PPC to local businesses is a *long* way off at best. (There are rumors of partnerships with Yellow Pages companies though.)
- In categories where "mail order" is impossible and you *have* to get it locally, the clicks are *cheap*. For example right here in Chicago, there are only six ads showing for the keyword "Brake Shop" and one of them is eBay. Nickel clicks, anyone?
- Web savvy local advertisers are *very* rare, and this is not going to change any time soon. Running a retail store and running an online store are two entirely different things. So for local yokels, it's like I always say, "In the land of the blind, the man with one eye gets to be king."

If you can accept the fact that many keywords will only produce a few local clicks a month, the ROI on what you do get is extraordinary.

GOOGLE ADWORDS VS. OTHER LOCAL ONLINE SERVICES

My friend Glory the dentist got a call from the local phone company a few weeks back, offering her the chance to advertise her practice online. Shoppers in town, they told her, would jump on the internet looking for dentists in the area, and her name and contact information would show up when folks clicked through to look at their directory.

Here was the deal: the phone company charges $0.25 for every click, and then posts a special private phone number that web visitors can use to call her office. Her cost per call: $15.00.

Glory wanted to know what I thought. I said a smart marketer like her, using Google, can get new customers far cheaper than paying $0.25 per click *plus* $15 for every phone call she gets.

And when I opened up my computer and showed Glory how Google advertising works locally, we did a search on "dentists" and, sure enough, there appeared the local phone company's Google ad (!) right up top:

Dentists & Dental Offices
Find a dentist here in town in
your online XYZ Yellow Pages
www.XYZYellowPages.com

In other words, they're buying clicks from Google wholesale, sending them to their directory, and selling those second clicks to dentists retail. Not to mention the extra $15 Glory would have to pay per phone call.

Sound like a good deal to you?

Didn't think so.

Now any advertising is a good deal if it brings you new customers at an acceptable ROI. You shouldn't reject an "acceptable" ROI from ad media B even if you get "extraordinary" ROI from ad media A. Still, Glory can bring local customers to her dental practice without having to go through the phone company's system.

She can buy clicks for the same price as the phone company—probably less—and take people directly to her own site rather than a directory where she's one of a dozen other listings.

She can put up a sensibly designed direct-response website that turns visitors into phone calls and appointments, *without* having to pay $15 for every call!

> A giant fraction of Google searches are local. Advertise your business locally, and you'll get traffic and customers for a fraction of the cost of other media. This may sometimes reach more people than Yellow Pages ads; it's more traceable than billboards; and it costs you less than mailings and fliers.

The fact that a service is charging some dentists $15.00 a call should tell you something. Heck, maybe you should start a service like this and only charge $10.00.

Google uses IP addresses and other clever technologies to figure out where people are when they search, and it serves up local ads. (Its targeting seems to be pretty accurate, too.)

Local Google is perfect if you're in any of these markets:

Real estate	Beauty salons	Heating / Plumbing /
Hotels	Telephone service	Electricity
Private investigators	Attorneys	Landscaping
Wedding planners	Bid auctions	Doctors
Storage	Cars & trucks	Counselors
Home furnishing	Printing	Restaurants
Dentists	Construction	Clothing
Churches	Movers	Photographers
Hospitals	Funeral planning	

YOU'RE REACHING TWO KINDS OF PEOPLE, NOT JUST ONE

It seems like we give the following advice to real estate people the most, but the idea applies in a lot of places. There are *two* kinds of people looking for your business:

1. A person who lives in your area—your city, your state—who types in "real estate" or "dentist" or "churches" or "restaurant," and expects that the results he sees will be area-only. You'll be there when he comes looking for you.

2. A person may not be in your area at all (or else Google's system can't tell where he is) but is still asking for your area's services. He goes to Google and types in "movers in Palo Alto" or "Palo Alto real estate" or "hotels Palo Alto," hoping to get Palo-Alto-only results. He may be traveling on holiday; he may be planning a move; he may be an investor.

He may in fact be from Palo Alto. But he could be down in San Diego. Or way out in Orlando. Or in Montreal. Or Sydney, or Tokyo. But he's still searching on Google for you, and he identifies Palo Alto by name.

Either way, you want to be there, ready to open the door when he comes knocking.

HOW TO REACH THE FIRST PERSON

Because you're aiming at these two kinds of people, you can set up *two* Google campaigns for them, not just one.

So here's how. When you're first setting up your campaign, choose your country, then choose your state/province or even a city or group of cities:

```
Campaign settings

General

        Campaign name

Audience

        Locations  ⑦   In what geographical locations do you want your ads to appear?
                        ○ Bundle: All countries and territories
                        ● Bundle: United States; Canada
                        ○ Country: United States
                        ○ State:
                        ○ Metro area:
                        ○ City:
                        Select one or more other locations

                        You can show additional location information with your ads. After you've created you
                        location information to the campaign.

        Languages  ⑦   What languages do your customers speak?
                        English   Edit

⊕ Demographic (advanced)
```

From this point forward, everything else you do in this campaign is the same as is described in the rest of the book, but your ads will only be seen in the local area you choose.

HOW TO REACH THE SECOND PERSON

(Warning—This Cuts a Huge Amount Off Your Bid Prices, and Google May, Uh, Prefer That You Not Know This)

If you were advertising for real estate in California, you'd set up a *nationwide* campaign—possibly even an international campaign—but with local terms like "Visalia real estate" and "Yorba Linda real estate." After all, there are likely people from all over the country—and maybe even outside the country—who are doing searches on these terms.

So you'd grab a map or a listing of cities from a website and create a keyword set like this:

California real estate
LA real estate
Healdsburg real estate
Villa Real real estate
Santa Monica real estate
Buy homes California
Buy homes San Francisco
Buy homes Bakersfield
Buy homes Sausalito

To do this the best way you would combine a large list of general keywords (the same ones you used on the regionally targeted campaign) with a large list of cities and towns, and then use a spreadsheet to mix and match them together.

Either way, you'll end up with a huge keyword list; 95% of them will never get searches, and the other 5% may only get a few. However, it doesn't cost anything to bid on these keywords if nobody clicks, and when people do click, they'll only be five or ten cents. Not much traffic, but what you do get will be bargain priced.

You should still buy generic keywords in your local campaign, but these local keywords in a nationwide campaign will bring very cheap clicks, mostly.

Your real estate Google account would be arranged like this:

Campaign #1: California Targeting Only
Group 1: Real estate
Group 2: Buy homes

Campaign #2: National Targeting—entire USA
Group 1: California real estate
Group 2: Buy homes California

Now you have both bases covered, and you'll be getting as much traffic as possible for your local market. The key is that you're not leaving out people in other geographic locations who are seriously looking for what you offer.

Under the geo-targeting tool's "Custom" tab you can also use your business's address or latitude and longitude, and target all searches within a radius that you select. Google even gives you the advanced option of choosing your own customized set of coordinates that you want to target.

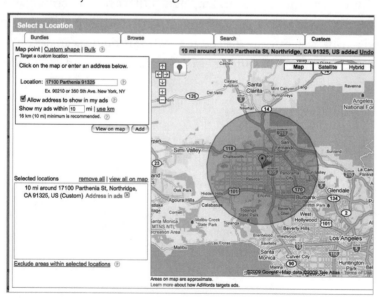

HONE YOUR CHOPS ON A LOCAL TEST CAMPAIGN BEFORE YOU GO NATIONAL

Age-old advertising practice is to test ideas in a smaller market before you spend big bucks to try them out in a larger one. Nowadays the risks of going national instantly if you have a good product may seem small—since, after all, you're paying for one click at a time and you can set a daily budget and turn your traffic on and off at will. But that doesn't undo the value of trying your product in one small geographic area first.

For example, if you sell advice to investors, you might start just with investors in New York State. The advantage? You don't need to worry nearly as much about your daily budget.

If your cash reserves are limited, you can choose this smaller market to start off in, and if in the first few weeks or months it's not profitable, you're not forced to shut the entire thing down for fear of going quickly bankrupt. Make the sales process profitable in a smaller market, and then go national.

At that point you're able to take on the big boys in the worldwide market because you know that the mechanism works like clockwork in the small market, and every dollar you send out comes back with more dollars attached.

(Oh—this is also an excellent way to keep competitors from knowing what you're up to, if they don't live in the cities you're targeting.)

HOW TO OFFER A SERVICE LOCALLY, BUT A PRODUCT NATIONALLY

Entrepreneur Frank Pasquale is a designer of handmade custom electric guitars. These are not the el cheapo variety you buy off the shelf at Wal-Mart. No. These are quality, handcrafted instruments that can sell for several thousand dollars apiece.

Frank lives in the remote suburban-Chicago village of Hampshire and his custom clients are always local, since for him any one project involves personal visits, selecting woods, looking over neck types and paint samples, and giving ongoing feedback about the product as he assembles and fine-tunes it.

But Frank uses Google to find his customers. He reaches musicians in Chicagoland who are doing general online searches for custom guitars, along with anyone around the country who may on occasion search specifically for guitar builders in the Chicago area.

Frank is in the process now of taking his local skill and spreading his knowledge literally around the world. That's the next step for him as his custom-work business gets off the ground. He'll be writing an e-book about custom guitar design, and he can sell it any place on planet Earth where people are searching and interested.

And this is not just an information business, either.

You can run your business locally, and at the same time make money teaching people worldwide how to do exactly what you do. And again and again you'll discover that they turn right back around and pay you to do it for them. After all, you're the professional. Your book proves it.

In Frank's case, people will buy his kit, and then turn around and hire him to design their guitar for them.

Which means this is going to generate customers and orders for Frank Pasquale's handiwork from around the country, and possibly even around the world—not just Chicago—as he instills in readers the confidence that *he knows custom guitars.*

Sometimes it's easier just to pay the expert to do the job than to try and do it yourself.

The next thing Frank may do is use his credibility from his book to hire and train apprentices to design custom electric guitars themselves. Frank can then send them out to do their own work, and he can set up and manage their local Google campaigns for them for a fee—which then, like his own ad campaigns, will run on autopilot.

You can take this business model and replicate it many times over!

Uncle Claude Sez

We usually start with local advertising, even if magazine advertising is best adapted to the article. We get our distribution town by town, then change to national advertising.

Whether you advertise few or many dealers, the others will stock in very short order if the advertising is successful.

CHAPTER 11

Slashing Your Bid Prices: How Google Rewards You for Relevance

"Which One Do You Think Will Get Us to the Martinis Faster?"

My friend and mentor Dan Kennedy was in a conversation over cocktails with an ad agency exec. The discussion was about two different ads that were each scheduled to run in a national magazine.

■ ■ ■

One was the classic, old-school formula with a compelling headline and dense, carefully-worded body text followed by a call to action and a clip-out coupon to be mailed in.

The other was the ultra-modern, ultra-sleek gigantic full-page ad with the irrelevant photograph and blurb at the bottom in tiny, whittled-down, vague text about how hip XYZ Company was. The usual ad agency fluff.

Dan pointed to the old-school ad and explained to the ad exec that it had been run before and was carefully tested and tweaked for maximum response, and was virtually guaranteed to make the client's phone ring. "How would you like to run this one against your corporate-style ad and see which one got more sales?" he asked. "What would your client think?"

The ad guy chuckled. "To be perfectly honest with you, Dan, I could run either one. Makes no difference to me. But if I have the choice of showing one or the other to the CEO, which one do you think is going to get us to the martinis faster?"

Glitz and puffery is the secret sauce in most ad agencies. The goal is not ROI or to make the client's phone ring. The goal most certainly is not to be relevant.

The object in an old-school ad agency is to goose the CEO's ego, get invited out for drinks, and get the guy to invite you back and write you another round of checks next month.

IT AIN'T HIS NECK UNDER THE GUILLOTINE BLADE

When you're the person laying out the cash yourself and it's *your own* business and *your own* risk and *your own* credit card that Google is dinging every month, you don't have time for your own ego stroking. Your customers don't have the patience for it either.

Nowhere is this more clear than in Google AdWords. Putting your own money on the line has a funny way of wising us up to what gets clicks and what doesn't.

> People are drawn to you when you're relevant. The formula for success on Google is relevance. When you're relevant, people will click on your ads, Google will explicitly reward you for it, your costs will drop, and your profits will grow.

HERE'S HOW GOOGLE REWARDS YOU FOR RELEVANCE

Traditionally, you get higher positions on the search page by bidding more. But when your clickthrough rate goes up, Google actually gives you better positioning without charging you more per click. It rewards you for being relevant.

Roughly speaking, the first position has always been given to the highest bidder. But Google has long maintained an ingenious little twist. Here's a simplified version of its formula:

Your Relative Position = (Your Bid Price) x (Your Clickthrough Rate)

The fuller version of Google's formula is your bid price multiplied by your Quality Score. More on the Quality Score later. Either way, in this case your CTR swings the biggest difference apart from the price you bid.

Which CTR, exactly? *The CTR of your individual keywords as they perform on Google alone,* not the total CTR of your ad groups, or the CTR of any of your ads; and not the CTR of your ads as they're performing on Google's search partner sites or AdSense.

If you have a high clickthrough rate, then you don't have to bid as much for the position. Example: I bid $1.00 and my ad gets a CTR of 1%. Your ad gets a CTR of 2%. You can get the same average position as me by bidding $0.50. If you bid $0.51 then you'll get the position above me.

If you're already in top position, Google will automatically charge you a lower bid price as your CTR improves. Not bad.

This really works. Our customers who buy our regular online book (www.PerryMarshall.com/adwords) tell us this all the time:

> *Before I purchased your program, I was averaging about 50 clicks a day, paying at least 25 cents each for them. But after implementing your strategies: 402 Clicks, average cost per click of 14 cents, average position of 3.3 with my ads. My traffic is much more targeted, so my conversion rate almost doubled. I don't think my first impression of Santa Claus was this good!*
>
> —Michael Mettie, Simple Streams, The Colony, TX

> *My name is Andres Cordova and I've been doing Internet Marketing for a little over 4 months now and I just have to say that your Definitive Guide to AdWords has been the best course I've bought because it has allowed me to spend a fraction of what I used to pay and get more than 5x the visitors for less money. And I particularly love your newsletter, it's always filled with quality content.*
>
> —Andres Cordova, Salinas CA

This isn't magic, even though it looks like magic. Our customers are just writing straightforward, relevant ads, and their cost per click is going down.

That's what will happen to you. It means you're coughing up less money to Google every month, and you're putting more in your own pocket every day.

WHAT IS "QUALITY SCORE," AND WHAT DOES IT HAVE TO DO WITH BEING RELEVANT?

AdWords ads are little salesmen. And you know as well as I do that you rarely get straight, unfiltered info from a salesman. It's even worse when the website it takes you to doesn't give you what it promised.

Google knows this, too. It knows its users are cynical about their sponsored ads. But it also knows that if it can slowly alter this trend by ensuring better websites after you click, more people will trust their paid ads, and click them.

Google won the first round of the search engine wars by making its organic searches more relevant than anyone else's. The owners became billionaires in the second round because their CTR-based ranking system made their pay-per-click ads more relevant than anyone else's. Far better user interface, too.

And they continue to kick the other engines' butts in the third round by having their paid ads send users to more relevant, higher-quality *websites* than anyone else's.

In summer 2005 Google introduced the idea of *Quality Score,* where it gave each of your keywords a secret Google-only-knows ranking based on how well your ad copy matched your keywords.

If your Quality Score was low, you were then forced to pay a high minimum bid of $1.00 and sometimes more, otherwise your ads wouldn't show.

Then a year later the burners got turned up higher: In July 2006 Google issued its first major "slap": your keywords' Quality Score was now based on keyword-to-ad-text relevance *and* landing page relevance both.

If your ad and website were not up to snuff, Google would deactivate your keywords, and require a minimum bid of $5.00, $10.00, and more in order to get your ads to show again.

Since then Google has updated and revised the Quality Score algorithm numerous times. It seems to grow ever more complex and unpredictable by the day. Nowadays it doesn't make your keywords "inactive" per se; instead it names a minimum bid that you have to pay in order, it claims, to show on the first page of search results.

But let's start with some fundamentals. Google's biggest penalty comes when you don't have a good website to send people to in the first place.

More often than not, until you pay that minimum bid, or fix your Quality Score, you'll show on page one of results, but only a tiny fraction of the time.

HOW DO YOU DIAGNOSE AND UNTANGLE THIS HAIRY PROBLEM OF QUALITY SCORE?

First off, if your keywords have been slapped with a "poor" Quality Score and Google is demanding bids from $0.10 to $2.00 to show fully on page one, start by seeing if you've got a mismatch between your keywords and your ad. If that's the problem, do Peel & Stick as we teach.

Here's an example of how this looks when done right:

If Google is demanding higher-dollar bids, such as $5.00, $10.00, and more, go dig into your website for answers.

Google used to penalize incompetent advertisers by *disabling* their keywords and not letting them show ads. Markets all across the spectrum became more and more competitive, and the players who couldn't write relevant ads and match them with keywords bombed out and got disabled, permanently.

And as the rains descended and the floods came, the incompetent advertisers would bang on the outside door of the Google ark begging to be allowed to pay more, to do anything at all just to get back in the game.

Since Google now has Wall Street to please, and with enough advertisers demanding to pay more, the decision makers in Mountain View got wise and said yes. Which now means you're free to run perfectly irrelevant, utterly ineffective ads and ad groups through Google. It'll just charge you 10X as much to do it.

"GOOGLE IS REQUIRING $10.00 EACH FOR MY CLICKS, TO SHOW UP ON THE FIRST PAGE. WHAT DO I DO?"

First, check your mind-set. No more "get people to my cheapo one-page site and force them to sign up." Now you have to give people content, or you won't be doing *any* business on Google.

Google tells you your Quality Score, ranked at one of three levels: Poor, OK, and Great. To see your Quality Score, click on "Customize Columns" link under the "Filter and views" dropdown menu and check the "Qual. Score" box:

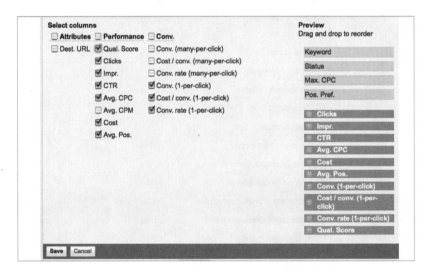

Along with that, in the "Status" column Google tells you if you're below its "first page bid." If you are in fact below it, then it's either 1) showing you on the first page of search results, but only a fraction of the time, or it's 2) showing you on pages 2, 3, and lower.

Either way, the goal is now no longer to get people to take action or leave. Instead it's to get people to stay there longer. Ways that do include:

· Avoid opt-in-only squeeze pages that force people to sign up or leave.
· Turn teaser bullets into paragraphs with information.
· Have an e-mail series? Put it on your site and make every installment of it accessible by links without signing in.

· Put up a sitemap that links to every relevant public page on your site.
· Post articles. Put the kids to bed, promise your wife you'll make up the quality time, and go lock yourself in your study and start writing articles and content like a banshee.
· Start a blog.
· Link to other good sites.
· Start learning the bare rudiments of search engine optimization (SEO). We highly recommend getting on the list of the folks at Planet Ocean (www.SearchEngineHelp.com). Also, see our chapter on SEO by Stephen Mahaney later on in this book.

MORE ON FINDING, DIAGNOSING, AND FIXING QUALITY SCORE

First, you want to know exactly what your Quality Score is. You can set your interface to show your Quality Score (see the screenshot earlier in this chapter), but you also want to know the actual 1–10 number grade that Google is giving each of your keywords.

Do that by mousing over the magnifying glass next to your keyword. It will give you some key details, and you can click through to see even more:

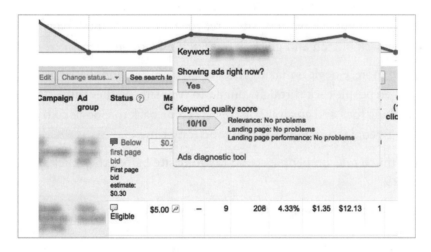

By the way, when you get a "bid is below first-page estimate" note, that does not necessarily mean that your Quality Score is low. I've found keywords with "great" Quality Scores (8/10 and better) where Google still tells me that I'm below a first-page bid. That's Google warning you of tough competition.

But of course I couldn't know that without getting the actual Quality Score number for myself.

Keywords slapped as "poor" (in the 1–3/10 range) usually, not always, call for major fundamental revamping of a whole website and sales process. "OK" keywords (4–7/10) can often get better quality scores by doing a better job of matching keywords to ads. This is not hard and fast, though, and you'll need to explore all the possibilities with your site, yourself.

Putting your keyword in the headline of your ad, however, is the best place to start. As we've been telling you.

Google's slaps are based on a series of factors, some of them sounding more like SEO than just simple pay-per-click. Here's a beginner checklist that you can start with to help diagnose what's causing your low Quality Score:

- Does the slapped keyword match your ad perfectly? Does it show up in the headline of the ad?
- Is your landing page clearly about that keyword, and is the keyword used repeatedly on the landing page?

Of course, you want Google to conclude that the entire *site* is about your keyword's topic as well. That yours is the best site people could go to in order to learn about the topic:

- Does your landing page link to other pages on your site (and other good quality sites) that are about that keyword as well?
- How *many* people leave your site after they hit your landing page? How many hit the back button and go back to search on Google?

More and more, Google is making its Quality Score decisions based on actual users' behavior. When people click through your ad to your site, do they think, "No, this isn't what I'm looking for," and go away? disappear? come back to Google to try again?

You want people to stay, and stay a good long time:

- How much *time* do people spend on your site before they click back or click away?

Great, interesting content is the best way to get people to arrive and stay put. Blogs, online calculators, audios, videos, and other "involvement devices" will keep people around longer. Do whatever you need to in order to keep people there in larger numbers and for longer times.

ACTING ALL UPPITY WON'T EARN YOU A PENNY MORE

Do you like to see impressive, amazing things? Do you like to see jaw dropping, astonishing situations and events?

Of course you do. Everybody does. And it only costs $10.00. That's right, for $10.00 you can go to a movie theatre and watch Jet Li or Denzel Washington or Angelina Jolie deliver two solid hours of stunning imagery, special effects, action, and thrills, splashed across the big screen in blazing color and Dolby Surround. And these days, with a few thousand dollars of audio-video equipment, you can see the same thing, maybe better, at home.

Yes, people like to be wowed and impressed; Hollywood thinks nothing of spending $100 million on a picture so they can give the people exactly that. And they do a great job of it.

But one of the worst things you can do is deliberately try to impress your customers. Why? Because when you try to impress instead of building trust, educating, and persuading, your would-be customer shuts you off. His guard goes up and he stops listening to you.

Help him solve problems and capitalize on new opportunities, however, and he's yours for life.

Most businesses these days are trying hard to impress. But impressing people never makes a positive contribution to customers' needs. Nobody cares how many billions of dollars of assets some company has.

Your customers would much rather know that you'll go to the mat for them when there's a problem. They'd much rather know that you're there to help them.

Your customers want to be spoken and written to in a conversational, layman's tone of voice that strives to build trust, educate, and persuade them, rather than dazzle and impress them.

This is why the best of the best Google ads are never the ones that jump off the page and knock you over. The ones that get the most clicks are simple, engaging, straightforward, and honest, and they speak in a voice that their unique market recognizes and understands.

If you want CEOs to buy you martinis, New York ad agencies might be just your thing. If you want to stand tough against your competitors and sell to customers who trust you, just be relevant.

Uncle Claude Sez

Ads are not written to entertain. When they do, those entertainment seekers are little likely to be the people whom you want.

That is one of the greatest advertising faults. Ad writers . . . forget they are salesmen and try to be performers. Instead of sales, they seek applause.

When you plan or prepare an advertisement, keep before you a typical buyer. Your subject, your headline has gained his or her attention. Then in everything be guided by what you would do if you met the buyer face-to-face.

Don't try to be amusing. Don't boast, for all people resent it. Don't try to show off. Do just what you think a good salesman should do . . . .

CHAPTER 12

The Most-Ignored Secret Behind the Most Profitable Marketing Campaigns in the World

This could be the most important chapter in the whole book.

Because this is the ingredient in marketing that trumps all others.

■ ■ ■

With this ingredient, *everything* in marketing gets easy.

Without it, people wander around in an aimless stupor for years.

What's this "thing," this magic ingredient?

It's having a good answer to the following question:

Why should I do business with you, instead of any and every other option available to me, including the option of doing absolutely nothing at all?

Another way of asking the same question is:

What do you uniquely guarantee?

When you have a really powerful answer to these two questions, your ads practically write themselves. When you have a really powerful answer to these questions, people will line up to buy from you.

When your business possesses a simple, unmistakable mission, it stands out in an age of obfuscated marketing messages and Byzantine corporatespeak.

Your answer to this question is your *Unique Selling Proposition.* A statement of value that's so clear and focused it's almost impossible to *mis*-understand it.

Less is more. Your business will grow, the world will sit up and take notice, and even your Google ads will write themselves, when you stand out from the crowd with a clear, simple, and utterly unique message.

WHAT IS A USP?

Your USP is that one thing special about you that your customer can't find anyplace else. It's your *unique selling proposition.* It's what you bring to the table that no other business does, or even can.

Your USP is about the uniqueness of your product, and it's more than that. It's your whole argument not only for just your product but also its accompanying services, why it's necessary in the first place, and the timing of getting the product and seeing your problem solved now, rather than later.

A lot of the difficulties people have with Google come not from doing Google AdWords wrong per se, but that their USP isn't clear or maybe isn't even unique in the first place.

If you have this right up front, everything from the keywords and ads to the price of your product—all that falls into place.

How to Identify Your USP

Your first step is to answer these four questions:

1. Why should I read or listen to you?
2. Why should I believe what you have to say?
3. Why should I do anything about what you're offering?
4. Why should I act now?

In fact, these questions create a powerful guideline for what to include in your Google ad *and* on your web page when folks click through. Answer them, and you've taken your message and made it that much more compelling.

We've all fallen on our faces attempting to be all things to all people. *You can't please everybody.* If your purpose is murky and if your sense of identity is vague, it confuses your customers and robs you of time and energy.

Perhaps the most famous USP of all is from Domino's Pizza:

Fresh, hot pizza delivered to your door in 30 minutes or less, guaranteed.

This isn't unique now, but in the early days of Domino's it most definitely was. A multi-billion dollar business was built from this very unique, simple statement of value.

Just look at what a focused USP does in streamlining the daily Domino's work routine:

- *Fresh.* They don't have to keep freezers full of prepared inventory. They keep all of the needed ingredients on hand, along with adequate staff to prepare the orders. They don't even claim that the pizza tastes good!
- *Hot.* They keep a disciplined time schedule, getting the pizzas into the oven in time with orders that come in. They keep the right containers on hand and the delivery guys make sure the pizzas are well packed.
- *Pizza.* No spaghetti. No lasagna. No fine wines. No burgers.
- *Delivered.* This isn't an eat-in joint. No servers or extra busboys, no extra chairs or tables.
- *In 30 minutes or less.* Everyone works fast.
- *Guaranteed.* When the customer hears this he sits up and pays attention. And the manager has financial incentive to keep the operation moving.

When you have this message defined and focused, it will *liberate* you. You become the specialist. People ask you to solve problems that you're not geared to deal with, and you simply refer them elsewhere. Nobody expects you to be an expert on anything other than your one niche.

You can certainly expand into other areas, and many businesses have multiple USPs. Every product in a retail store has its own USP. But in each case it needs to be unique and it needs to be clear.

A good USP will fit in a Google ad—or at least the most important part of it will. Here's an ad that turned up on a search for "pizza delivery":

1-800 PIES 2 GO
Great Pizza Delivered to your Door
Free call Fast Delivery Great Pizza
www.1-800Pies2Go.com

SAY IT IN JUST ONE SENTENCE: YOUR ELEVATOR SPEECH

You'll arrest the rabid interest of people in seconds with a good USP. When a guy asks you in the elevator what you do, and you've got fourteen seconds before you get off at the next floor, this is your answer. It's your "elevator speech." Craft it right, and the guy will probably perk up and ask for your business card and website.

Here are some great examples:

> **I sell the world's best comprehensive health insurance plan
> to businesses with ten employees or less.**

Google ad:

> ### Health Insurance
> Comprehensive Health Plans for
> Businesses with 10 Employees or Less
> www.SmallBizHealthInsurance.com/10

> **I help high-tech companies grow sales and eliminate waste
> with highly targeted web traffic, marketing, and publicity.**

> ### Generate Leads
> Make Customers Call You First
> Don't Sell Harder—Market Smarter
> www.PerryMarshall.com

> ### B2B Guerilla Marketing
> Eliminate Cold Calls & Ad Waste
> Instant Web Traffic & Free Publicity
> www.PerryMarshall.com

> **I teach you how to find the love of your life in 90 days or less.**

> ### Find Love in 90 Days
> Discover Your True Love & Life Partner.
> Based On 30 Years of Research.
> www.90DayMatch.com

Imagine how people will take notice of you when you have a quick answer like that. We're all drawn to a simple, clearly defined, gutsy message. Hammer out your own, and you've got a verbal business card that's irresistible.

YOUR USP MAKES A GREAT GOOGLE AD

Last summer I went searching for a solution to my increasingly slow computer. I typed "my computer is slow" into Google, and this surprising ad popped up:

> ### Slow Computer?
> The Problem is Registry Errors.
> Scan Your PC Now—Free Trial
> www.RegistryFix.com

Registry errors are a common problem with Windows. Software that repairs these errors is available all over the place. But no advertisers that I've seen are as clear and gutsy as the guy who wrote this simple ad.

It got my attention. So I clicked. As did thousands of others.

This advertiser sells software to fix registry errors. That's it. The diagnosis is uncomplicated, the offer is compelling—a free and quick, no-obligation registry scan—and the result is a faster computer.

Can't beat that for clarity.

Can you take your message and whittle it down to one short sentence, enough to fit in a Google ad? Can you restate your USP to diagnose a problem, and position yourself as the solution? It's amazing to us how many advertisers could, but don't.

Be different. You'll get the clicks.

BIG ASS. BIG-ASS FANS.
HOW TO BUILD AN UNFORGETTABLE PERSONALITY
AROUND YOUR USP

It was one of the funniest ads I've ever seen.

The naked truth? It could easily be knocked off. But the company gets love letters. It gets hate mail. And all the while Bill Buell and company have created a product with broad appeal and an incredibly unique identity in the marketplace. This is their amazing story.

HVLS, Inc., of Lexington, Kentucky, builds large, slow moving fans for giant spaces like warehouses, dairies, and factories. Its initials stand for *high volume, low speed*. But it's not known to most people as HVLS. Most folks know it as Big Ass Fans. And it's taking its world by storm with some of the savviest guerilla marketing we've ever seen.

You read it right—it sells fans. Great big ones. Fans with blades literally wider than your house. Factory-sized fans, fans that take your breath away.

But Big Ass Fans' marketing is not just "cute." HVLS's growth is literally in the *triple digits*. In a lousy economy where titans like Allen-Bradley and ABB are having their worst stretch in decades, Big Ass Fans is rising like a rocket.

This isn't a terribly exciting product. It's not a magic portable DVD player. It's not some satellite receiver with built-in GPS. It's just a fan.

But Bill Buell has created a personality around this product so powerful that it grabs people's attention immediately and *catapults* his advertising effectiveness into the stratosphere. Big Ass Fans is now a permanently recognizable brand.

More importantly, there's a real economic argument here.

Let's say you've got a warehouse equipped with a standard fan, circulating air at 10,000 cfm (cubic feet per minute). Run it for one hour and it would cost you 5.6 cents.

But suppose that you needed to circulate 125,000 cfm of air—13 times that amount. Using 13 standard fans would cost you $0.75 an hour. Run those for 24 hours and you've got a one-day electric bill of $18.00.

But run just one Big Ass Fan, and you'll circulate the same amount of air and do it for $0.88 a day. Sound like a good deal?

Here's how it breaks down over time:

	1 Day	1 Week	1 Month	1 Year
13 Standard Fans	$18.00	$126.00	$540.00	$6,570.00
1 Big Ass Fan	$0.88	$6.16	$29.12	$321.00

This is now part of Big Ass Fans' USP. It doesn't just shock you into buying its product. It *proves* that this is an investment.

The question now becomes, can your warehouse afford *not* to put in a Big Ass Fan?

In Bill Buell's industry, folks think it's a crime to stand out, to look different, conspicuous. Advertisers in industry magazines and trade journals work hard to keep their own ads looking just like everyone else's ads.

Which, of course, is marketing suicide.

We talked with Bill on the phone about this very question. "Most folks look at my ad," he explained, "and they think to themselves, 'Whoa—if I wrote ads like that, they would look totally different from everyone else's.'" Bill's reaction? *"Of course* your ads should look different from everyone else's. How else will they get noticed? That's the whole *point!"*

Want to dominate your market? Take your USP, add some serious chutzpah, and give it an unforgettable delivery.

WHY A GOOD USP MAY SAVE YOUR LIFE, LITERALLY

In her landmark book *Nickeled and Dimed: On (Not) Getting By in America*, daring journalist Barbara Ehrenreich tells of a risky personal experiment she undertook: abandoning her city, her identity, her education, and professional qualifications for three months, she attempted to live on $6.00 per hour working as a Wal-Mart employee, waitress, and maid in an unfamiliar city.

Ehrenreich discovered how it's barely possible to survive on those wages. She had to work two jobs, she constantly lived on the verge of homelessness, with no insurance and no safety net. And, not surprisingly, she was treated with little respect. She experienced the worst of everything.

While Ehrenreich has shown great insight into the daily grind of America's "working poor," she has offered little in the way of answers or solutions, other than a poignant appreciation of the hard-working waitress who pours your coffee at Denny's, and the goodness of leaving a generous tip.

You see, here's the real problem:

How is it that a person can go to school for 13 years, graduate with a diploma, and be qualified for nothing more than waiting tables or stocking shelves at Wal-Mart? Is $6.00 an hour all the value that a person gets from a modern high school education?

Sadly, that seems to be the case. There is a missing ingredient, however.

If you have a USP to offer the world, you're not a commodity any more. The book *Nickeled and Dimed* is not just about low wages, but about being a commodity. One hundred twenty-five pounds of "human capital." An awful state to live in.

One of Ehrenreich's jobs was working as a maid. In that industry if you want to be a bona fide cleaner of homes or businesses you have to get bonded, and there are a number of hurdles you have to overcome. But what would prevent that same person from creating a clever USP, printing up a compelling flier, distributing it, and getting five or six families to employ her directly—for $20 per hour instead of $7—without having to go through the official hurdles?

It's a free country, after all.

Aristotle Onassis once said, "The secret of business is to know something that nobody else knows." Don't let yourself become a commodity. Discover how to do something valuable that few others can do. That's not something you learn in a classroom of 30 kids. And the funny thing is, while you *will* learn that in a marketing seminar, unlike a traditional education nobody can give you your answer, your USP, on a platter. Your challenge is to identify it for yourself.

The lesson in all of this? The concept of a *unique selling proposition* is not merely a marketing technique, but in fact is a fundamental life skill, an essential ingredient in all human endeavors. It's as important as Reading, Writing, and 'Rithmetic.

And it's your ticket out of the rat race.

Uncle Claude Sez

A person who desires to make an impression must stand out in some way. Being eccentric, being abnormal is not a distinction to covet. But doing admirable things in a different way gives one a great advantage. So with salesmen, in person or in print . . . .

There is refreshing uniqueness, which enhances, which we welcome and remember. Fortunate is the salesman who has it.

CHAPTER 13

Converting Visitors to Buyers
The Single Biggest Website Mistake Marketers Make

We got an e-mail with the following rant:

Why can't people just give me what I want?

I went searching for "hedge funds" yesterday. Only one of the AdWords ads had that exact phrase in it (only one—imagine that!) so I clicked. The ad had made it look like I would get some very clear directives on how to learn more.

But no. The ad took me to some stupid corporate homepage, which had no hedge fund information whatsoever. I went clicking everywhere around the site. Still nothing. I finally gave up and went and did something else.

I want to know *more about hedge funds*! For crying out loud, I'm ready to pay money to learn this stuff. Why can't these corporate idiot web designers figure that out?

■ ■ ■

This is so common it's not funny. If millions of people are searching for what I've got, why would I set up a site, buy clicks, and then not give them exactly what they're looking for?

Maybe those hedge fund experts figure that guys surfing the web will just call them on the phone. *Wrong!* They could have given him what he was looking for *and* collected his contact information and stayed in touch with him for months afterward. He was ready to do business.

They weren't.

So he left, money in hand.

> The internet is instantaneous: give people what they want the instant they crave it. Otherwise they'll spend their money with your competitor.

When your AdWords ad leads perfectly to a landing page that gives people what they want and provokes action, you've got a winning ad campaign. It's a very simple formula.

BRYAN TODD

For example, I have a book that I sell online that teaches people how to master Mandarin Chinese more quickly. It's ideal for folks living in mainland China or Taiwan. So I post this Google ad:

Want to Learn Chinese?
5 Crucial Principles You Must Know
To Master Chinese, and Fast
MasterChineseFaster.com

. . . which takes people to this landing page where they can read about my five-day course that teaches these five principles. And they can sign up right there:

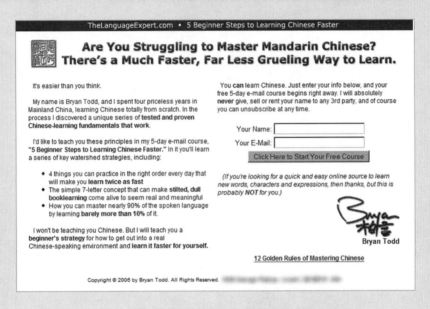

On many days a 30% signup rate for my e-course is not uncommon.

This principle works again and again, no matter what your market. Tell people exactly what you're going to give them, and deliver immediately.

Uncle Claude Sez

The advertising man studies the consumer. He tries to place himself in the position of the buyer. His success largely depends on doing that to the exclusion of everything else.

CHAPTER 14

How E-Mail Transforms Those Expensive Clicks into Long-Term, Profitable Customers

N o discussion about Google AdWords would be complete if I didn't show you how to turn that expensive one-millisecond click into a long-term relationship. When someone clicks on your ad, Google charges you $0.50 regardless of what happens next. If the guy leaves after five seconds, he's gone, and you'll probably never get him back without paying *again*.

■ ■ ■

Fifty cents for five seconds of someone's attention—dang, that's $600.00 an hour! Kind of depressing if you look at it that way.

On the other hand, if that person gives you their e-mail address, you can communicate with them on a regular basis for little or no cost.

If you're trying to sell a $1,000 product, which is easier to get from your prospects—a $1,000 order or their e-mail address?

The more complex your sales process, the more important it is to break it up into bite-sized steps. Which is why, the main Google AdWords page at www.perrymarshall.com/google is an e-mail opt-in page:

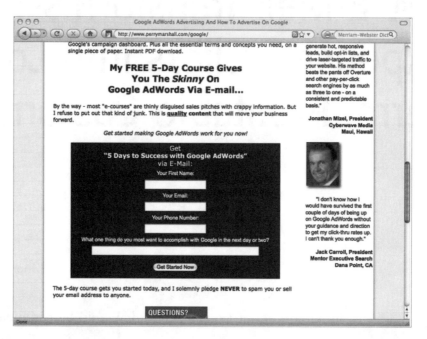

Visitors can either opt-in or leave. I figure if a person's really interested in Google AdWords—i.e., likely to buy my *Definitive Guide to Google AdWords*—they'll at least give their e-mail address first.

This is better than only getting e-mail addresses from people who buy the book on the first visit. And it's better than having only one shot at selling them our services.

HOW TO PUT PERSONALITY AND PIZZAZZ INTO YOUR E-MAIL MARKETING

In a day when much of the manufacturing industry is downsizing, cutting management, laying off employees right and left, and moving in a panic to India and China, B&B Electronics in Ottawa, Illinois, is knocking over growth records right and left.

They're hiring more staff to handle their growing number of incoming catalog orders and mounting list of willing buyers.

Most people would never think to utter the phrase "infectious personality" and "electronics manufacturing company" in the same breath, but B&B is both.

They refuse to surrender to the dull, corporate geek stereotype. Instead they have loads of fun with it. B&B regularly courts their growing customer list's inboxes with witty, lively messages that celebrate the stale, geek image of the Dilbert-cubicle engineer. Marketing director Mike Fahrion graces customers with his regular "Mike's Politically Incorrect Newsletter" rant column.

A techie's girlfriend recently wrote B&B to thank them for turning the engineer stereotype on its head:

Hey Mike,

This is the hapless girlfriend who shares an e-mail account with a techie who subscribes to your newsletter.

The amount of dry, poopey e-mails that we get in our inbox is criminal, and it's pathetic that the other electronic types are perpetrating the geek image that's out there by sending those incredibly boring messages.

I mean, come on! "All you've ever wanted to learn about C++, Extensive Layer Management Plug-In for mental ray Pipeline"? BRUTAL!

Thank you for the sense of humor in your newsletters.

Mike—I think you need to start a "how to write a cheese-free newsletter course." I can think of many companies that need your help!

Signed,

Disgruntled Dish

Does B&B owe its stellar growth in a stagnant industry all to their e-mail? No, but it's a vital ingredient of their carefully thought-out marketing strategy.

> Use e-mail correctly, and your customers will stick around three times longer. It's the most personal online medium there is. With it you can sell to your customers again and again by building trust and creating an entire business around your own unique personality.

Mike understands how to use e-mail effectively, which is why he hired Perry to ghostwrite his Politically Incorrect newsletter.

Whether you're B&B Electronics or Martha Stewart, capturing a person's e-mail address turns a one-time click into an opportunity to build a relationship that can work for you again and again and again.

Buying Google traffic is only the first of many important steps in our marketing process. If we had to credit our own success to just one thing, it would be the use of e-mail and autoresponders.

HOW THE POWER OF YOUR E-MAIL LIES IN BEING PERSONAL: SIX KEYS

Run-of-the-mill advertisers have little respect for the personal nature of e-mail. They don't realize how easy it is to turn off otherwise receptive prospects to their message, just by violating that.

You need to write to the person as one person. Unless the person you're writing to is part of a group where he or she personally knows each of the other members, then the last thing you want to do is write as though you're talking to a crowd.

This is you, an individual, talking to your customer, an individual.

1. A "From" Field That Shows You're a Real Person

If the text of your e-mail messages needs to address your customer as an individual, chances are that same principle will apply to other details in your e-mail. Take the "from" field, for example. Consider the different impressions these "from" lines create:

> Bill Kastl
> William Kastl
> William D. Kastl
> Nakatomi Corporation
> William D. Kastl, Nakatomi Corporation
> Nakatomi Sales Department
> Bill Kastl, Nakatomi Sales

You want to be warm and personal without looking like spam. This is a challenge, since spammers are themselves always trying to make their messages look like they're from some forgotten old friend. The key is to say something that is so specific to their particular interests they know no spammer would ever come up with it.

Pick a "from" field that your customers will understand, and stick with it.

2. A Provocative Subject Line

The most important thing about e-mail is that its success or failure is all about **context.** E-mail subject lines work *not because they follow standard copywriting formulas* but because *they tap into what specific people are interested in at a particular time.*

If I showed you generic examples of e-mail subject lines, it would be almost impossible for them to not sound like spam.

So let's take examples from a specific context that *you* understand: Google AdWords. Here are the subject lines of some of the e-mails I've sent out to my Google AdWords customer list:

· When Google is NOT the Best Way to Get a Customer
· Are Google Employees Spying on You?
· Google's "Don't Be Evil" and all that
· Five Insidious Lies About Selling on the Web
· Hurricane Katrina: I'll Match Your Donation

These headlines do not assault the reader with cheesy-sounding promos, but they do hint very strongly at a story. They provoke curiosity rather than scaring people off.

3. Everybody Loves a Good Story

B&B Electronics sells industrial communication hardware via catalog and the web. A "boring" geek business if there ever was one. But when Perry writes their monthly newsletter, he turns that dull, geek image on its head and interrupts a dreary day of engineering with wry humor.

His method? Storytelling.

Subject: **ZIGBEE AND THE GEEKS' REVENGE**

Leslye was the girl who made my heart go pitter-patter in junior high school.

I was always sure to take the long way to Social Studies, down the stairs to first floor, past her locker, then back up to 2nd. Just checkin' up.

I was not the boy who made her heart go pitter-patter. She liked Sam, and maybe Rodney too. She wasn't interested in me. And she never discovered that I liked her. It was my little secret.

Now maybe you didn't run the sound system in Junior High like I did. Maybe you ran the film projector instead. Maybe you programmed Apple II computers in BASIC and belonged to Chess Club.

Still, you and I were geeks, and the pretty girls took no notice of us.

But it's 2009 now, and we geeks rule the world. We're the people who really know what's going on. All the pretty boys and their material girls have viruses on their computers and they can't function without us. They're at our mercy.

And the latest Geek Revenge these days is . . .

ZigBee.

ZigBee is sort of like wireless instant messaging for sensors and smart devices. You drop ZigBee nodes wherever you want, no cables necessary, and the more nodes you have, the more communication paths there are and the more reliable your system is . . . .

This is a little wonky. It doesn't surrender to the stereotype that engineers are dull, lifeless geeks who only understand ones and zeros; no. It *celebrates* it. It turns it into the central message. It plays with the concept and has no end of fun with it.

More importantly, though, while it celebrates the engineer stereotype, at the same time it smashes it to pieces.

Engineers make buying decisions based on emotion no differently than the rest of us do.

Storytelling *does* work when marketing to them, no differently than people in any other profession. Plus, every geek out there has suffered the heartache of unrequited love.

Every time B&B sends out an e-mail blast, they get e-mails back from customers saying "Your newsletter is the only one I read every time it comes" and "I always look forward to getting e-mails from you guys."

WHY WE CHOSE ENGINEERS AS AN EXAMPLE FOR E-MAIL MARKETING

Most people stubbornly insist that you can't use storytelling and humor to sell to "logical" people like engineers and scientists. Most people also think that business-to-business marketing has to be dreadfully serious.

Well this shoots holes in both beliefs, because we're doing both at the same time here—using emotional, human-touch e-mail marketing to sell business-to-business products to engineers and scientists.

Does this work in other markets? You bet it does. Bryan has sold more books on learning Chinese and ignited more feedback and fan mail through this one message than anything else he sends out:

Subject: **WOMEN WHO HOLD HANDS; MEN WHO HUG**

William kept brushing against me as we walked down the street.

Now I'm a guy like he is—and I'm straight, too—and I found this a little unnerving. This was back during my first month living in mainland China, William was my new friend, and he had some habits that were awfully strange.

And when we'd go out walking somewhere, he always rubbed his shoulders up against me. I kept thinking I was crowding him, so I'd move to the right. Then he'd move right too, get closer and rub up against me again.

Sooner or later I figured out that this was just his way of being friendly. No, not "friendly," just friendly—you know, normal, nice-guy friendly.

It's that classic issue of personal space. Every culture has different rules. My Chinese guy friends rubbed shoulders with each other, and with me, as they walked down the street. Americans don't do that, unless they're in a relationship.

Younger women in China hold hands.
Sometimes regardless of age. Arm in arm, hand
in hand, they saunter together down the street.

Ah, but do they HUG you?

None of my friends ever did.

At least, not until I was with a couple of
guys being visited by a lady pal of theirs from
Shanghai . . . .

This e-mail is part of Bryan's regular autoresponder, and it doesn't even explicitly promote his book. But it gets a *reaction* from people. It turns the spotlight in a sensitive yet eminently funny subject.

It paints Bryan as completely and totally human. Not a peddler, not a salesman, not a pushy marketer, but as a regular guy whose experiences his mainland readers all share.

Most importantly, he *trains* people to read his e-mails by convincing them that he's always got something interesting to say.

4. People Can't Forget You When They Hear from You Often

Get an autoresponder series going and you can win the hearts of customers for life:

- We like five-day sequences. Five is a good number. Prime numbers like three, five, and seven are good.
- After that five-day sequence is done, keep in touch at a slower rate. In our "Nine Great Lies of Sales & Marketing" e-course (www.PerryMarshall.com/9), messages continue every few days and taper out for more than two years afterward. (You read it right: two years.)
- Your unsubscribe rate should be 3 to 10%. If it's more than that, your message isn't matching your market. If it's less, congratulations.
- Want to squash refunds and returns? After someone buys from you, send them a series of messages that show them how to use your product more effectively and shares features they might have missed. When we do this, it cuts returns by half or more.
- When people complain that they've missed a day or two from you, it's a sign that your content is good *and* that the spam filters are doing their job.

5. If You Violate the Expectation of Relevance, You Damage Your List

Let's say you're a chiropractor and you've just launched a new herbal remedy. It's a fantastic product, and you want to tell your customers. What should you do? Should you blast your entire list with it?

Odds are, you could maximize your sales total for that day by doing so.

But you're going to pay a price. All the people on your list who aren't interested in herbal stuff are now going to be *less responsive* to everything else you do—even if they don't unsubscribe. You've just taught them that you like to send out e-mails about stuff they're not interested in.

Which means they're that much less likely to read your next e-mail.

It's a nasty mistake to treat everyone on your list the same unless they really are. If you've got a back pain newsletter, it's likely only a few people on that list would ever be interested in a knee pain newsletter.

The typical marketer will treat everyone the same—when he gets a back pain subscriber, he'll also send knee pain stuff, neck pain stuff, herbal stuff, environmental stuff, whatever.

The smart marketer will not. The smart marketer will have different lists for each topic—different sublists.

So if you're the chiropractor, you build an herbal sub-list, and then sell the herbal remedies just to those folks. That way you maximize the value of every single list you have.

In e-mail—and by extension, direct mail and other forms of communication—that means that some of your prospects and customers don't ever want to hear from you (the bottom 5 to 10%). They, of course, do not matter. They can unsubscribe. But for the people who do:

- Some of them (maybe 50%) would like to hear from you no more than a few times a year.
- Some of them (20%) would like to get your three-, five-, or seven-day autoresponder sequence for a few days, then only hear from you if something really important happens.
- Some (5 to 10%) would like to get all your newsletters, and if you have e-mail lists for six different problems or products, they'll want to be on every single one.
- Some (1 to 2%) would like to hear from you every day.
- A tiny handful (less than 1%) would literally read ten e-mails from you every day, if you were willing to send them.

6. The Human Touch Sells

Don't hide behind your e-mail. Use it to express more of yourself. You're not a faceless corporation; you're a person. Show that side of you, and people will remember you. And buy. And tell others about you.

Express a personality that people can instantly recognize. This is free branding. When you introduce new products or make changes in your marketing program or message, now you can attach those to a name—your name or another person that your business is known for—and now your name itself has even more meaning and credibility.

A MEDIUM THAT WILL NEVER GO AWAY

When you communicate with your customers in multiple media rather than just one, it greatly solidifies your power in the marketplace.

There's power for you in adding offline marketing to your arsenal. Communicating with your customers via direct mail or fax takes you out of the ephemeral, fly-by-night online world and plugs them into you by an entirely new medium—a medium that is harder to break into but potentially more rewarding and enduring.

You can bank on the fact that the guy in the blue-grey uniform who comes to your house every day is going to *continue* coming to your house every day pretty much as long as the earth keeps rotating on its axis.

A customer who finds you offline and goes to you online is usually more valuable to you than a customer who knows you only online. In the same way, a customer who knows you offline through physical mailings and physical products as well as online is going to be a much more valuable customer than one who only knows you online.

OPT-INS: MORE THAN JUST AN E-MAIL ADDRESS?

Most opt-in pages only ask for a name and e-mail address, but is that all the information you want? Many if not most businesses should also collect physical addresses and fax numbers. Asking for this information, even requiring it, makes your database much more valuable.

It also gives you a valuable communication medium besides just e-mail. What if you accidentally get on a spam blacklist, if your e-mail service goes belly up, or e-mail suddenly gets a lot more expensive? It's a mistake to rely solely on e-mail.

THEY CAN KNOCK OFF YOUR PRODUCT, BUT THEY CAN'T KNOCK OFF *YOU*

Anybody can have a TV talk show, but there's only one Oprah. Anybody can rant about the Democrats, but there's only one Rush Limbaugh. Products can be replicated and ideas can be stolen, but personalities cannot be duplicated.

Use e-mail to express your own personality and you'll have a unique bond with your customers that nobody can take from you.

Uncle Claude Sez

A person who desires to make an impression must stand out in some way. Being eccentric, being abnormal is not a distinction to covet. But doing admirable things in a different way gives one a great advantage.

That's why we have signed ads sometimes—to give them a personal authority. A man is talking—a man who takes pride in his accomplishments—not a "soulless corporation." Whenever possible we introduce a personality into our ads. By making a man famous we make his product famous. When we claim an improvement, naming the man who made it adds effect.

CHAPTER 15

The Winning Method the World's Smartest Marketers Stole from the Wright Brothers

The boneyard of modern civilization is littered with "great" marketing ideas that never got off the ground.

Think of the billions and trillions of dollars that those companies spent developing products, only to find out that their products weren't what people wanted in the first place.

■ ■ ■

Let's *not* assume you're a corporation with billions of dollars to spend. Instead let's assume you're a regular guy who quit a cushy job to pursue an entrepreneurial vision. As you calculate it, you've got to start making a profit in six to nine months or else you'll run out of money.

If that's you, then you can't afford to make a mistake. You can't spend three months developing a product and later find out in month six that the product has to be totally redesigned. That'll kill your business and send you back to the J.O.B. with your tail between your legs.

We're going to make sure this never happens to you.

How can you prevent this? By testing your product idea and even your website itself on the cheap, using Google, *before* you've spent a lot of money on it. With the internet, you can find out if a product idea will succeed or fail, for a few hundred to no more than a few thousand dollars.

If you do this, you will be sure that the product you develop will be well received.

HOW THE WRIGHT BROTHERS' SAVVY TESTING METHOD MADE THEM "FIRST IN FLIGHT"

The year: 1903. The place: a houseboat on the Potomac River, USA.

Just weeks before Wilbur and Orville Wright were to fly the world's first airplane at Kitty Hawk, North Carolina, Samuel Pierpont Langley, a well-funded engineer and inventor, was launching an airplane of his own—with the assistance of an entire staff.

Langley's assumption: put a big enough engine on the thing, and it will fly. He focused all his effort on that one project: creating an engine powerful enough for the plane to go airborne. On October 7th, 1903, Langley tested his model for the very first time.

The plane crashed immediately after leaving the launch pad, badly damaging the front wing.

Two months later, just eight days before the Wright Brothers' successful flight, Langley made a second attempt.

This time the tail and rear wing collapsed completely during launch.

Langley was ridiculed by the press and criticized by members of the Congress for throwing away taxpayer dollars on his failed projects. Can you imagine the cynicism? I'm sure some sneering reporters believed that nobody could or would ever fly. Disillusioned by the public response, Langley abandoned his vision.

Wilbur and Orville Wright, meanwhile, had a completely different approach: build a glider that would glide from a hilltop with no engine at all. They focused their energy on balance and steering. Power was almost an afterthought. Only after the glider worked by itself would they try to put an engine on it.

After three years of tedious experimentation the glider was working well, so they commissioned bicycle shop machinist Charlie Taylor to build them an engine. It was the smallest engine he could design—a 12-horsepower unit that weighed 180 pounds.

And on December 17, 1903, at Kitty Hawk, North Carolina, Wilbur and Orville Wright made history.

The Wright brothers changed the world and became famous historical figures, while few have ever heard of Mr. Langley. Their approach of making the plane fly *before* applying high power was the winning idea.

Langley had spent most of four years building an extraordinary engine to lift their heavy flying machine. The Wrights had spent most of four years building a flying machine so artfully designed that it could be propelled into the air by a fairly ordinary internal combustion engine.

– Smithsonian Magazine, April 2003

Skill comes by the constant repetition of familiar feats rather than by a few overbold attempts at feats for which the performer is yet poorly prepared.

– Wilbur Wright

Samuel Pierpont Langley died in 1906, a broken and disappointed man.

PEOPLE WHO TEST, FLY. PEOPLE WHO RELY ON BRUTE FORCE, DIE.

You don't want to die a broke and disappointed man or woman. You want to die rich and famous.

Right?

Then there is a direct comparison between the Wright brothers and your career as an internet marketer.

The search engine is the motor. Your website is the glider.

A motor without a good set of wings does you no good. When you put an engine on a glider, you have a plane. When you feed traffic to a website that can "fly," you have a business.

And as smart marketers like Uncle Claude have known for over a century, you get the wings to work through careful, systematic testing.

This is not a new concept. For more than 100 years, smart, savvy marketers have followed these time-tested principles of proven good sense, and made their dollars go many times further.

In 1923, Uncle Claude said:

Advertising and merchandising become exact sciences. Every course is charted. The compass of accurate knowledge directs the shortest, safest, cheapest course to any destination.

We learn the principles and prove them by repeated tests . . . . We compare one way with many others, backward and forwards, and record the results . . . .

Advertising is traced down to the fraction of a penny. The cost per reply and cost per dollar of sale show up with utter exactness.

One ad compared to another, one method with another. Headlines, settings, sizes, arguments and pictures are compared. To reduce the cost of results even one per cent means much.

So no guesswork is permitted. One must know what is best.

Building a business online doesn't have to be guesswork. It's not a crapshoot. It's a *science*. Wise men and women before us have taken the risks, tested the limits, learned the hard lessons for us, and laid down a clear path that we can follow with confidence.

Whether your business is all online, or only partly so, the foundation remains the same: Start small, test carefully, make modest improvements, get deeper insights into your market, test some more, and you'll *know* that your business is going to grow.

This well-worn path builds a sales process that works. And when you have a persuasive website, you have a glider. Just like the Wright brothers, all you need to do is put a lightweight engine on it and you can fly.

Add Google traffic the smart way, and you've got a business that soars.

Google AdWords can bring you a lot of traffic, and that traffic is valuable to the extent that your website can convert the traffic to leads and sales.

When you're getting started, Google is like a lightweight engine that you can turn on and off instantly. You can test your glider safely without crashing, killing a potential joint venture partnership, or blowing a wad of money.

MARKETING MISERY IS *NOT* NECESSARY

Thousands of people go to bed every night wondering *Why? Why can't I make any sales? Why can't I earn any real money at this?*

This is not necessary, but it's a lesson that the scorched Dotcoms in 1997–2000 learned the hard way. They were a lot like Langley. They focused on the engine instead of the wings. When it didn't take off, they just poured more gas into the engine. When that didn't work, they put it on a rocket launcher and forced it up into the air.

You don't have the time or the money to pour into product ideas and sales messages that, in hindsight, were "almost right." Your spouse won't let you blow the grocery money or college savings on a lark.

Reality is a great teacher, if you let it speak its piece. The people who click on your ads will tell you what they want, if you ask them. They'll show you what they want, if you watch them.

Uncle Claude Sez

The time has come when advertising has in some hands reached the status of a science. It is based on fixed principles and is reasonably exact. The causes and effects have been analyzed until they are well understood. The correct method of procedure has been proved and established. We know what is most effective, and we act on its basic law.

Once a gamble, advertising has become, under able direction, one of the safest business ventures to undertake. Certainly no other enterprise with comparable possibilities need involve so little risk.

CHAPTER 16

How to Get Customers to Eat Out of Your Hand

Get the Biggest Money from Your Market When You Give Your Customers Exactly What They Want to Buy

Next time you roll out a new product, you can have a 75% chance of success or better by using Google to measure your traffic. You can know exactly how much demand there is for your idea. You can test your headlines and copy and have your potential customers tell you exactly what kind of product they're looking for.

Google makes this far less expensive and far less risky than ever before.

■ ■ ■

HOW WE USED GOOGLE ADWORDS TO PICK A TITLE FOR A SEMINAR

Do you know what's wrong with most "market research"? It's not market research, it's opinion research. Opinions are what people *say*. Markets are about what people *do*.

In his landmark book *Blink,* author Malcolm Gladwell talks about this very issue: People's buying decisions are usually an impulse act, and the reasons they *tell* you after the fact for buying a certain item or liking a particular product may have nothing whatsoever to do with their real reason.

Focus groups won't tell you the real reason. In-depth surveys won't get to the bottom of it. Often the only way to know what attracts customers is to give options and let them act in real time. Then go with what works, even when you don't know their personal reasons why.

Here's one such example of powerful, real-time market research on the internet.

PERRY MARSHALL

How Google Quickly Assessed the Viability of an Event Name . . . for Two Dollars and Seventy-Eight Cents

I'm the marketing and publicity director of TruthQuest, which is a local nonprofit group that hosts speakers and discussions on a variety of hot topics in religion and theology.

After the smash success of *Lord of the Rings,* its sequel, *The Two Towers,* followed suit the next winter. We found ourselves a speaker, Professor Jerry Root of Wheaton College, who could talk about this movie and the philosophical point of view of its author, J.R.R. Tolkien.

No matter how great the speaker may be, it doesn't matter if nobody shows up. So the title of the event was crucial.

Somebody suggested a preliminary title: "Is *Lord of the Rings* Christian?" But I didn't like it. Not intriguing. Too easy to say "No" or "Yes" and forget about it.

The more marketing I do, the less I trust myself even to pick a good title. So our group brainstormed four titles and let the world vote on them. I used Google AdWords and had an answer in just 18 hours.

What Happened When We Ran the Overnight Test

I took our proposed titles and made four ads, all rotating simultaneously. I purchased the keyword "Tolkien," as well as "Tolkein"—a common misspelling that people often mistakenly search on.

(Clickthroughs on misspelled words are often two to three times as high, and the words are less expensive—because there are so many other vendors who aren't bidding on them. *One out of every seven searches misspells the name "Tolkien"!*)

I started running the ad on Google at about 3 P.M. on a weekday and stopped it at 8 A.M. the next morning. Here's what the ads looked like, along with their results:

The Two Towers
Tolkien, The Two Towers, and
Spiritual Symbolism
tolkiensociety.org
11 Clicks | 1.0% CTR | $0.06 CPC

Lord Of The Rings
and The Spiritual Powers
of Hobbits
tolkiensociety.org
8 Clicks | 0.7% CTR | $0.06 CPC

Spirituality of Tolkien
Hidden Messages in
The Two Towers
tolkiensociety.org
20 Clicks | 1.9% CTR | $0.05 CPC

Tolkien Spirituality
Is There Hidden Christianity
In The Two Towers?
tolkiensociety.org
16 Clicks | 1.5% CTR | $0.06 CPC

Keyword	Clicks	Impressions	CTR	Cost
tolkien	48	3,878	1.2%	$2.43
tolkein	7	252	2.7%	$0.35
Overall	55	4,130	1.3%	$2.78

What We Found Out

1. As you can see here, clickthrough rates were dramatically different for different titles. The winner was "Spirituality of Tolkien: Hidden Messages in *The Two Towers.*"

2. This was *vastly* better than doing a "focus group" or a survey of our friends. Why? Because when someone reads about this in the newspaper or on a

flier, their decision either to continue reading or to ignore it is made *on impulse*. They don't sit and ponder it. The decision to click on a link is equally impulsive.

3. This is a *great* way to come up with titles for magazine articles, white papers, books, and names for new products. And believe me, the votes you get will surprise you. What you *think* sounds cool is probably not what your customers think is relevant.

You can use this exact method to test the marketability of almost *any* idea you have. You can take it a step further than I did—bringing visitors to your own website and further testing their response to different offers.

HOW TO BE SURE THERE'S A MORE PROFITABLE MARKET FOR YOUR IDEA BY DEVELOPING A PRODUCT *AFTER* YOUR CUSTOMERS TELL YOU WHAT THEY WANT

Let's say you're thinking about writing a software program for doing automotive repairs. It's for do-it-yourself car enthusiasts, and it does engine diagnostics that help increase your fuel efficiency by five miles per gallon.

If a guy bought your software (which you haven't written yet), he could buy a cable at Radio Shack, take his computer into his garage, hook it up to his car, and your software would collect a load of data and display it on the screen. Your program would then tell the guy what to tweak in his engine.

Sounds like a great idea. But how do you know there's a market for this?

You can find out if there's water in the swimming pool before you dive in. You certainly don't want to spend weeks writing software if nobody's going to buy it. So here's what you do:

1. *Write an e-book, white paper, or guide.* Call it "How to Use Engine Diagnostics to Improve Your Car's Fuel Efficiency by Five Miles per Gallon." In it you tell people how to do it the hard way. The whole routine that takes you three days, including the spreadsheet and the connector from Radio Shack. (I have a free e-mail course on writing white papers at www.perrymarshall.com/whitepapers.)

2. *Head over to Google, and bid on starter keywords.* Find all of the major terms related to engine diagnostics.

3. *Post an ad* like this:

DIY Engine Diagnostics
Simple Procedure Improves
Your Car—5 MPG or Better
www.AutoDiag.com

On your landing page, you have a sales letter that tells them about your e-book. You can also follow up with a series of e-mails that talk more about this.

4. *Get ideas and feedback from your readers.*

5. *Sell the e-book.* Or even give it away for free. But not without a plan. While you're marketing your e-book, you're going to take the next step with your buyers.

6. *Test your customers' response to your actual product idea.* What do they say back to you? Are they interested? Do they pester you to find out when this will be available? Do they offer to pay you for it now, hoping to get first dibs on it when it comes out? If so, you know you've got a winner.

7. *Sell your product*, and the dollars will come rolling in.

You've listened to your customers, you've put together a product in line with what they ask you for, you've proven to yourself that they're interested; now when you give them exactly what they want, you'll make the cash register ring.

WHAT YOU LEARN WHEN THIS DOESN'T WORK THE FIRST TIME OUT

Now what happens if it's a flop?

Don't cry in your milk—learn your lesson and get on with something else. You can come up with a new idea and test it for no great sum of money.

And what if the idea is only marginal?

Play with it. Change your ad, change your landing page, fiddle with the title of your report or e-book, adjust the price if you sell it, give visitors incentives in exchange for lots of feedback, and try again. If it won't work, then move on. If you can clear out the bugs, then run like the wind.

Did you know that infomercials also run on this same premise? It costs $50,000 to $100,000 to produce an infomercial and run it for a few days. If the producer can get 80% return on investment (i.e., only lose 20%) the first time out, he won't scrap the project. He'll play with the offer, the upsells, the testimonials, and other ingredients until he gets it above break-even. And he's not afraid to cut his losses if he has to.

When you test ideas that don't work, *fail fast.* Get it over with as quickly as possible. Spend the money, get the results, cut your losses, and move on.

"Wait a minute," you might be thinking, "I don't have hundreds of dollars to blow on pre-testing. I can't afford to do that."

The reality is, you can't afford *not* to. Spending those dollars and going into the red now could save you *thousands* of dollars later in botched advertising and mediocre returns, and can prevent you from having to start again from scratch.

BRYAN TODD

The Insights You Get When Customers Vomit All Over You

I spent more than four years in mainland China, during which time I went from not even knowing how to say "hello" to becoming conversationally fluent in the language. It saddened me as I watched many of my western friends there struggling with the language and getting nowhere.

I learned through trial and error a host of practical, working methods for acquiring the language. Multiple times during my stay there my American and European friends would tell me, "Wow—you need to share your whole method with me, because whatever it is, it's obviously working."

So I listened. And after returning to the United States I sat down to write a book that would teach other English speakers to do just what I did.

I then decided to take our marketing advice: I wrote a series of autoresponder e-mails and bought Google traffic first, planning to sell the book to customers later.

I set up my Google campaign, sent traffic to my new website, www.MasterChinese Faster.com, and let it go.

Here are two of the responses I got:

> You have shown me absolutely nothing. You have wasted my time and paper printing off your worthless e-mails. I learned more in five minutes from a Chinese business website than I could ever expect to learn from your time-wasting activities.
>
> D.M.

You have not provided me with any practice Mandarin lessons, which is what I wanted. Instead you provided generic information, as a "carrot" to buy your course. This is a scam.

F.P.

Oh, crap! Here I am in the middle of writing a book about learning the language living in China, while these people are in their home country looking for simple online lessons.

Thank God I hadn't created a whole product yet.

But get this: they *did* tell me exactly what they were looking for. The first guy above left me the URL of the Chinese business site he had mentioned, so I could go and compare. The second guy told me specifically that he wanted "practice Mandarin lessons." Others weighed in, too.

These people wanted online lessons. I didn't have the resources to put something like that together at the time. But I logged it away to pursue in the future.

Now what about my e-book? Should I cancel the project?

No. I knew from experience with friends that I had something of tremendous value. But how was I going to find the folks who really needed it?

I finished the book and set my ads to show only in Taiwan and Mainland China—and not even in Hong Kong, where Cantonese and English are more common than Mandarin. I turned on the traffic again.

When Your Machine Finally Kicks In

And that's when the positive e-mails started pouring in. Grateful readers who had moved to China and Taiwan from the United States, Israel, Germany, Australia, United Kingdom, New Zealand, India, and from all over the globe wrote in to tell me that they were finding my e-mail course to be helpful and relevant.

More importantly, *they were buying the book* and telling me that they were using it. I even found myself doing late-night telephone consultations to Beijing with my customers, helping them improve their Chinese-learning strategy even further.

In reality, the book is an invaluable resource regardless of what language a person is learning. The principles are universal and apply anywhere in the world. Still, focusing on China and Taiwan paid off.

One buyer sent me this:

> At about midnight last night, I paid for and downloaded your products. I thought I would take a quick glance before going to bed.
>
> It is now five o'clock on Sunday afternoon, and I haven't been to bed yet. I read the entire document twice; your bonus article three times. During this time, I experienced a gamut of emotions; everything from the knowing smile, kissing the computer screen, wildly punching the air, and dancing around the room.
>
> Your product is excellent, Bryan, and worth every cent I paid for it. For the price, I could not have had a better night! Don't even think about returning my money, as I love your work, and I am looking forward to any stuff you do in the future.
>
> —Andrew V.

When you find your market, *boy, do you ever find them*! Giving people exactly what they need and then having them turn around and thank you for it is the true joy of marketing.

The market has spoken. The book is selling. I'm making a profit. People like Andrew are writing testimonials, which in turn sells more books.

My customers keep telling me they want actual learning materials and the actual experience of studying with a person. So I'm hard at work now, putting together a unique international Chinese learning program that incorporates the principles that I already teach.

When Your Market Speaks and You Respond, It's Money in the Bank

Start small with Google, and when your market talks, listen. You'll knock your head against a few walls in the early going, but there's no better education to be had.

In fact, behind every angry rant you hear is someone who didn't get what they really wanted. Go with what your prospects tell you they want. And don't ever stop asking. Especially when your *existing customers* talk. That's as good as money in the bank.

Since I lived in China for four years, I listened for *four* years as friends and acquaintances complained about their struggles in learning the language. That taught me *what* I need to create for people.

Then I spent two weeks listening to my Google visitors in order to discover where I needed to market it.

Then Andrew used the book. It improved his Chinese. He wrote back to tell me about it. His testimonial resulted in more sales. He went on and told friends and coworkers. Word traveled around. More people bought.

That's exactly what people will do for you when you hit their sweet spot.

Uncle Claude Sez

Almost any questions can be answered, cheaply, quickly, and finally, by a test campaign. That is the way to answer them, not by arguments around a table. Go to the court of last resort: the buyers of your product . . . .

We establish averages on a small scale, and those averages always hold. We know our cost, we know our sale, and we know our profit and loss. We know how soon our cost comes back. Before we spread out, we prove our undertaking absolutely safe.

CHAPTER 17

Knowing Your Numbers Equals Money in the Bank

How Google's Conversion Tracking
Tells You What's Working

Josh was burning up the pages on Google. He had a fine-tuned herbal supplements AdWords campaign that was breaking new CTR records literally every week. Traffic was screaming. Product was moving. People were buying. Dollars were changing hands.

But then the credit card statements came in.

■ ■ ■

Josh compared his credit card statement from Google with his sales reports. *The ship was leaking!* He was losing money, lots of it, fast.

The left hand didn't know what the right hand was doing. He had no tracking system set up. No way to trace sales back to clicks, no way to know where to plug the leaks.

Josh called us in a panic.

So we went over to www.Hypertracker.net and set him up with an account there. He tracked every sales dollar back to the ad group it came from. He had put in place a system that was lean, mean, dirty. Every penny going out accounted for. Every dollar coming in measured for profit down to the cent.

With this newfound knowledge Josh beefed up his Google advertising even more, trimmed off the fat, and in a ferociously competitive herbal supplement market (where new competitors show up daily and soon drop off like flies), he went on to solid profitability.

Now Josh can take his supplements business wherever he wants. He can reinvest his profit and expand, or he can put it on autopilot and pursue other ventures. Josh has succeeded because he keeps close tabs on every number, all the time.

> You're a smart Google user when you know your numbers: How much each click is worth, what you can afford to spend to get a customer, and the Return On Investment (ROI) for each ingredient in your AdWords mix. This is a well-oiled machine that can generate profit for you night and day for years.

WASTED CORPORATE ADVERTISING DOLLARS VERSUS YOUR PROFIT-GENERATING TRAFFIC MACHINE

If you called up your stockbroker and asked him, "How much is IBM selling for today?" what would you think if he mumbled, "Oh, IBM's been fine," and dodged the rest of your questions?

You'd get a new stockbroker! You want to know exactly how much your stock is worth, in dollars and cents. That's the only way you know if you're making money or not.

The same applies to the operation of any aspect of your business—your website, your mailings, your employees, your phone and utilities, everything.

You may have heard people say, "I know that half of my advertising dollars are wasted; I just don't know which half." If you were Coca-Cola and you did image advertising on a mass-marketed consumer product, that might be the hard reality of things. But you're not Coca-Cola. You can do far better.

The mail-order business has known this secret for decades: *One really good ad in the right place can make money for you month after month for years, with no changes or alterations.*

That's because when you use rigorous methods to identify advertising formulas that work, then you're going to do as much of it as you possibly can. More, if you're in a recession.

If advertising is the great hidden waste in corporate America, effective results-accountable advertising is one of the great secrets of small business success.

Business has never been better for us, because we put in tracking mechanisms a long time ago. We can glance at a few numbers and see where we're at. We teach our clients how to succeed in marketing themselves and their businesses the exact same way we market ourselves and our business.

You can track your own Google clicks and advertising dollars using the same systems, the same mechanisms, the same techniques, and the same criteria that we use.

HOW TO SET UP GOOGLE TRACKING SO YOU CAN PERFECT YOUR ADS AND GROW YOUR BUSINESS EVEN MORE

Google makes it kindergarten simple for you to track your conversions and sales all the way back to every keyword in your list. You can turn up traffic where it's the most profitable for you, and trim back dollars where they're being wasted.

Tracking clicks to sales is not optional, by the way—it's mandatory if you want to get all the profit that's available to you. In competitive markets it's the only way to survive.

There's a host of conversion programs and subscription services you can buy that do conversion tracking, split testing of landing pages and sales letters, web analytics, and more.

In general, if you're giving Google your money, it's better to give somebody else the job of reporting your results. However Google's tracking is effective, and it's integrated with the AdWords system itself.

HOW GOOGLE'S CONVERSION TRACKER WORKS

1. When you search for "astronomy" our ad shows up on the right:

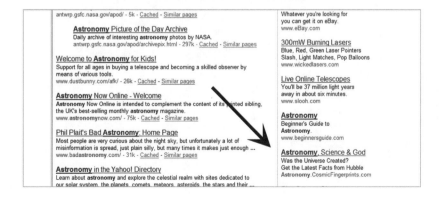

Click on the ad, and Google sticks a little "cookie" in your Internet folder. It's like stamping your hand at the amusement park: it tells Google you've been there.

2. Google sends you to our opt-in page. Enter your name and e-mail address:

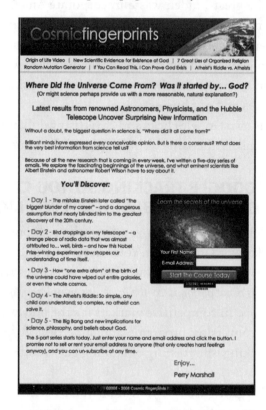

3. Our site sends you to a thank-you page. Google gave us a small piece of JavaScript to include in its source code.

Remember that "cookie" Google stuck in your internet folder? Google remembers that cookie, sees this JavaScript when you land on this page, and Presto! it records this as a conversion.

4. We've programmed this particular thank-you page to automatically send you on to another page on our site after about ten seconds.

Google's conversion tracking is simple to set up. On the toolbar at the top of your campaign summary page, click on "Tools," (or "Opportunities") and select "Conversion tracking" from the tool list you're given. Click to create a new action and Google will let you define the action you want to track:

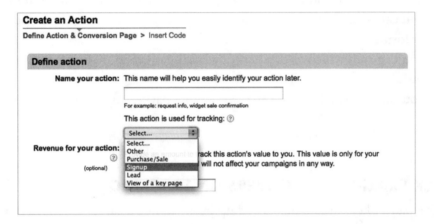

From there you can generate a simple piece of JavaScript that you'll stick in the code of your thank-you page where the only people who see it are the ones who have signed up or made a purchase:

Now as people opt in to your site, or as they buy, Google will tell you how well you're turning clicks into sales or actions, and which keywords generate conversions better than the others. And you can tell which *ads* you're writing are turning into more conversions as well.

Want to make your engine hum? This is where you tweak and test more, and hone your advertising to perfection:

- You can bid more on keywords that are highly profitable, and get even more good traffic from them.
- You can delete irrelevant keywords that are wasting your money.
- You can trim spending on ad groups and campaigns that have thin margins.
- You can identify whether content-targeted advertising is making you money, or losing it.
- You can spot which sites you're advertising on that are bringing in the most cash.
- You can tell which ads are attracting more paying customers.

This is where the profit is in Google AdWords!

QUICK EXAMPLE OF CONVERSION TRACKING

Here's a pair of keywords that showed up in the same ad campaign. Both bid at the same price. Both ran off of the same ads. But I knew I had a limit where I could not go over $1.10 cost per conversion—otherwise it would be losing me money.

One succeeded, one didn't. So I deleted the keyword that didn't:

		Keyword	Cost / Conv. (many-per-click)	Conv. Rate (many-per-click)
✓	●	mandarin	$1.08	19.32%
☐	●	[mandarin]	$0.36	23.95%
☐	●	[learn mandarin]	$0.85	27.03%
☐	●	[mandarin language]	$1.11	24.14%
☐	●	"mandarin language"	$0.64	40.00%
☐	●	mandarin language	$0.72	25.00%

When I did this, I made more money the following month. Google gave me the information I needed to streamline my marketing engine even more.

OUTSMART THE LAW OF DIMINISHING RETURNS: WHY THE MORE YOU PAY, THE WORSE YOUR TRAFFIC MAY GET

If you've got keywords that are doing screamingly well, do you just up the bid price on them and aim for the top positions on the page?

It sounds logical, but experience sometimes tells otherwise. Don't assume that you'll make the most money by being in the top positions. Very often, the opposite is true: you'll *lose* the most money by being in the top positions.

It's because of 1) the price you pay to get into those positions, and 2) the low quality traffic that you'll get from them.

One of our clients, John Jaworski of X-Streamers, sells confetti and party supplies for large events and venues. He was doing conversion tracking just like we've described here, and words like "party confetti" and "wedding confetti" were doing just fine. But he was paying $0.65 per click for a high-ranking position on "confetti" and had gotten 1,200 visitors . . . with zero sales.

Some people would consider $0.65 to be cheap. Compared to the $10 and $20 prices you pay for keywords in some markets, that's a bargain. Nevertheless, we advised John to cut his bid price by 90%, and get his listing on page *two* of the search results instead of page one. He dropped his bid to $0.07.

You might think that would have killed his traffic and sales. Amazingly, the opposite happened: his traffic started *seriously* converting!

This is not unusual, and for big-market, high-traffic categories (i.e., the top few hundred most searched terms on the web), even the page-two and page-three listings can get you decent amounts of traffic.

Real savings and money well spent comes in finding that "sweet spot" between paying a *low price* for clicks (which generally improves the conversion rate) and still getting a *good position* (which increases your traffic). You have absolute direct control over this because you set the price. And as you watch your campaigns over time you can move that CPC up or down to hit the perfect middle ground between price and position.

You'll know you've hit that "sweet spot" when your net profit is the highest. This is something you can set and tweak individually for literally every single keyword in your entire account.

(Realistically you only need to do this for the top 10 to 30 individual keywords, which for most people will represent 95% of the traffic.)

BIGGEST BOOM OR BIGGEST BUST: ADSENSE AND CONTENT-TARGETED TRAFFIC

AdSense is Google's program that lets site owners display syndicated Google AdWords ads on their sites, and earn a few extra cents of their own each time visitors click through.

Unlike regular search engine traffic where ads show based solely on the keywords you typed in, AdSense ads are *content-targeted,* i.e., Google shows them based on the content of the page and of the site. Here are ads shown when you search on an online dictionary for "migraine."

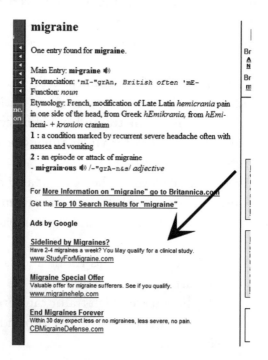

Rather than appearing on sites like AOL or Earthlink, content-targeted advertising puts your ads on sites like Dictionary.com, Amazon.com, the *Los Angeles Times* website, and so on.

Making money as an AdSense partner and putting Google ads on your website is a whole 'nother topic for another book. But this section is about how to take advantage of this if you're the advertiser.

You can opt to turn content-targeted traffic on or off, so that your ads either show on sites like these or they don't. Another option Google makes available is Placement Targeting, where you can choose to pay per-impression rather than per-click, and choose which sites you want to show up on, and which ones you don't.

To AdSense, or not to AdSense? Separating it from search traffic and carefully tracking your conversion numbers will give you the answer you want.

This invariably depends on your market. For some advertisers in some markets, AdSense is nothing but money down the drain. Huge numbers of clicks result in pitiful sales. For other advertisers, AdSense traffic is their bread and butter.

Why is it this way? Because the people who search on Google are proactively searching for solutions and are often in the frame of mind to spend money to have their problem solved.

Visitors to sites like *The New York Times* or Dictionary.com, on the other hand, are more likely in search of news or quick factual information or the definition of a word, and are less likely to be in a buying frame of mind.

WHEN THE CONTENT NETWORK IS GOOD, AND WHEN IT'S NOT

Here are three different scenarios—you're probably in one of them now:

1. *Your product has broad appeal, at least to certain people.* They don't necessarily have to be searching for it in order to be interested. It might be about a problem that was bothering them just yesterday. It scratches an itch that people persistently have. It could possibly even be an impulse buy. AdSense is a good place to advertise.

2. *Sometimes Google Search brings you ignorant people and non-buyers instead of enthusiasts.* Example: If you want to advertise your charitable cause to Buddhists who might be willing to donate money, you'll never reach them bidding on the word "Buddhism" on Google. Buddhists already know what Buddhism is and they already have their favorite hangouts. So they're never going to search for it. So unfortunately the keyword "Buddhism" only brings you college students writing reports about Buddhism. If you bid on Buddhism on the Content Network, however, your ad will be seen by devout Buddhists who frequent Buddhist websites. In this example the Content Network will bring you much better traffic than search.

3. You're trying to target a certain profession or population with an offer they don't often search for. Let's say you're a dental practice management consultant—every dentist in the world is your potential client. However, only a few dentists actually search for "dental practice management." Plus you can't reach them by bidding "dentist" because most people searching for "dentist" want to get their teeth fixed. The Content Network can reach dentists via dentistry sites.

Google shows your ads on its content network by default, so if you don't want to pay for AdSense clicks, you'll need to go in and manually turn it off.

To do that, from your campaign view click on "Edit Campaign Settings." On the right hand side you're given category options for "Networks." To turn off AdSense, uncheck the third box, and your ads will no longer show on Google's content network partners.

YES, A HIGHER CTR STILL HELPS YOU

Getting a high CTR means you pay less money.

Remember how we told you that your position on the page is a function of your bid price times your clickthrough rate? That's a simplified explanation of Google's whole Quality Score formula, but it's fundamentally true. The higher your CTR, the higher up on the page Google will place you, without charging you more for each click.

That can only help your bottom line. As your CTR goes up, either you'll be able to get more traffic without having to pay a higher rate for it, or you can lower your bid prices and keep the same volume and quality of traffic but pay less.

Sound like a good deal?

YET ANOTHER COUNTERINTUITIVE WAY TO TWEAK YOUR NUMBERS AND SAVE MORE MONEY

More than 80% of your sales will come from fewer than 20% of your campaigns.

Some keywords and ads are naturally, almost automatically, going to bring in good, consistent sales, while others simply never will.

When you know which ones are which, you can put smart money and effort into those campaigns that produce, and take your time and money away from the ones that don't.

It might even be 90% of the traffic that comes from 10% of the keywords. Most of the time the most productive 20% of keywords will be obvious to everyone, and there will be bidding wars.

One way around this—and it is an extreme measure—is to turn the 80/20 principle on its head. If you can get by with a smaller amount of traffic, you can cut your costs dramatically.

KNOCKING YOUR COSTS DOWN BY 95%: AN ACTUAL EXAMPLE

We've been buying traffic with the keyword "Ethernet switches" and a plethora of variations. We're bidding $0.50 per click.

Let's say I go to Google and want to find out what happens if I double the bid to $1.00 per click. Google will give me this estimate:

Current Clicks/Day:	11.7	Current CPC:	$0.33
Forecast Clicks/Day:	14.0	Forecast CPC:	$0.50

Our cost per click will go up by 50%. When we crunch the numbers, what actually happens is that we'll get 20% more traffic but for 76% more money.

So what if we go in the opposite direction and drop the bid price to $0.05? Here's what Google predicts:

Current Clicks/Day:	11.7	Current CPC:	$0.33
Forecast Clicks/Day:	6.4	Forecast CPC:	$0.05

This shows that we will get half the traffic at $0.05 as at $0.50, but pay only *one tenth* as much for it!

Caveat: I am certain that some of these keywords will now get much lower CTRs. *We may very well lose 80% of the traffic, not just 50%.* But we'll still be paying out much less money than before.

So by turning the 80/20 rule on its head, you get one fourth the traffic and you only spend one-twentieth as much money!

Reminder: You can only "invert" the 80/20 rule if you're bidding on *lots* of keywords and their variations. Use "" and [ ] keyword matching options on phrases to further specify your bids—it puts you ahead of advertisers who don't use them.

As you can see, "points of diminishing returns" are more of a problem when you're bidding too much than too little.

With Google you can do this. Every ad is an on-screen salesman at some level, and paves the way for real buyers to come in and spend real money with you.

Some ads get high CTRs but turn away good customers. Other ads may get mediocre clickthroughs up front but end up bringing in just the right customers who buy and buy again. So you go with the ads that make the eventual sales.

(The online supplement has links to more winning ads, and has MP3 seminars you can load into your iPod and listen while you exercise, drive, or work around the house: www.perrymarshall.com/bookbonus.)

THE SAVVY MARKETER'S WISH COME TRUE: HOW TO PERFECT YOUR SALES NUMBERS AND GO ON AUTOPILOT

For almost 30 years a business called LT Sound has sold a "Vocal Eliminator," a forerunner of the Karaoke machine. It's been running classified ads in *Popular Science*, music and entertainment magazines, audiophile periodicals, and more.

The Vocal Eliminator is a small unit you can play your CDs through. It eliminates the original vocals and inserts your own as you sing. Like Karaoke, but with your regular CDs.

Here are two ads for this product, an early version and one that's run continuously for more than two decades:

The owner of the business, Lacy Thompson, has tested these ads for years. He knows his numbers. He knows which ads pay and which ones don't. He knows which magazines get a response, and which ones don't. He knows which sizes, which copy, which descriptions—which *everything* pulls the best response.

The older ad above was published in *High Fidelity* magazine in October 1978. You'll notice how the mailing address is "LT Sound, Dept. HF." The newer ad ran in *Popular Science* in December 2004. Sure enough, readers of this magazine wanting the free demo are told to write to "LT Sound, Dept. PS-1." In other words, these ads are carefully traced back to the magazine they appeared in.

Lacy Thompson keeps the money flowing by knowing his numbers. And now he's got a machine that runs almost on autopilot and puts cash in his bank account month in and month out, winter and summer, year after year.

The product has been redesigned a few times, but the business has not essentially changed in 30 years.

Is this a "dream" business? No, but it ain't a bad business either way. Steady. Predictable. The FTC and FDA won't be going after Lacy for anything. It's a lot better than most peoples' jobs, and there's no pink Kool-Aid to make him frustrated with his lot in life.

If he wants to grow this business by introducing other products or exploring new distribution channels, he can certainly do that. And being that his advertising is largely offline, he's more immune to competitors suddenly showing up than if he were only online.

Marketers who can do this are the marketers who know their numbers. Are you one of them? Once you learn how to do it you'll control your game.

Savvy marketers keep an eye on the numbers that matter: How much each customer is worth, what they can afford to spend to get each customer, and the return on investment for each ingredient in their marketing mix. This is true online and offline, for internet startups and brick-and-mortar businesses alike.

Uncle Claude Sez

Never be guided in any way by ads which are untraced. Never do anything because some uninformed advertiser considers that something right. Never be led in new paths by the blind. Apply to your advertising ordinary common sense . . . .

The only purpose of advertising is to make sales. It is profitable or unprofitable according to its actual sales. It is not for general effect. It is not to keep your name before the people . . . . Treat it as a salesman. Force it to justify itself. Compare it with other salesmen. Figure its cost and result. Accept no excuses which good salesmen do not make. Then you will not go far wrong.

Take the opinion of nobody who knows nothing about his returns.

CHAPTER 18

The One Magic Number That Defines the Power of Your Website

Every business and every industry has a basic measure of success. Retail is real estate, and the real estate in your local mall is leased on a square-footage basis, so in retail sales the measure of the store's success is sales per square foot.

■ ■ ■

On Google, traffic is charged for on the basis of dollars per visitor. So success is also measured in dollars per visitor. If 100 people come to your site and you get $200 of sales, then your *value per visitor* is $2.00.

This is the most fundamental measure of your website's success. Your mission in life is to have a high value per visitor, or *visitor value*.

If you have a high visitor value, you'll be like the hottest and most fashionable spots at a high-brow mall: Nordstrom, Lord & Taylor, Starbucks, Sachs Fifth Avenue, and Macy's.

If you have a low visitor value, you're destined to be like the strip-mall stores: Dollar General, T.J. Maxx, Piercing Pagoda, and the like.

If your visitor value is even lower than that, you're on the slag heap. Eking out a meager existence at a flea market. Or hawking your excess inventory on eBay.

> The marketers who make the real bucks are the ones whose websites have the highest visitor value, which is the average sales value of each click they get. When you grow your visitor value, it means more money getting deposited into your bank account. Plus it means more affiliates and joint venture partners will come seek you out, because you can advertise more aggressively and pay more money to everyone.

Profit is your goal. That's why you're in business in the first place. But your profit alone doesn't tell you how sleek and effective your sales process is. You might just be getting lucky with unusually cheap click prices.

Visitor value is a powerful measure of what your clicks are actually worth. It's a measure of how smart your website is, how effective your sales copy is, how powerful your offer is.

How do you calculate visitor value? Simple:

$$\text{Visitor Value} = (\text{Your Total Sales Value}) \div (\text{Your Number of Clicks})$$

So if you make 50% margin on a $1,000 product, and one out of every 100 visitors buys, then your visitor value is $10.00 and in theory you can spend up to $5.00 per visitor to buy the traffic and still break even.

If one out of every 1,000 visitors buys, then your visitor value is $1.00 and in theory you can spend up to $0.50 to buy the traffic.

We know this is an oversimplification of what margins are and how they work. So don't write us and complain. (Every now and then some accountant sends us a scorching e-mail about how we forgot to include depreciation or amortization or some such thing.)

But the point is clear: visitor value tells you what your clicks are worth, and what you need to do about it.

DOLLARS MEAN MORE THAN PERCENTAGES

Let's say you sell a book online, and you've got two prices: your short version for $9.00 and your full, expanded version for $29.00. At the end of August you make some tweaks in your sales page, and then you watch your numbers through September. Here's what you find if you just measure percentages of sales:

	Clicks	Number of Sales	Percent Conversion	Sales Amount
August	3,447	45	1.3%	$1,241
September	3,921	82	2.1%	$1,260

Hey, this is great! You had more clicks, you sold almost twice as many units, your conversion rate jumped up and your sales dollars in September improved over August, right?

Wait a minute.

This isn't an improvement at all. Your tweaked sales letter actually hurt your cause. Now visitors are spending less money, and your clicks are worth less than before:

	Clicks	Number of Sales	Percent Conversion	Sales Amount	Visitor Value
August	3,447	45	1.3%	$1,241	$0.36
September	3,921	82	2.1%	$1,260	$0.32

Your conversion percentage went up, but people are just buying your cheaper version now. Now your sales process is less profitable than before and you're less attractive to affiliates, since they'll now make less money sending visitors to you.

Don't miss this: When you're split testing landing pages, opt-ins, and sales, you're not just going after high percentages. It's the *dollars* that you care about.

That percentage thing is a one-dimensional view of your traffic.

Visitor value reduces a *multi-dimensional* process to a single number. When you try things, you learn those kinds of secrets, combining percentages with dollar values to establish how much you can bid for your clicks. Once that's settled you move on to adjust for your own ultimate big number: your net profit.

ULTIMATE GUIDE TO GOOGLE ADWORDS

Heck, you could *double* the value of your clicks just by offering similar products at higher price points. This is something sales percentages alone don't tell you.

Buying web traffic reduces a complex process to a simple question: *How much can you afford to pay for a visitor and still make a profit?* At first, you may not know how many visitors you need to make a sale. But you can find out pretty fast: just buy traffic and test it.

QUICK AND DIRTY CHECKLIST FOR IMPROVING YOUR VISITOR VALUE

- ❏ Create an effective sales page that follows the time-honored classic formula:
  1. An attention-getting, benefit-driven headline
  2. A statement of unique value
  3. An unbeatable offer
  4. A clear and specific call to action
  5. An easy way to respond

- ❏ Continually test new headlines.
  Headlines have the biggest influence on whether your visitors continue to read or not, and will make the biggest difference in your sales.

- ❏ Offer something clear and specific on the landing page.
  Tell visitors where to go, what to do, and why it will help them. A site full of pretty images and polite puffery won't sell nearly as well as a simple, clearly written page that tells people what they'll get if they respond today. Most of the main pages on website www.perrymarshall.com have a specific offer and call to action.

- ❏ Continually change your offer to test response.
  You may well find that by changing the payment terms, including a free bonus gift, offering free delivery, or adding an option to gift-wrap the item, you double your sales!

- ❏ Add an opportunity for your visitors to opt-in.
  Offer a report, coupon, discount, white paper, e-book, book, CD, software, consultation, or problem-solving tool in exchange for their name and e-mail address.

HOW TO USE SPLIT TESTING TO BOOST YOUR VISITOR VALUE

Google AdWords is so revolutionary because it has made split testing so unbelievably easy. Now you can test two or more ads against each other and systematically beef up your clickthrough rates over time. The process is simple, the numbers are easy to read and understand, and winners and losers are clear.

170 · 18 / THE ONE MAGIC NUMBER THAT DEFINES THE POWER OF YOUR WEBSITE

But this can also be applied to your entire sales process. You can split test two similar landing pages, two sales letters, two different e-mail series, two purchase pages, two thank-you pages—everything.

This is will multiply your sales and exponentially increase your profitability.

Google doesn't have the guns to do this automatically with your web pages. And your webmaster may charge an arm and a leg to set up your own proprietary system for doing that.

Not a problem. There's a host of online services and downloadable programs that you can use that will run tests like these from outside your website, but which give you all the numbers and data you need to win the game of visitor value.

One that we've been using successfully for years is Hypertracker. We put together a video tutorial at http://video.hypertracker.net that shows you how to set up this type of account to split test and track multiple sales pages, multiple opt-in pages, and more.

The best part is, if you have multiple price points for certain products, that's not a problem at all. In fact, that's the *strength* of this kind of tracking and testing. Hypertracker and other services like it can track and measure sales of different products and different dollar values, and give you the figures you need in order to discover the visitor value of your Google campaigns.

PERRY MARSHALL

The Greatest Asset You Can Have Is a Marketing Machine You Can Turn On at Will That Continually Spits Out Money

My first successful sales letter was for a training program called "DeviceNet Boot Camp." Engineers would come to our training class for $1,500 and we would teach them how to use a new technology.

That sales letter sold a quarter million dollars of training in a year and a half.

Dang, that felt good! Knowing that every time we mailed out a couple thousand of those letters, we would get $10,000 to $20,000 in training revenue. Plus, about half the time we sent out mailers for the class, we would also get requests for custom, on-site classes.

Not only did this become a profit center for our company, it positioned us above all our competitors as experts, because we offered specialized training.

All from a four-page, folded self-mailer sales letter. We got $8.00 of registration money for every $1.00 we spent sending out those letters:

Is that a great asset or what?

When you have three, four, five assets like that—especially a combination of Google campaigns, e-mail promotions, teleseminars, and direct-mail pieces, you have the most liberating, profit-producing thing a business owner can have.

Uncle Claude Sez

A rapid stream ran by the writer's boyhood home. The stream turned a wooden wheel and the wheel ran a mill. Under that primitive method, all but a fraction of the stream's potentiality went to waste.

Then someone applied scientific methods to that stream—put in a turbine and dynamos. Now, with no more water, no more power, it runs a large manufacturing plant.

Advertisers will multiply when they see that advertising can be safe and sure. Small expenditures made on a guess will grow to big ones on a certainty.

CHAPTER 19

Beating the Competition When It's Most Brutal

How to Win Even If You're Not a 900-Pound Gorilla

J oe Spratley is a former Dilbert-cube occupant who struck out on his own. He found himself going head-to-head with his old company—Joe vs. the $50 million giant.

He discovered our website and e-mailed us asking if our methods would work in his business. We assured him they would, and even gave him advice for what to do if it worked *too* well. He listened, bought the toolkit, took notes, and went to work.

■ ■ ■

We got this letter from Joe shortly afterward:

Last week I had an incident that made your kit worth every penny that I paid for it. My old boss, who I haven't heard from in over four years, e-mailed me to say that people at my old company are starting to get worried because I'm getting a high profile. This from a $50 million corporation!

All I've used so far is Google AdWords and the web.

I just had to laugh. A two-person business has a $50 million corporation worried!

You don't have to be terrified of big players, on Google or in any advertising medium. It's a level playing field. If you follow our formula, you'll keep your toughest competitors at bay and make your biggest foes nervous.

> Your profits can grow even in the face of the toughest competition on Google. If you're slightly better in your use of keywords, slightly better in your visitor value, and slightly better in your customer follow-up, you'll move out ahead of your competitors, no matter how big they are.

Here are the ingredients of a successful strategy:

IT STARTS WITH KILLER AD COPY

The best of the best advertisers in any market are paying solid bid prices, *and* they're writing killer ad copy that would bring in high clickthrough rates regardless of their positioning. Google rewards good, relevant ad copy, you'll remember, by moving you up on the page as your CTR improves. Your bid price, however, does not change.

Below that "best of the best" are the unwashed masses of mediocre advertisers and copywriters who simply get where they are by bidding lots of money. The fact that they're there and that even on the first page of search results are businesses with big-budget mediocrity, means that you can nudge up through their ranks simply by split testing and slowly but surely arriving at better and better ad copy.

The Most Recession-Proof AdWords Advertisers Have Carefully Chosen the Best "Hill to Die On," and Tweak It to the Hilt

In the first chapter we described to you Glenn Livingston's Bull's Eye method for choosing the "keyword center" of your business, i.e., choosing the one single broad-matched keyword that you're going to optimize your entire online business around. The best AdWords advertisers do precisely this. They've chosen the search term with the highest possible chance of representing their ideal buyer, and they've adjusted their site, their landing pages, their ads, their offers, their autoresponders to fit it. See Chapters 2 and 3.

Remember that you can filter out unwanted searches by using negative keywords. Not just dozens or hundreds, but *thousands*. Do this and you've already got an edge on your competition.

Know Your Visitor Value and Bid the Price Where You're Most Profitable; Don't Assume That the Top Positions Are the Best

We ran this estimate in one market. We first tried to see if we could pull anything good out of the "keyword bargain bin." We created a list of multiple combinations for the existing keywords, and then went to Wordtracker and generated a list of over 200 related words.

We told Google that we were bidding $0.10 on them and here's what we got:

Clicks/Day		Average Cost-Per-Click		Cost/Day		Average Position	
current	forecast	current	forecast	current	forecast	current	forecast
	2.3	—	$0.10	—	$0.22	—	10.8

We don't like that—it suggests only a couple of clicks per day and positioning on the second page of search results. If we changed the bid to $0.35 a click, here's what we got instead. Still not impressive:

Clicks/Day		Average Cost-Per-Click		Cost/Day		Average Position	
current	forecast	current	forecast	current	forecast	current	forecast
	5.8	—	$0.21	—	$1.20	—	8.9

At $1.00 a click:

Clicks/Day		Average Cost-Per-Click		Cost/Day		Average Position	
current	forecast	current	forecast	current	forecast	current	forecast
	14.0	—	$0.78	—	$10.85	—	6.8

At $2.00 a click:

Clicks/Day		Average Cost-Per-Click		Cost/Day		Average Position	
current	forecast	current	forecast	current	forecast	current	forecast
	22.4	—	$1.53	—	$34.09	—	3.4

Despite Google's Traffic Estimator often being freakishly inaccurate when it's forecasting your average position, it looked like the range for success here—i.e., getting a reasonable amount of traffic at a reasonable position on the page—would be $1.00 to $2.00 per click for many of these phrases.

That's what it would cost. Are our clicks really worth that much?

Whether $2.00 a click is your actual visitor value or not, don't be fooled by the lure of those topmost positions . . . unless you've already got a serious back end sales machine that can support it. So often advertisers have been able to make positions five through ten on a page wonderfully profitable and deliver a surprisingly good amount of traffic.

But it's ultimately visitor value (VPV) that matters. Develop a higher VPV with a killer sales process, and you can bid more.

Go right now and do a Google search on "home business." This is just one of a hundred examples of keywords that draw ferocious online competition. As of this writing, the top position is going for $6.32 a click.

You could certainly pay $6.00 a click to be on the first page of search results, but is every click on average actually worth that much to you? If you have a fantastic sales process, and yes, your clicks are worth more than that, then staying on page one is not an issue.

But again, don't be lured by the siren song of those very top positions. In most markets the top spots attract tire kickers and looky loos who don't turn into buyers, and those top positions come at disproportionately high prices.

You need to test this. Sometimes the number-one position *is* the best position. But don't assume so.

Share Customers and Create Partnerships

The savviest online marketers don't look at their competitors as competitors, they look at them as partners. We all know that the other guy's site is only a click away, right?

On the internet, there's no such thing as "owning" a customer or having a captive customer. Mature marketers know this so they become affiliates of their competitors and sell competitive products to their own list, and vice versa.

Approach the top bidders and invite them to become affiliates of your site. You pay them a commission for promoting you to their customers, and now you're able to multiply your visibility.

Get the Customers That the Big Boys Can't Get or Don't Want

Try buying exit traffic from your competitors. Buy exit pop-ups from them for example.

Or position yourself on the content network as the "alternative" in related markets, bidding on the most popular keywords but offering a unique angle. Something different:

> **An Alkaline Alternative**
> Lithium: The Rechargeable Solution
> Saves You Time, Money & Frustration
> AlkalineAlternative.com

Market Offline as Well

If you have only one medium by which to communicate with your customers, you're always in serious danger of being shut off. There are times when asking for additional contact info on an opt-in page beyond just a name and e-mail address—such as telephone number, street address, fax number, and so on—is the only sensible thing to do.

Bring customers offline who found you online. Run your business and stay in touch with your customers in print and via direct mail. Offer a print newsletter and create a unique continuity-based back end that your competitors don't know about.

Members of our Renaissance Club (www.PerryMarshall.com/club) receive a monthly newsletter and CD from us in the mail. It's print and that creates a second level of trust with us.

You get from us a physical newsletter in your mailbox, something you can hold in your hands and take with you to read anyplace. We don't concentrate solely on Google AdWords in the newsletter; we also deal with topics from every corner of the direct marketing and business world.

It gives our customers a whole new dimension of a relationship with us, and a level of insight into doing business that extends far beyond Google.

The mailman delivers this every month, without exception. Google may not be around in 5 or 10 or 20 years, but the postal workers will. When you're in touch with your customers through multiple media, you've added yet another layer of invincibility to your business.

You can also advertise in offline media and bring customers *online* from there—through magazines and print ads. Customers who go online from offline are far better quality than online-only customers.

Build Your Back End

The smartest businesses make their money on back end. Customers buy and buy again, and the business owner is not afraid to lose money on the initial product sale, knowing that he'll more than make it up later on in his relationship with the customer.

It's the same with clicks. If you have a killer back-end sales process, you're free to barely break even, or lose money, on the initial Google click, and get that money back later. Which means you can bid more.

It's harder and harder all the time to complete a one-time sale straight off of a click. As the pay per click market has matured, doing that has become like riding a bicycle uphill in tenth gear.

It's almost a given in most markets, especially information markets, that your first step is simply to collect an opt-in. This gives you permission to develop a relationship with people instead of just getting a quick sale. When there are a lot of bidders, the merchants who develop ongoing relationships and accomplish more than just the first sale, will be the ones who thrive.

SEA LIONS, SUNFISH, AND JULIUS CAESAR: NATURE TEACHES YOU HOW TO WIN OUT OVER YOUR COMPETITION

Out in the wild, as with Google, it's not always the biggest and the strongest and the toughest that survive, that beat out the competition.

There's a saying in biology: *Runts make love, not war.*

Take the North American freshwater bluegill sunfish. The large males are always there defending their territories that the females come to in order to spawn. The smaller males—the runts of the group—behave just like females and flirt with the big males. The trick works. Along comes a real female, the courtship dance begins, the runt males join in without the big ones realizing it.

The genetic material is, uh, released, and in the midst of all of it the sneaky, cross-dressing little guy contributes his share and passes on his DNA.

Julius Caesar had constant headaches of this sort to deal with. A young man named Publius Clodius once disguised himself as a woman to gain entrance into the women-only Feast of the Good Goddess.

Rumor had it at the time that even Caesar's own wife Pompeia fell prey to the trick . . . and he divorced her for it.

Cooperative conniving is everywhere in nature. Smaller sea lions form packs and fend off the large males by sheer numbers. The smaller black-winged damselflies sneak in and get the girl while the big boys are off hunting or frolicking. Poorly endowed peacock males form leks and together manage to win mates even despite their bigger competitors, through their collective displays.

Should you steal your competitors' business? Should you play dirty like the animals do? Absolutely not. But Barnes & Noble serves Starbucks coffee, right? The principle comes from nature: Dig for deeper niches, share your customers, pick up business that the 900-pound gorilla doesn't want, and partner with others like yourself. You'll survive and your business will grow.

Uncle Claude Sez

Advertising is much like war, minus the venom. Or much, if you prefer, like a game of chess. We are usually out to capture others' citadels or garner others' trade.

We must have skill and knowledge. We must have training and experience, also right equipment. We must have proper ammunition, and enough. We dare not underestimate opponents. Our intelligence department is a vital factor . . . . We need alliances . . . . We also need strategy of the ablest sort, to multiply the value of our forces.

CHAPTER 20

Persuasive Ad Copy:
The Ultimate Silver Bullet

How to Mint Money with the Printed Word

M any skills engage when you run an internet business: HTML and web servers and all the techie stuff; graphics, pay per click, search engine optimization, recruiting affiliates, setting up joint ventures, testing and tracking; analyzing web traffic, avoiding spam filters, developing products, managing projects and teams, setting up blogs, and managing discussion forums. The list never ends.

■　■　■

But head and shoulders above all these things is the one skill trumps them all:

Copywriting.

How effective your Google ads are all depends on copywriting. Whether anyone buys from your website has more to do with copywriting than anything else.

If you crank out persuasive copy, everything else will ride its coat tails. Really good copywriting is the *only* thing in the above list of skills that you cannot easily hire done. Webmasters—dime a dozen. Pay per click and SEO people, not always great but readily obtainable. Products—dime a dozen.

But good copy isn't cheap. An "A list" copywriter will typically charge $5,000 to $20,000 to create a single package or sales letter. Not only that, it's no small task to "hire a voice" for your company anyway. The best voice is yours.

STRIKING OUT ON MY OWN:
"I need to get good at copywriting really really fast."

When I left the Dilbert Cube in 2001 and hung out my shingle, my copywriting skills were more than adequate for corporate client work—writing press releases and product descriptions and magazine articles. However I wanted to sell information: toolkits, books, e-books, and the like. I wanted a sales-on-autopilot business, not a consulting project business.

At the time my copywriting skills were not up to the task. I needed a mentor.

For years John Carlton had been the hotshot freelancer the Los Angeles ad agencies snuck in the back door to do the work their staff writers couldn't pull off. He had just begun to mentor rookie copywriters like myself, and his name was getting out. I heard he was taking new students.

I joined John's *Insider's Club* and started sending him stuff.

John would rip my letters apart and bust my chops. Then he'd bandage my damaged body parts with some words of encouragement and instruct me on how to reassemble my message for killer persuasion power.

Then . . . the first letter he made me rewrite went from 1% response (not quite breaking even) to 2% (solidly profitable). I was elated!

John's guidance got me over the hump. I can attribute my business "escape velocity" to his tutelage. His help was essential to moving my rocket ship from launch pad to orbit.

(It's kind of like space travel: your capsule either escapes the earth's gravity and circles our blue planet on its own momentum . . . or else it burns up in the atmosphere and sprinkles a 300-mile trail of scorched metal parts across southern Mongolia. The latter was not an option, at least for me.)

Well, then a couple years later John and I were together at a seminar, and he introduced me to his number-one student, Harlan Kilstein. Harlan followed John's advice to the letter and went from zero to charging $8,000 per project in 18 months. (At the seminar, John was complaining to me about how much money Harlan was making, just by ripping off all his great ideas.)

What follows is a shift of gears from the rest of the book, a transcript of a conversation between Harlan and John. As you'll see, these guys don't take themselves terribly seriously . . . but *you* should. You should scour this chapter and adapt some of these superb examples to your own promotions.

The interview is a riot. Enjoy and prosper.

(Oh, and by the way, this is only about a third of the total interview, condensed for the book. An uncut version is available in PDF at www.perrymarshall.com/bookbonus.)

Harlan: Hey John, I'm holding yet another book written by an "online writing expert" who says writing for the web is entirely different than any other kind of writing. He claims web copy demands a different approach, a different voice, and a totally different attitude. "You can't write online in the same way that you write a sales letter . . . ."

John: He's got a lot of balls for someone who's so obviously clueless. Toss that book.

There are circumstances online that will limit your choices of what to write, either because of limits on space (such as Google Adwords), or bans on certain words that will get you tossed off search engine searches, or get your e-mail shot down as spam.

But these limitations are physical, such as the number of actual letters you can use in a given space. They do not mean the fundamentals of great direct response copywriting are changed. In fact, these limitations really mean that you must understand and apply those fundamentals even more diligently.

Abandoning great salesmanship would be like firing your sales staff. You'll murder your bottom line.

So whoever is writing that stuff about needing a different voice online is not a copywriter or a marketer—I'll bet on that.

Harlan: Now, you've called me on a weak hook a bunch of times, and insisted I beef it up. How important is the hook online?

John: What makes or breaks a sales letter is the compelling hook.

It's not just important. It's the difference between copy that gets read, and copy that gets passed by.

Anyone who has followed my work knows how I have come up with some of the most outrageous and notorious hooks in modern advertising. Like—just to take the golf market—the one-legged golfer, the skinny geek who can drive the ball farther than anyone, the blind golfer, and on and on.

Outrageous? Sure.

But here's the kicker: These are all based on true stories connected with the product. (And by the way, they were never picked up by anyone else in the campaign. I had to use my best Sales Detective tactics to uncover these hooks . . . and then I had to twist some arms and put my reputation on the line—as well as risking the success of the entire project—to force the clients to run the ads once I had the hook in place.)

The Google Ad gets the first click, then the hook draws readers into the letter. It has to be so compelling and so motivating they cannot drag their eyes away from the ad. A great hook goes straight to the passionate sweet spot of the reader, and sets up camp.

A world-class hook, like a life-changing event, will linger inside a reader's head for a very long time. In a good way, of course . . . if he buys.

If he demures . . . well, he may be haunted by what he passed up.

Curiosity, desire, a challenge to your world view . . . a great hook actually violates your sense of reality on some level, or causes some inner conflict from the incongruity of what you're reading. To the degree that you are compelled to continue reading to find out what the heck this story is all about.

If you golf, I defy you to read this headline, and not care about the story behind it.

How in the world does a one-legged golfer play better golf than you? What ARE these amazing secrets?

I've taught my Insiders to think of the offline prospect as a slothful, somnambulant blob welded to the couch . . . and so averse to moving that he wouldn't get up to save himself if the house were burning down.

This may be a slight exaggeration of the actual situation . . . but not by much. Getting another human being worked up enough to take money out of his wallet and give it to you . . . is easily among the most difficult interactions you will ever face.

So the image of the half-awake blob is actually close to what you're really facing when you're trying to initiate a sale.

Your job—your ONLY job—is to get that blob so excited and agitated that he can't sleep or do anything else until he's gotten off his lazy ass and ordered your product. Because you've put an itch on him that won't go away.

The average time on a site is less than seven seconds. Top marketers keep track of these stats. Seven seconds is what it takes for a surfer to register an impression from the landing page of your site. That's not enough time to make a buying decision. It's enough time to decide, *naw, I don't want that.*

If your site were a retail store, this would be equivalent of watching people walk in the front door, take two steps in, and then turn around and leave.

That's a lost opportunity.

So, to keep that analogy, you better be darned sure that what a prospect sees first grabs his attention and draws him INTO the store.

Yet most websites—and, downtown, many stores—actually drive people away.

Now, Malcolm Gladwell has explained in his book *Blink* exactly how people make decisions in a fraction of a second and I'm going to prove this even more so later on.

For right now, think of your hook as an actual fish hook flying out of your computer to grab your prospect and hold him in place while your ad invades his consciousness. He won't be able to click away from your site in no stinking seven seconds. His attention has been nabbed.

Take a look at this site Harlan swiped from my One-Legged-Golfer.

There's a really big promise in the pre-head and he's just getting warmed up. The headline is an exact parallel of the one-legged golfer headline hook. Only, this hook is the secret weapon of movie and TV stars and the names going up and down the side of the page prove his claim.

Your pen really does become mightier than the sword. Mightier than the best salesman you've ever met, too.

Harlan: Sometimes people ask me to look at their site and the first thing I see is there's no headline to be found. And I'm sitting there wondering why would anyone stick around and read this? Then I find out, no one is buying and it's easy to tell why.

John: The headline on the site has to tell the reader exactly what you're gonna get if you stick around and read.

Just imagine standing next to a passing crowd, say, at a football game as the joint empties. People are rushing by, eager to get to their cars or the bus or whatever, to move on with their busy, hectic lives. Their mind is still half on the game, half on the job of going home.

This is the state of your target audience much of the time—distracted, and urgently moving past you.

So, what do you say to get their attention? You can't write from your heels. You can't whisper, or be incoherent.

Rather, you need to deliver a solid punch directly to their passionate sweet spot.

> *Learn these amazing moves just from watching... and be able to use them to save your life tonight!*
>
> **"How A Bad-Ass Bouncer Caught The Eye Of The Nastiest Undercover Division Of The U.S. Military... Why They Chose <u>Him</u> *Over Spec Op Soldiers* To Do The Most <u>Dangerous</u> Job They Had... And How <u>You</u> Can Now Learn This Guy's Secrets To Instantly Dominating *Anybody,* Of Any Size Or Any Skill-Level, As Easily As Taking Candy From A Baby!"**

Let's go through my headline off Bob Pierce's www.trsdirect.com site. It's a study in grabbing the specific attention of a specific audience.

The pre-head promises that you can learn this just by watching . . . I'm feeding the slug factor there. He doesn't want to work at anything and I'm telling him just watch this and you'll be able to save your life tonight.

So we're hitting the most important themes: it's simple, quick, and easy to get started.

Now let's move down into the headline. We have a bad-ass bouncer which brings all kinds of imagery to mind . . . and now, oh wow, he's also part of the Nastiest Undercover division of the military . . . and at this point the slug is already leaning into the computer screen and that's when I reach out and grab him and yank him into my letter.

Next: You're going to be able to dominate anybody as easy as taking candy from a baby. I've got a huge claim there—the classic "Big Promise" of old school salesmanship, the key to setting up a quick sale—and to someone who's interested in the fighting/defense market, I've hit one of his most tender and influential hot buttons.

He doesn't even know what the product is yet but his insides are already saying I want it.

Or check out this puppy:

> *Want to start <u>winning</u> motocross races almost <u>immediately</u>... even against stronger, more experienced, and better equipped riders?*
>
> ## Astonishing "Insider" Short-Cut Secrets to <u>Instantly Faster Times &</u> <u>Total Bike Control</u> Finally Revealed By The One Expert Many Motocross Pro's Want To *Keep Hidden!*

Notice the subtle and not-so-subtle juxtaposition of seemingly opposite concepts. If you're a motocross biker, you're going to thrill at the promise of winning almost immediately . . . even against much better riders. Hot button, punched.

And while you're still taking that lovely image in, I also promise you the insider secrets revealed by a credentialed motocross expert so powerful, other professionals don't want you to even know he exists.

Aw, the secrets promised here have got the reader sloppy with desire right out of the gate . . . and we're way under seven seconds.

If you're in this target market, you're gonna read a lot more of this ad, at the very least. Because this is exciting stuff, and it SPEAKS to your heart-of-hearts and deepest wishes.

Harlan: Let's talk about bullets. Here are some of yours . . .

- How to "empty" your mind of all nonsense as you tee up—the "Zen" secret that will allow your body to ***naturally "let it rip"*** and instantly turn your swing into a *nuclear-powered windmill!* (You'll be the **only** guy on the course who *never* worries about his drives!)
- The tiny physics-related adjustment that will *automatically* "square up" your club at impact . . . ***giving you the accuracy of a guided missile, every time you swing!***
- How to naturally allow that amazing "**lag**" everyone talks about (but no one knows how to tap) into your swing, *without* effort and *without* worrying about your movements! (The sudden distance you get on your drives will **SHOCK** you!)

John: All of these bullets feature what I call the "One Two Punch" tactics of piling benefit on top of benefit. You get a benefit by getting this product but there's a benefit on top of that benefit.

Most rookie writers stop at a simple recitation of a bullet. "How to get your mind in shape to hit a good tee shot." Yawn.

Go deep. Put yourself in a state where you're on the spot to drive home your point as succinctly yet specifically as a man convincing his wife to leave a burning house.

"Honey, wake up. We have to leave." Don't think so. No urgency, no sense of amazement or alarm, no insight to information that changes the way you perceive the situation.

It's more like "We have two seconds to get out of here! Flames are licking at the door already, the roof's ablaze, and if we don't leave right now we're goners . . . ."

Let's look at the first bullet. If you're a golfer, when you're up at the tee, you've got all kinds of crap going through your head. So emptying your mind is going to give you an advantage, sure . . . but I'm not stopping there.

In fact, we're just warming up. Because, if you'll let us share this stuff, you'll quickly turn your swing into a nuclear powered windmill. What's more—my God, it just gets better and better!—you'll never feel anxious about your drives again. Ever.

The image is specific. The benefit is simple: Better skills than the other guys, professional-level secrets that keep you calm, and the end of nervousness over this rather difficult game.

There are two kinds of bullets—open and blind. But both employ the tease concept—one by being specific, one by being mysterious.

Here's an example of blind bullets from my infamous Total Bike Control letter:

- *Clutch control secrets for maximum traction in any kind of dirt!* (Plus—the ONE simple clutch tactic you must use to be first out of the gate! Even most pro's don't know this secret!)
- How to use your size to total advantage! (Jeff is 6'4"—usually considered a huge disadvantage in motocross. This "disadvantage" forced him to study bio-mechanics, which led him to many of his most sought-after "advantages." Doesn't matter if you're a squirt, still growing, light or heavy on the pegs . . . Jeff will quickly show you how to eliminate all problems and use your size to gain speed and agility on the track.)
- *Instantly pick your best line through any dirt with just a glance* (even if you come up on new ruts unexpectedly)! Most rookies guess, and pay dearly. Pros know how to always hit the best lines . . . *and now you will, too!*

Notice none of these bullets gives the information the buyer is looking for. They're thinking, how the devil DO you instantly pick your best line through any dirt with just a glance? How DO you use size to your advantage? It's driving them nuts. I'm teasing them. I'm pushing their buttons.

And the *only* way he is going to get this curiosity answered is to order. I'm not going to tell him the answer until he buys the book. But he can't stop reading the bullets. It's driving him nuts.

But then, from time to time, I'll throw him a curve like these bullets:

- How to use nasty-ass ruts to your *advantage*—to gain speed, pass other riders in a blink (or force them outside), and *slash minutes off your total time!*
- How to use simple pivot and alignment tactics on the bike to keep your stamina at peak levels . . . *and finally be the MASTER of your bike!* (Easy, once you see how overlooked grip techniques and better forearm angles take the stress out of "fighting" with your bike.)
- *Instantly eliminate drift and bogging from too-wild clutch/throttle useage!* (The most common mistake rookies make . . . which murders your chances of winning! Easy fix.)

Just looking at these bullets, you can figure out what they are about, but I use powerful visual adjectives to paint a picture for the reader.

Often I will even give away the entire secret, just spell it out:

· *Braking around corners for maximum traction!* (Hint: Stay back in the seat and use your weight to come forward, over the tank, and unload as you carry your speed through each corner.) Crucial stuff for serious riders, explained in such simple terms you will understand *instantly*. (And be able to use it *tomorrow*!)

It's good, in fact, to give something away now and again. (But not when you're dealing with sex—in my Rodale Sex Letter I didn't give away any information, because it was an opportunity to go wild with the tease.)

If I were selling a book on home health tips, or gardening (which I've also done for Rodale), I'm always sure to include specific tips in detail. The sales piece becomes an information-heavy resource for the reader, who keeps it around for the advice and tips.

But the best stuff is always blind. You gotta get the product to relieve your curiosity.

This combination of open and blind bullets works like magic on readers. It teases them, cajoles them, and flirts with them until they buy.

Harlan: So why not just write blind bullets?

John: Because the open bullets serve the purpose of keeping the reader in the ballgame. Their appearance convinces him the whole thing is believable. If I only had blind bullets, their suspicions are up and they don't know whether or not to believe me.

Now there's one more ingredient I use in almost all my copy: subheads. The "official goal" of a subhead is to provide a mini-headline, typically a benefit for the next section.

Here's a subhead from an old Gary Bencivenga letter in my swipefile:

What I Learned
About the Rich and
Powerful When
I Worked at the CIA

So what Gary's done here is provide a mini-headline for the next section but it's so compelling, you just gotta read more. No one in the world can stop at the headline without wanting to know what's coming. And that is the whole goal of a subhead.

Here's another Gary Bencivenga subhead:

**A Major New
Economic Trend Is
Now Solidly in Place...
It Will Fool 9 Out of Every
10 Investors and Affect
Everything You Own**

The financial reader is looking at this and wondering . . . what is this new economic trend (and how come I don't know about it yet) . . . and then Gary hits below the belt forcing you into the next paragraph, ". . . and Affect Everything You Own." That's expert level force-marching readers to go further on into his copy.

Harlan: Another aspect setting your copy apart from most others are the pithy testimonials. Many people have testimonials that go on for paragraphs at a time. Your testimonials are a sentence or two and they are extremely tight.

> "John has created millions in profit for us. We pitted his ads and letters against big-city ad agencies, PR firms, and writers with lots of awards . . . and John slaughtered them all. He consistently hits 'home runs' for us—a 20-to-1 return in profit is not unusual. He has saved our butts on several occasions."
>
> -Robert Pierce, president, Tactical Response Solutions

John: A good testimonial is specific "Thanks to one idea you gave me John, I made $64,212 in one week." It stretches the limits of credibility and pushes believability to the max—"I was an alcoholic in the gutter and I was just elected governor." You aim for that "Whaaaaa?" reaction.

Plus, to be effective, a testimonial has to be exciting so the reader doesn't fall asleep during the testimonials. Boring copy anywhere in your pitch will murder your results.

It doesn't get read.

Here's a good testimonial from a letter Harlan wrote. You've got a celebrity doing the selling for you. And Harlan got cute with the subhead leading off the testimonial but it works in this case.

> **"My Name Is Bond – James Bond"**
> "Arthur Joseph started as a teacher of mine years ago. Over these years, he has become a good friend whose teachings of Vocal Awareness have become a constant in my life. He enlightens with compassion and understanding of the human spirit and above all else, it works."
> **– Pierce Brosnan**, Actor

Warning: *Never forge testimonials.* Good grief, especially when you're dealing with markets that are under constant scrutiny by federal "alphabet" agencies, like the FDA, FCC, SEC, etc.

If your product is any good, you can get testimonials. Just ask. Actively solicit them from satisfied customers. Most will welcome a little help in being pithy and succinct—so interview them, and help them craft their story simply and effectively. With lots of specifics and credibility and believability.

And if your product sucks so bad, you can't get any testimonials . . . find another product. Or fix the one you have. Just don't muddy the waters for everyone else by marketing crap.

Harlan: You've been doing something incredibly sneaky with your subheads for years. Here's an example out of your Rodale letter.

> ✔ A step-by-step "fingertip" guide to *the 16 most sizzling "hot spots" on her body* (pages 94-95)...
>
> Including At Least *FOUR*
> She Probably Hasn't Discovered *Herself* Yet!

You break the paragraph in mid-thought and forcibly yank the reader into the subhead. It's impossible to bail out at the end of the paragraph. Your subheads represent the second half of a blind bullet so you force someone who is scanning your copy to want more.

John: You betcha. Sneaky, and wicked-good stuff.

In the example below, I interrupt the bullet to add "and you're gonna love this"—which keeps punching at their curiosity hot buttons to the point they can not make sense of what I wrote unless they go on and read more.

But here, I sucker-punch the reader by beginning my next paragraph with the word "And." Good old-fashioned "bucket brigade" stuff.

Remember when your teacher told you never to begin a paragraph or a sentence with the word "And?" Well, forget that piece of advice. The word and connects you to what came before. So in the example below, not only do I pull the reader into the subhead, I drag them into the next paragraph as well.

> What Bill McKinney focuses on... and you're gonna love this... is...
>
> ### Whacking The Stuffing
> ### Out Of The Ball!
>
> And that means... you only need to pay attention to the CONTACT you make. And no, it's not hard. It's extremely *easy*, in fact. Once you know the secret.

In the example below, the subhead gives a stunning benefit. You can master these killer skills just by watching a video. No practice. No effort. It's a slug's wet dream.

> Everything is so dead-on simple...
>
> ### You Can Master All Of It...
> ### Just By Watching.

And here's one of my favorite examples. This is from the famous "nickel letter" we sent out. My boys questioned why they had to mail so many nickels, because it was costing them a fortune . . . until the orders started flying in the door.

Their staff remembers the nickel letter to this day. Notice how the subhead jumps out at you. And contrary to what your English teacher told you, my next paragraph is so dramatically short that it forces you into the next subhead.

> In less than a second, he suddenly realized he was about to be jumped by **three experienced streetfighters...** and if he didn't do something right *NOW*...
>
> ### His Life Wasn't Worth
> ### Much More Than That
> ### Nickel In His Pocket!
>
> Well, what would you have done? You know, in your heart, you run the risk every day of being in the same situation... cornered by punks who want to do you (and your *family*, too, if they're nearby) **serious harm!** It's not even connected to robbery anymore — they don't want your nickel, they want the thrill of stomping your face into hamburger.
>
> It could be in a parking lot downtown, in a movie theatre, outside your local Seven-Eleven...
>
> ### Or In The Cool Darkness
> ### Of *Your Own Bedroom,*
> ### Late At Night!

The goal of copy is to keep the reader interested, involved, and dying to find out what comes next. Move him along, as if he were sliding down a greased chute. On the ride of his life. And he doesn't get to ride unless . . . he comes along with you. Mint money by stringing words together, it's the most powerful skill a marketer can have.

■ ■ ■

The above content is only about a third of the conversation between Harlan and John. The full version is available in PDF at www.perrymarshall.com/bookbonus.

You can get a highly informative free tutorial on John's website at www.Marketing Rebel.com. And if you want to see Harlan's handiwork, visit him at www.Over night-Copy.com.

Uncle Claude Sez

Always bear these facts in mind: People are hurried. The average person worth cultivating has too much to read. They are not going to read your business talk unless you make it worth their while, and let the headline show it.

People will not stand to be bored in print. They may listen politely at a dinner table to fanciful stories and personalities, but in print they choose their own companions, their own subjects. They want to be amused or benefited. They want economy, beauty, labor saving, good things to eat, and wear.

There may be products which interest them more than anything else in the magazine. But they will never know it unless the headline or picture tells them so.

The writer of this chapter spends far more time on headlines than on writing. He often spends hours on a single headline. For the entire return from an ad depends on attracting the right sort of readers. The best of salesmanship has no chance whatever unless we get heard.

CHAPTER 21

Untapped AdWords Copy Ideas to Spark Your Creativity and Boost Your Response

In an ad-writing rut? This will get you out of it permanently.

Here's a list of ideas designed to help you think through all of the possible dimensions and directions you can take your advertising message.

■ ■ ■

Huge, huge disclaimer: Just because you see a particular type of ad in this list doesn't automatically mean we recommend that you copy its ideas. You've got to use your own critical judgment. Many (not all) of these are in fact actual Google ads by real advertisers, and some of them contain punctuation mistakes, bad grammar, stupid offers, lousy salesmanship, and more. Plus a number of them send you to websites that sell complete junk and do a crappy job of it to boot. We're not advocating any of that. We're just giving you examples of approaches that people take.

So start your motor, turn on your creativity, and dig in.

MOVE PEOPLE BY THEIR SENSES
Words and Phrases That Evoke Taste

> Designer Paint Collection
> Luscious Bold Colors
> Delicious Earth Tones
> www.paint.com

Words and Phrases That Evoke Sound

> Street Fighting Secrets
> Smack! Bam! Splat!
> Your Fist Against His Jaw
> www.StreetFightingSecrets.com

WORDPLAY AND CLEVER LANGUAGE CATCH THE EYE
Rhyme

Be creative with this, but beware that Google's editors could decide your ideas are too far over the top, and disapprove your ads.

> Stop Spam
> Create a Jam
> Turn Evil Men into Ham
> www.SpamClam.com

Haiku

Haiku is the old Japanese poetic form that involves succinct expressions and powerful word pictures. It consists of three lines; the first and third have five syllables, and the middle line has seven.

> Anger Management
> Smash! Punchbowl is in Pieces
> Learn Some Self-Control
> www.SpringfieldCounseling.com

Metaphors

> Will Your Wedding Be
> A Carnival of Utter Confusion,
> Or the Happiest day of your life?
> TheWeddingOintment.com

GET YOUR URL NOTICED

The URL is the second thing people notice after your headline. Find out whether making it more readable or more noticeable helps your cause or hurts it; uncover all the possible ways you can display your website location, how specific or general you should be, and which variations swing the biggest difference.

Which Domain Name Should You Use?

Choosing a more generic domain name can be useful for suggesting that you offer a wide selection of other products. Choosing a more specific domain name tells users that you're highly specialized.

> 15" Woofers
> Extraordinary Sound Response
> Top Quality Driver Design
> www.SpeakerExpress.com/woofers

> 15" Woofers
> Extraordinary Deep Bass Response
> Top Quality 15" Woofer Design
> www.15InchWoofers.com

Capitalizing Your URL

You can't capitalize the whole thing, but you can capitalize initials. Sometimes this makes your URL more readable, especially if it's longer or made up of multiple words.

- www.adwordsstrategy.com
- www.AdWordsStrategy.com
- freegift.weddingsurprise.com
- FreeGift.WeddingSurprise.com

PUNCTUATION

Question Marks

Google won't allow double or triple question marks (e.g., ??, ???) but you can test to see if using multiple question marks in a single ad catches users' attention better than just one.

Sexually Transmitted Info
Warts? Herpes? Blisters? AIDS?
Symptoms-Diagnosis-Treatments
www.STDmisery.com

Exclamation Point

Google will only allow you one exclamation point in your ad, and never in your headline. Test and see what effect exclamation points have.

Work From Home
Take control of your future;
We'll put you in business today!
www.epowerandprofits.com

Dashes

Don't confuse dashes, which have a space before and after ("Fresh strawberries - Low Prices"), with hyphens, which connect two words without any spaces ("Fresh-picked strawberries"). Dashes used the right way can catch the eye and even replicate spoken emphasis.

The Universe
Was it Created by God?
Or Does Science Say Something Else?
www.CosmicFingerprints.com
15,404 Clicks | 0.6% CTR

The Universe
Was it Created by—God?
Or Does Science Say Something Else?
www.CosmicFingerprints.com
21,615 Clicks | 0.9% CTR

Notice that the second ad got a 50% higher CTR than the first!

PROVE YOU MEAN BUSINESS WITH SPECIAL CLAIMS AND OFFERS

Trial Offer

> Hoodia 750 Appetite Supp.
> Rapid Loss of Weight
> 30 Day Guarantee, Buy 2 Get 1 Free
> www.lab88.com

Results Within a Certain Amount of Time

> Learn German in 10 hours
> After a weekend you will have a
> working vocab & grammar.—Newsweek
> www.unforgettablegerman.com

A Portion Goes to Charity

> Diamond Engagement Rings
> Free Shipping and 30 day Returns
> 3% donated to her favorite charity
> www.IDoFoundation.org

MAKE YOUR TERMS OF BUSINESS UNEQUIVOCAL

Filter

Use your ad copy to filter out visitors you don't want, or to prevent clicks from people you know won't buy from you. This will lower your clickthrough rate, but your conversion rate will go up.

> Guaranteed Sales
> We do the work—You get paid!
> $1995 to start your new life.
> porterdirect.kokorio.com

A person who's not willing to plop down $1,995 upfront won't even bother clicking on this ad.

"You Don't Have to Meet Certain Conditions"

> Home Loans, Bad Credit OK
> Bad Credit? Good Credit? No Credit
> 4 out of 5 applicants approved.
> Refinance-Home-Loans.us

TAKE ADVANTAGE OF CONTROVERSY

Use the controversy that does or could surround you and your website to attract more visitors, or more of the type of visitors you're looking for.

Sponsor a Discussion

> Euthanasia
> Is it morally correct?
> Discuss with other youth.
> NewzCrew.org

Make Bald-Faced, Controversial Statements and Claims

> Global Warming: a Hoax
> It's Anti-Business Liberal Paranoia
> Uncover & Discover the Media Lies
> www.globalwarmingbaloney.com

Have a Little Humor

> How To Destroy a Village
> Get the truth about the Clinton
> administration. Below retail price.
> www.conservativemall.org

BE A HELP IN CRISIS
Speak Directly and Solve the Problem

> Bad Marriage?
> Learn How To Stop Arguing, Improve
> Your Relationships and Self-Esteem
> www.PositiveConflicts.com

CHOOSE A TONE

Sarcastic

Spanish? Oh, Please.
Just What You've Always Wanted:
Another Dopey Spanish Program.
www.LoserSpanish.com

Hyped

Make Money NOW
Fire your Boss-Dump your JOB
You Deserve to Earn $-Your Terms!
www.businessforsuccess.net

Compassionate

Let Go Of Your Grief
Grief Is A Voice In Your Head.
Learn To Find Peace & Comfort.
www.jeffputnam.com

TRY OTHER FRESH APPROACHES

Shocking Incongruity

Tired of Sissy Men?
Meet a man with morals and
discipline of a warrior. Free!
www.worldcombatdating.com

Reverse Psychology

Do not use my program
Use other fake programs.
I love being richer than you all!
www.richjerk.com

Famous Quotes, Phrases, Lyrics

"Go Ahead, Make My Day"
Dirty Harry's Streetfighting Manual
For Hard, Leathery, Remorseless Men
www.DirtyHarryManual.com

Headline Humor

Backwards Bush Keychain
Because counting backwards makes
the time pass quicker.
www.backwardsbush.com

For more examples of winning ads and unusual ad copy ideas, get the online supplement to this book at www.perrymarshall.com/bookbonus.

Uncle Claude Sez

There is uniqueness which belittles and arouses resentment. There is refreshing uniqueness which enhances, which we welcome and remember. Fortunate is the salesman who has it.

We try to give each advertiser a becoming style. We make him distinctive, perhaps not in appearance, but in manner and in tone. He is given an individuality best suited to the people he addresses.

CHAPTER 22

Potential Customers Are Already Looking for You on Google But Don't Realize It

Here's How to Capture Them and Force Them to Pay Attention

E very year at Christmas time the Salvation Army sends out troops of bell ringers to stand on street corners and at entrances to grocery stores and shopping malls ringing brass bells, collecting donations, and saying "God bless you" to every kind soul who chips in.

■ ■ ■

There's no lack of Christmas advertising and soliciting already going on from relief organizations and charitable societies, from signs to TV ads to billboards to phone calls and more. So why the bell ringers?

They're there to divert your attention. A ton of folks who wouldn't go looking for the Salvation Army otherwise will cheerfully give a donation if they're reminded of it on the spot.

It's the art of getting you to "turn the corner." Making you interrupt what you were doing, or looking for, or chasing after, and head down a different path. This is a vital skill if you want to reach into new, profitable markets and pluck out the big plums.

> There are people searching online who desperately want the solution you offer. They just don't know about you yet. Use this little-understood "turn-the-corner" Google strategy to tell them about your solution, and they'll buy from you.

Our client Scott teaches a very contrarian approach to solving acne and other skin conditions. He argues that they are a symptom of another problem, far from being merely skin-deep.

A messed-up complexion, he says, is a sign of toxins in the body. Eat a solid diet and clean up your colon, says Scott, and you've just rid yourself of a major root cause of adolescent and young adult skin problems.

Scott says he can solve your acne, but he's a nutritionist. Which means that if his approach works, it will solve not just acne but a whole spectrum of health problems—problems that Americans and Europeans spend millions, in some cases billions, of dollars every year to fix.

Most people who go to Google in search of a solution to acne are looking for some product they can glop on their face and get rid of the symptoms. That's not what Scott offers. Does this mean that he shouldn't try advertising to them?

With the level of ferocious competition on Google now, he's swimming against a powerful current. Doesn't mean he shouldn't try, though.

Granted, if Scott has a big enough back end and other revenue streams from his business that can subsidize this, then he can turn this into a loss-leader. (That's what most of the top advertisers are doing anyway.)

But he damn well better make sure his landing page and site are about acne, dealing with acne, sharing his solutions to acne, addressing the root causes of acne. Otherwise Google will zap him, as clickers will bail.

He's got what he argues is a *real* solution to acne, and people are searching for it, so I told Scott to run it up the flagpole and see what happens:

Serious Acne Alternative
Why Your Acne May Actually Have
Nothing at All to Do with Your Skin
TheAcneAlternative.net

Most people assume that acne is just a skin problem and nothing more. So the ad attacks that assumption head-on. That may be the only way to get people's attention in his market.

Again, Scott is a nutritionist, and his best prospect is always the person who is already nutrition minded. Still, his solution to acne could add to his sales and bring friendly new faces into his fold. Those are customers that he can't get any other way.

So in Scott's market, "acne" is what we call a *turn-the-corner keyword*.

It's the same reason that this ad works, when selling to people searching for "alkaline batteries":

The Alkaline Alternative
Lithium: The Rechargeable Solution
Saves You Time, Money & Frustration
AlkalineAlternative.com

If you're selling lithium batteries and you know that your product is a valid alternative for certain applications that use alkaline batteries, then bang your gong and tell the world.

THIS WORKS BECAUSE YOU'RE SELLING RESULTS, NOT PROCEDURES

After all, what people who search on "alkaline" really want is long-lasting power for their electronic device. If you provide that in a different type of battery, then go on Google and tell them.

If you sell acetaminophen and you know your product can relieve headaches and pain for the people who are looking for ibuprofen, then tell them.

You may already be doing this unconsciously. Now it's time to do it *consciously*. Don't limit yourself. Think of any and every problem that you offer a solution for, and then do whatever you need to do to catch the attention and sell to the people who wouldn't have thought of you but still want your solution.

Know which of your keywords are turn-the-corner keywords, and know that you need to employ a special strategy to make them work. Use seductive copy. Take a different angle, a different attitude, a different message.

People *will* buy.

MORE TURN-THE-CORNER EXAMPLES

Notice the assortment of imaginative ways that these advertisers are catching people's attention and getting them to "turn the corner":

Be Contrarian

ADD Secret Revealed
Find Out How ADD Can Lead to
Genius, Creativity & Great Success.
www.ADD-ADHD-Success.com

Most folks who search on ADD are just trying to "deal with it"; they don't think of it as a powerful asset.

You find this ad on the content network when reading about "hemp." How's that for contrarian?

What Would Jesus Wear?
Fairly traded, sweatshop-free
unique gifts & accessories.
www.jesuswearsfairtrade.com

Be Controversial

Intelligent Design Truth?
Read why there is strong evidence
of an intelligent Creator.
ChristianityToday.com/ctmag/

This ad came up in a search on "evolution." It may not use the keyword in the headline (as we usually teach it should), but it boldly plays to the modern debate.

The Happy Capitalist in an Otherwise Intellectual Debate

Charles Darwin T-Shirt
Not a fan of intelligent design?
Try some intelligent fashion!
www.therealretro.com

Most folks who search on "Darwin"—which is where this ad showed—aren't looking for T-shirts. But a lot of them will gladly consider the idea once you suggest it.

Warn

Flatulence: The Facts
Don't Treat Your Flatulence
Until You Have Read This Report
www.infobasset.com

Be Deliberately Ambiguous (This One's Perry's)

Organized Religion—2010
7 Great Lies Of Organized Religion
"A Hard Look at Past & Present"
CoffeehouseTheology.com

Be the Ambulance Chaser

Vioxx Injury Lawyers
Class Action Lawsuit Attorneys
Finch McCranie, LLP
www.Product-Liability-Lawyers.org

This ad came up in a search on "Vioxx."

While You're Doing That, Why Don't You Also Consider . . .

If you're searching for "Switzerland vacation," you might see an ad like this:

Traveling Switzerland?
Add Vienna to Your Swiss Itinerary
Breathtaking Scenery, Rich History
www.Austria-SwissTour.com

YOU CAN REACH THREE KINDS OF PEOPLE

This approach is how you're going to reach folks that you might have overlooked. It's built on three possible scenarios:

1. There are people who'll gladly buy what you offer, but they don't know about you, or they aren't thinking about you at the moment;
2. You've got an alternative solution to a common need;
3. You've got a completely contrarian approach to a problem, which defies conventional wisdom.

Go after the folks who want your solution, but don't know it yet. You'll win over new customers that your competitors are overlooking. *Hit the right need and you could multiply your sales tenfold.*

TURN-THE-CORNER VS. QUALITY SCORE

Again, let's be fair and address the issue of Quality Score. That's the single biggest issue with using this method, and you need to pay heed.

If people don't want what you're offering, they ain't gonna buy it from you. If they're not already looking for some close-at-hand version of what you're selling, you're in for an uphill battle. So choose your battles wisely.

When you bid on keywords, use them in your ad copy. That adds a challenge if the keyword term is not what you're selling. Your Quality Score will get dinged if there's not a clear match between your keyword and your ad.

Your landing page has to be about that keyword you've bid on as well. Clearly and unmistakably.

Sometimes you gotta cut your losses. We used to run this ad regularly, on the keyword "Overture":

Beat the Overture System
Discover the AdWords Alternative
Access 100 Million People in 10 Min
www.PerryMarshall.com/adwords

It worked, for a long time. Would not work now. Overture was the first notable pay-per-click advertising system, but it's not around in name anymore, and the costs and quality score requirements to bid on "Yahoo" (who bought Overture out) are too prohibitive now. The Yahoo crowd's not low-hanging fruit. So we've stopped bidding on that.

A fair-handed "is XYZ really the right solution for you?" approach on your landing page and site, where you discuss the merits of XYZ vs. your unique alternative to XYZ, is probably a far better place to start testing the waters.

PERRY MARSHALL

Selling Prevention When People Only Want a Cure: When Turning the Corner Falls Flat on Its Face

In the late '80s, an infomercial was shot for the quintessential product that every parent should have: a video designed to help parents talk to their teenagers about drugs. Dan Kennedy, who told me this story, was hired to write the copy.

It was such an altruistic, appealing project that everyone wanted to help with it. It was hosted by First Lady Nancy Reagan; there were dozens of prominent Hollywood stars on the cast; the production values were outstanding; and it was nothing less than a beautifully produced, impressive, and inspiring infomercial aimed at making America a better place for kids.

It was the advertising equivalent of the Milk of Human Kindness.

The company behind this infomercial was so proud of themselves, they almost busted their buttons.

They bought the airtime and ran the infomercial. Guess how many orders they got?

Zero.

Absolutely none. The phones were silent.

Frantic, the producers called the number on the screen just to make sure there wasn't a problem with the phones. No—the problem wasn't the phones.

Nobody wanted to buy a video about talking to their kids about drugs. And they especially didn't want to sit their teenager down on the sofa, pop in the video, show it to them, and have a discussion about it.

Nancy Reagan couldn't convince them. Hollywood couldn't convince them. A team of professional copywriters couldn't convince them.

Why not?

Because the whole concept behind the video was *prevention*, not cure. It was entirely too easy for the viewer, who was in no pain whatsoever—not yet, anyway—to think, "Fred and Doris need this, not me. My kids would never take drugs. Talking to little Missy about it would be an awful conversation anyway."

It's awfully hard to sell a solution to a problem somebody's in denial about.

Chicken Soup for the Dysfunctional, Lust-Infested, Drug Addict's Soul

On the other hand, if you run a detox center or halfway house, it's similar to owning a funeral home. Yeah, you need to be at the right place at the right time, and yes, you probably need an ad in the Yellow Pages, but getting some customers through your front door is more or less inevitable.

It's hard to sell virtue and goodness in and of itself. That's why there's such a drastic difference between non-profit businesses and for-profit businesses. It's why there are so many novels about murder, mayhem, lust, betrayal, and hell, and so few about goodness, hope, utopia, and heaven.

Now don't get me wrong. I'm not degrading the goodness of genuine prevention. I'm just telling you that if you want to sell prevention, it's much better to sell it as part of the cure for a problem someone is having now, than trying to convince a person who's never had the problem in the first place.

Copywriter John Carlton, who appears elsewhere in this book, has this running debate with Joe Polish, a guru of the carpet cleaning industry. Joe runs ads about carpet mites in rugs and pillows, and his ads make the phones ring.

John, on the other hand, argues that the *real* reason that Suzy Jones replies to the ads about dust mites and calls the carpet cleaner is that she's got company coming over in six hours and she doesn't want her friends to see the spot where little Jeffy puked.

In other words, Suzy's going to have the carpet cleaned before the party, not after. Waiting till afterward would be prevention. Doing it before the party is cure.

Uncle Claude Sez

Prevention is not a popular subject, however much it should be. People will do much to cure trouble, but people in general will do little to prevent it . . . .

One may spend much money in arguing prevention when the same money spent on another claim would bring many times the sales.

CHAPTER 23

How to Grind Down Your Competition

A Google Lesson from Han Solo

H arrison Ford, a.k.a "Han Solo" and "Indiana Jones," was working odd jobs back in the mid-1970s when he was asked by George Lucas to fill in doing readings for the part of Han Solo for *Star Wars*.

■ ■ ■

Ford wasn't even being considered for the part. Lucas actually had his eye on Nick Nolte. Kurt Russell and Christopher Walken were prime candidates for the Han Solo role as well.

But during these test readings Lucas realized that the man perfect for the role was right under his nose. Harrison Ford was in the right place at the right time. George Lucas decided he wanted him for the part, and the rest is *Star Wars* history.

Did he just get lucky? Ford told *Us* magazine back in 1981,

Right from the beginning, I believed that staying on course was what counted. The sheer process of attrition would wear others down. Them that stuck it out was them that won. That was my belief then. It still is.

According to Ford it was *attrition* that was the key to landing the big roles. Celebrity status and million-dollar title roles came his way because he hung in there long after other actors had given up and gone back home. Movie history vindicated his decision.

> Sometimes the secret to success is grinding your competitors down, making incremental improvements over time until you're ahead of them.

The secret to staying power, the secret to long-term sales numbers that your competitors will never beat, starts with always testing two ads against each other, two opt-in pages, two sales letters, deleting the losers, and beating the winners.

BRYAN TODD

Split-Testing + Attrition = Success: Brian K. Wins by Attrition and Surprises Even Himself

Some months back a gentleman named Brian, who had a website that sold custom gift products for children, joined our coaching program (www.BobsledRun.com). We had several productive one-on-one sessions together where we examined every element of his whole sales process and suggested changes and new approaches and small tweaks here and there.

A few weeks into the process Brian was on the verge of giving up the ghost simply because of the amount of work involved in keeping his whole operation running, along with his perception that there were no significant changes that he could ever make that would push this site over the top into serious profitability.

Perry and I managed to talk him out of quitting.

Just recently, though, we had Brian on a group call again. He raised an innocent question about conversion rates on websites, not realizing how far out of everyone's league he had actually progressed: "I'm averaging maybe a 5% clicks-to-sales ratio on my whole website. I feel like I could do a lot better and wonder if anyone else on the call struggles with this too."

There was silence on the line.

"Uh, did you say 5%?" one of the callers asked.

"Yes, that's right. Why? Is that kind of low?"

More silence. Perry piped up: "Five percent is really, really good!"

One in every 20 of Brian's visitors was saying yes and buying from him. Just a few months before, Brian had been averaging less than 2%—1 in 50. What made the difference? There was no point where Perry or Bryan or Howie gave some single Eureka-moment piece of insight that allowed Brian to make the leap from 2 up to 5 of every 100 visitors buying.

No, rather it was Brian's very calculated, systematic, methodical approach of simply split-testing our new ideas against his existing old ones and keeping the one that worked better. He did this tirelessly over the course of six months and more than doubled the response on his website.

To Brian, this seemed totally commonplace, simply because the process had been so gradual. So unremarkable.

And it really is not rocket science. Of all the secrets that Brian and others in our Mastermind Club learn, this is the least glamorous, and yet the single most profitable. You can do this with any sales process, and every piece of it, and see gradual, unmistakable improvements over time. The answer lies in split testing.

Google Makes It So Easy

What makes Google so elegant is your ability to do such painlessly easy, real-time split testing of different ads. Take an ad that's getting a CTR of 1.1%, write a second one with smarter copy, and run it live against the first one, and discover after a few days or weeks that you've now got a CTR of 1.4%. Then delete the old ad and try another copy idea to run against the new winner. That one gets you a CTR of 1.6%.

You repeat this process over and over again, and find that you're eventually, after several weeks or months, pushing CTRs as high as 2.5% or better. Maybe even close to 3%.

Are you patient enough to do this? I'd virtually guarantee that most—not all—of your competitors are not. They're eventually going to tire of split testing, if they haven't already, and conclude that what they've got going is adequate.

If you are patient enough, you can do what Brian did. He was ready to throw in the towel in March and by September had doubled his traffic, simply through his patient, methodical, Little-Engine-that-Could mind-set of never giving up while making just the slightest incremental steps forward.

When you combine the power of split testing with the force of attrition, you'll come out the winner.

NOUVEAUX SKIN CARE COMPANY GETS AN UNEXPECTED TURN IN ADVERTISING

Julie Brumlik, who sells an exotic skin care product using Google, happened to have a huge advantage coming into the game: Her product had already proven itself and she had been able to get celebrity endorsements, even winding up on Oprah's show.

When she joined our personal coaching program, we advised her to use her keywords in her ads—especially the headlines. This was based on good experience; she tried it, and did fine. But split testing new ideas all the time will sometimes bring you new insights that even beat otherwise sound advice.

Julie followed her hunches and tried a different approach:

> **Wrinkles Instantly Vanish**
> Oprah, Melanie, Goldie, Demi, Nora,
> Beyonce, Marisa and Dr. Weil Agree
> CelebrityBeautySecret.com
> 2.0% CTR

As seen on Oprah
Age-Defying natural product line
for skin care. Erases wrinkles!
CelebrityBeautySecret.com
2.2% CTR

10% improvement. Not bad.

Don't miss this though: Julie tried this new "As Seen on Oprah" headline and it worked for *some* of her keywords. But not for all of them. The only way to know is to split test in each ad group and see where it works and where it doesn't.

It's no exaggeration to say that *every keyword literally represents a different market.* Julie's approach appealed to women who respect Oprah. In a number of cases it worked but not in all.

Some keywords represented markets where the headline appeal to Oprah turned the trick. In other cases it was a flop. That's the real world for you.

PERRY MARSHALL

The New Army of Generation-X Marketers

A new breed of direct marketer is emerging: The one who's learned by the first-hand experience of split testing rather than the second-hand tutelage of gurus. And he learns fast, too, because with Google and the internet the answers are all but instantaneous.

When you start to join this new and elite crowd, you'll find paybacks on a level you'd never have imagined.

This creates unexpected problems sometimes. One of our coaching students grew his business from $7,000 a month to over $100,000 a month in 12 months. A couple of months after that I got this e-mail from him:

> Hey Perry,
>
> I have been dealing with my merchant account
> provider for the last 2 days.

The Bad News: They are tying up some of our funds.

The Good News: We apparently "broke the bank," so to speak.

We went from $103,000 in February to $175,000 and counting in March. Should end up around $190,000 or so.

This is all a little scary. Hopefully I will not have any problems but, needless to say, I am applying for another account at another provider.

Thanks for all the help!

I love getting e-mails from people who have problems like this! It proves that the commies haven't killed the Entrepreneurial Spirit in America yet.

And this guy is no old-school copywriter. I doubt he even knew what copywriting was a few years ago. He got these enormous results by steadily testing and improving his website.

Most niche marketers don't have big enough numbers to easily test lots of stuff, and they certainly don't have a whole staff of bean counters to help them do it. So they rely heavily on gurus, "best practices," and copywriting courses and seminars.

And many of the best niche copywriters I know, people like John Carlton, Gary Halbert, and Scott Haines, haven't had tons of their stuff split tested the way we're talking about today.

Their craft is really the result of lots of experience and intuition. These guys are good enough that most of the time they can crank out a winner the first time out.

Internet marketers who split test are mastering their trade faster than ever, and the best marketers discover what works with a combination of old-school tutelage and constant testing. The ultimate answer to every marketing question is test it. Answers have never been so easily within your grasp.

Now hang on, because the power of this is even greater than it appears. It's exponential.

The Improvements Don't Just Add Up, They Multiply!
How to Get Massive Compound Interest on Sales and Profits

If internet marketing is some kind of magic show, I'm about to reveal to you the secret trick of the whole thing. This is what's truly important! Let's say your sales process looks like this:

1. Your AdWords ad
2. A landing page that offers a free report or white paper in exchange for name and e-mail address
3. A sales letter
4. Your order entry page, or "action form"

We want to split test each of these four steps. We not only test the AdWords ads, we split test two different landing pages, two different sales letters, and two different order forms. What happens when we do this?

$$2 \text{ AdWords ads} > 2 \text{ Opt-in Pages} > 2 \text{ Sales Letters} > 2 \text{ Order Forms}$$

A challenging goal would be to double the effectiveness of each step. This is not impossible. And you don't have to be a genius—you just need to try some sensible things.

So if we double the CTR of the AdWords ad, and the landing page, and the sales letter, and the order form, our improvement is

$$2 \times 2 \times 2 \times 2 = 16X$$

A 16-fold improvement! Notice that the improvements multiply, cascading from beginning to end. Every improvement is magnified in the end result.

If you can triple each step, you get

$$3 \times 3 \times 3 \times 3 = 81X$$

You can make improvements early in the process faster and easier than late in the process—you have more trials. An aggressive but not unrealistic set of improvements would be:

$$6 \times 3 \times 2 \times 1.5 = 54X$$

If you go into a competitive market on Google—such as anything computer related, weight loss, martial arts, make-money-on-the-internet, real estate, web hosting—these are hyper-competitive categories that are very hard to win in.

It's not unusual to start out losing money at a 4:1 ratio—i.e., for every $4.00 you give Google, you only make one dollar in gross profit. Not fun.

But now you double each of these four steps—and you improve your numbers by 16X—now you're making $4.00 of profit for every $1.00 you give Google. That's pretty amazing. Continuous split testing unlocks the whole thing like the key to a safe.

And like I said, let's take a common scenario—a sixfold improvement on AdWords, a threefold improvement in your opt-in page, a twofold improvement in your sales letter, and a mere 50% improvement in your order page (order pages are extremely sensitive to small changes—that sale hangs by a thin thread!)—now you've got as much as a 54X improvement in conversion over what you started with.

Expanding into Other Media: Profiting from the Winner-Take-All Phenomenon

The top dog has a disproportionate advantage over the others. The top three players in any market get more business than all the rest combined. This is true on Google as well, and there's a snowball effect.

You enter a market, you start split testing right away, and you use sound marketing techniques, copywriting, and all of the tools at your disposal.

How fast can you go from zero to dominating a market? Answer: As fast as you can split test.

So You Have a Killer Sales Process. Now What?

What you've done so far would have been very hard to do in the offline world—and two or three years ago not a whole lot easier in the online world—because there was never a consistent, controllable source of traffic. Pay-per-click traffic, however, is generally consistent, and it's always 100% controllable. Within two to three months (as opposed to two to three years) you've tested several dozen variables and eliminated all but the best. You've polished a sales process to the point where it delivers killer results.

You're making a killer ROI on your sales process. And because you're so effective at turning visitors into dollars, you can afford to pay more for your traffic than all your competitors. You're getting unstoppable.

What now?

Now we go out with our growing war chest and buy all the traffic we can get, using the Expanding Universe Theory of Internet Marketing.

You've started out with Google AdWords and refined your marketing machine. Now you take the same messages and sales process and roll out your product in this order:

1. Google AdWords
2. Search Engine Optimization
3. Other PPCs such as Yahoo and MSN
4. E-mail promotions
5. Affiliates
6. Banner ads
7. Social Media
8. Press Releases
9. Direct Mail
10. Print Advertising

Items two through ten are more expensive and less controllable than Google. Get it right with Google first, where you have total control, then do e-mail.

Then get help from affiliates. Don't let any of these other things or people be your guinea pig—if it works on Google AdWords first, then you can invest in these other things and be fairly certain it will work.

I can't overemphasize how powerful this is. Usually search engine traffic represents only a tiny percentage of the people who are potential customers for you.

When you roll out to items two through nine, you may make five to fifty times as much money as you were making with AdWords. And remember, no longer is it necessary to risk more than a few hundred dollars on a marketing campaign!

AFFILIATES: THE MOMENTUM KICKS IN

Affiliates want to make money, and the Holy Grail for an affiliate is a program that consistently sends him very good dollars in exchange for his traffic. You never want your affiliates to be blind test subjects for your experiments.

Friends come and go, but enemies accumulate!

Do your experiments with PPC traffic first. Then verify it with e-mail promotions and inclusions in e-zines. Now that you have rock-solid numbers, take it to your affiliates.

Everybody's trying to turn their traffic into dollars. Affiliate marketing is as 2010 approaches what MLM was in the early 1990s—a craze. (It works far better, too.)

You'll never read about this in *The Wall Street Journal*, but anywhere from 10 to 30% of all Internet traffic is driven by affiliates. It's an invisible empire.

Affiliate marketers are not always rational, and there's a lot of ridiculous hype about affiliate marketing. But there are thousands of capable marketers trolling the web every day, looking for good affiliate programs to promote.

If you're the guy with the content and the efficient sales process that spins off dollar bills, the world's your oyster.

Good affiliate relationships are extremely profitable. And more affiliates breed more affiliates. The snowball effect multiplies, and you eventually hit the point where you're getting so much traffic you can't make it stop.

AMERICA'S SECOND HARVEST WINS BY ATTRITION AND WE DONATE TO HURRICANE KATRINA VICTIMS

Our business supports micro-enterprises and AIDS orphans in impoverished countries, from Haiti to Africa. Need knows no political boundaries.

One U.S. organization stood out from the crowd, however, and I parted with a donation based solely on their brilliant marketing approach. America's Second Harvest has an ingeniously simple message: they purchase un-bought groceries from supermarkets before the products reach expiration and distribute them to the needy.

Their costs of doing this are ridiculously low, and they hit you with a clear and simple claim:

Every $1.00 you give provides four bags of groceries!

How could you not give to a cause like this, when you know your dollar is stretching that far?

I gave once and continued to receive mailings from America's Second Harvest. They don't just send plain, dreary letters begging for money every time. Actually, no two mailings ever look alike.

Each one comes in a different shape and size. One is a large, lumpy, clear package. Another is a postmarked lunch sack. Still another is a full-color brochure on how to volunteer with the needy in your local community.

Always full of pictures, always interesting, always fresh. At Thanksgiving in November they wowed me with a matching promotion offer to buy 300 Thanksgiving meals for just $20.00.

How could I not give?

Then when Hurricane Katrina devastated the Louisiana gulf coast in late 2005, we were bombarded left and right with requests from all across the United States to donate.

Even though I had prioritized giving to third-world causes, sure enough, a letter came—from America's Second Harvest, saying that they were in the thick of feeding hurricane victims through their program, and would I please contribute.

It was a no-brainer. By this time the ASH letters were a welcome and regular part of every week, and I trusted them. My first gift to them had been small, but they kept at me. So when disaster struck and they were there again like a familiar visitor, I gave big this time.

The people behind the ASH effort are no slackers. They understand that you win by attrition. Others drop off the radar but you stand strong, and you win. You always win. This is true with Google; this is true with any marketing effort you put forth.

Harrison Ford landed the part of Han Solo through attrition and a fair share of luck. For you it doesn't need to be luck at all. You've got Google's outstanding system for split testing, and the flow of traffic from all over the world to vet your sales funnel.

Uncle Claude Sez

Advertising and merchandising become exact sciences. Every course is charted. The compass of accurate knowledge directs the shortest, safest, cheapest course to any destination. We learn the principles and prove them by repeated tests . . . . We compare one way with many others, backward and forward, and record the results.

When one method invariably proves best, that method becomes a fixed principle . . . . One ad compared to another, one method with another. Headlines, settings, sizes, arguments, and pictures are compared . . . . So no guesswork is permitted.

. . . We test everything pertaining to advertising. We answer nearly every possible question by multitudinous traced returns. Some things we learn in this way apply only to particular lines . . . . Others apply to all lines. They become fundamentals for advertising in general. They are universally applied. No wise advertiser will ever depart from those unvarying laws.

CHAPTER 24

No More Bitslinging: How to Literally Create Wealth with Your Customer List

My friend Paul Colligan would be a retired millionaire today if he had thought of this.

■ ■ ■

MTV's *Spring Break Weekend 2000* was sponsored by the hosts over at www.GotAJob.com. Paul at the time owned www.GetAJob.com—only one letter different. He hit pay dirt.

Nearly naked bodies cavorting around on the screen, and MTV tells them all, "Go to www.GotAJob.com!" and by the time those people get to their computer, they don't remember which is which.

Paul was able to cash in on the literally *thousands of visitors per hour* who came to his site by mistake. He was making money hand over fist, all the while getting a Mach-2 lesson in online marketing.

What Paul didn't realize at the time, however, was that he was making another very, *very* expensive oversight:

If he had simply collected names and e-mail addresses from those hundreds of thousands of visitors, he would have a goldmine that he could go back to for years to come.

He didn't. So the money he made—and it was terrific money—he made just once. Had he known to collect names at the time, he would be a multi-millionaire today. He would have built an *asset*.

(Today he does do that, and in fact teaches a method of affiliate marketing called "Affiliate Rancher" at www.AffiliateRancher.com.)

Do you want to create a growing asset that you can go back to again and again?

> Create your own site with your own good content. Collect contact information, and build a growing list of customers who appreciate hearing from you. By far the single most valuable asset you have as a marketer is your own well-maintained customer database.

Doing this the right way can make you recession proof. It can guarantee income for you year in and year out, whether you're selling your own product or you're an affiliate of someone else.

You may be a masterful salesman, but if all you do when people click through to your site is sell to them straight, you'll get no more than 2 or 3 out of every *100* visitors to buy. That means the other 98 leave and never come back. If they do come back, you have to pay for their click again.

But create a reason for your audience members to give you their name and contact information, and you're in near-permanent touch with 10, 20, maybe even 30 percent and more of your visitors. You can speak to them again and again, and convince them over time to spend money with you. You don't have to rely on that one-time first sale.

It doesn't have to be complex or difficult, either. For years we've been sending Google clicks to the signup page of our white papers course, with virtually no changes. It feeds us new interested prospects day in and day out, who we then follow up with, and itself requires almost no extra attention or management.

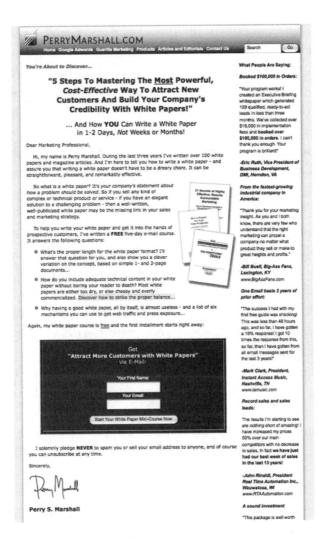

A good opt-in page includes:

1. The benefit-driven headline
2. A statement of what problem will be solved
3. A description, often with bullets
4. Explanation of how to get it
5. A promise not to violate trust
6. Simple information fields

Even if your site sells products that people would only buy on the first click, you can still give people an opportunity on whatever page they land on to give you their contact information in exchange for a newsletter, a series of free buying tips, a free report, or anything else of value.

With those people you can stay in touch again and again.

We've been collecting opt-ins since 2002, and today we have hundreds of thousands of loyal readers, subscribers, and customers with whom we communicate regularly. The e-mails we send out are interesting, informative, content loaded, and motivate customers to act.

We don't hit them up with constant offers, but we do make services and products available at the right time, and they respond. When you do this, you can send out a promotion and get back $10,000 in new orders in a matter of two or three hours. Your customers deliver if you do.

That is an asset!

If your business writes software, your source code is like the family jewels. You've probably got a safe somewhere in your home or office with that code locked inside, and if you're smart, you've also got copies at a remote location.

If your product is that valuable, then imagine how valuable your customers are. It's easier to get a product than to get a customer. Your customer list takes *years* to build, and merits even more reverence, security, and protection than your product itself.

It's simply amazing how many businesses are sloppy about their single most valuable piece of intellectual property: their customer database. I don't care what you do, what you make, or how smart you are; the most valuable thing you own is your list of customers.

The second most valuable thing you own is your list of *prospective* customers, those people who have expressed interest in your product or service but haven't bought just yet.

Do you capture the name, address, phone number, and e-mail of every possible person you can who visits your site? Do you stay in contact with them, letting them know what's new and always reinforcing your sales story every time you contact them?

If you know your customer list is the most valuable thing you have, then maintaining it and growing it will be your number-one priority. Just doing a good job of this will put you well above the average.

HOW YOU CAN BUILD WEALTH THE SAME WAY THROUGH AFFILIATE MARKETING

In affiliate marketing, it's no different. Even if you sign up as an affiliate and send thousands of paying customers every month to someone else and merely get a commission, you can still build an asset of your own doing this very thing.

As you buy clicks on Google, offer those people something of your very own, something of genuine value that nobody else can replicate. Collect contact information from as many of those visitors as you possibly can.

Traditionally—if you can call five or six years of history "traditionally"—affiliate marketers have mostly thrown up banner ads or link exchanges, bought PPC and other traffic, and tossed it back to the original owner in the hopes that a sale will be made and he can get a few bucks off of it.

Paul Colligan calls people who do that "bitslingers." They buy traffic and get the dollars from it, but nothing else. They add nothing of value to the mix. They're just brokers of clicks, and little more.

Want to be more than just a bitslinger? Build an asset, a site people want to come back to, and a customer list you can communicate with again and again.

What could you do to take a valuable product and add some value of your own to it? Here are some suggestions:

· Offer a tutorial.
· Do a substantive teleseminar on a topic that would be a natural, unassuming segue to the affiliate product or service that you're promoting.
· Set up your own site that provides a multi-day e-mail course about your topic, and promote your affiliate program that way.
· Offer a free guide.
· If you're promoting multiple competing programs, offer to show people a price and quality comparison and choose for themselves.
· Create audio recordings on the subject.
· Hold a contest.
· Provide a free software download.

We do this with products we promote. One of them is Hypertracker. We've been using this service for years to do split testing and to grow our own sales, and now we encourage our customers to use it and services like it as well.

The technicalities of a program like this can be a little daunting. So we put together a tutorial on how to use Hypertracker at http://video.hypertracker.net. It explains the services, makes it easy to understand and use, and folks can sign up for a free trial.

Most importantly, we don't just tell our customers, "Hey, go use Hypertracker." We don't push it like banshees. We first teach them something of value that will help them improve their own sales process.

WHY IT'S ALL BUT IMPOSSIBLE TO DO SUCCESSFUL AFFILIATE MARKETING ON GOOGLE ANY OTHER WAY

There was a time when you could run to Google, buy clicks, and send them through your own affiliate link straight to your host's website. Successful affiliate hosts loved this, because it meant they could very well dominate their market as almost every Google ad on the page promoted their website.

Google saw things differently. Stranglehold setups like that ruined the whole experience of using AdWords and made Google look bad. So they put a stop to it. The policy now is that only one advertiser per destination URL can show up on any one page of AdWords listings.

This does not mean, however, that you can't have your affiliates showing up on the same Google results page as you. It simply means that they can't just buy traffic and send it straight to your website.

Google has continued to crack down on pure affiliate traffic:

- Sites that are clearly just façade pages that send visitors immediately on to a merchant site will get slapped with low Quality Scores.
- Sites that review multiple products where the owner is an affiliate of one or several will get slapped.
- Sites that clearly have affiliate links plastered all over the landing page will get slapped.

So your affiliates—or you yourself, if you're an affiliate for another host—need to come up with real, original content on a substantial website of your own, if you want to survive.

When you do this, everybody wins. You add value to the market, and those visitors who sign in become an asset for you.

Uncle Claude Sez

Making a sale without making a convert does not count for much. Sales made by conviction—by advertising—are likely to bring permanent customers.

CHAPTER 25

How to Get High Rankings in Google's Organic (Non-PPC) Search Results

Pay-per-click traffic is great, and you have 100% control of it. However, if you have a listing on the left side of Google instead of the right side, it'll often generate at least twice as much traffic, and sometimes better traffic. Plus that traffic is free.

■ ■ ■

Search engine optimization can really pay off big time. Ignore SEO at your peril!

Before doing SEO, you need to pick your battles. Your PPC work tells you which keywords are valuable and how valuable they are; now you can selectively choose keywords to optimize for.

The following chapter is by Stephen Mahaney of Planet Ocean. I read Stephen's *Search Engine Newsletter* every month as soon as it comes out. From the beautiful state of Hawaii, here's Stephen Mahaney with a brief but highly relevant tutorial on search engine optimization.

■ ■ ■

Believe it or not, the secret to building a high-ranking website can be boiled down to three simple steps:

1. Build a site that's easy for search engines to find and index.
2. Make proper use of the keywords that customers use when searching for your product or service.
3. Locate the so-called "important" websites that are similar in topic to your own and get them to link to you.

Although Search Engine Optimization (SEO) can seem mysterious, especially if you're just starting out, 90% of it is really just focused on finding ways to achieve these three simple steps.

Of course, while these steps may be easy to understand, they can be a bit more challenging to accomplish. That is why smart marketers often start out by using the pay-per-click marketing model, such as Google AdWords, to begin their campaign. Then, once they know they have a winner, they branch out into organic search because, after all, those clicks are technically free.

In other words, if your system is working in AdWords, it's also very likely to be cost effective (i.e., profitable) in organic search as well. The catch is, of course, that scoring at, or near, the top of the organic search results can take time and patience, while a well-run AdWords campaign can drive traffic to your site almost instantaneously—albeit, for a price.

In any case, by understanding the fundamental building blocks of SEO, you'll be better able to focus your efforts on productive actions without wasting time and energy on strategies that have no effect, or worse, could even harm your page's position in the organic search results.

Remember this: SEO is not a magic art. To rank well in the organic search results, you simply must focus on building a great site, finding the words your customers are searching with, and getting the right sites to link to you.

Or, in SEO terminology: You need to build a search engine-friendly site, employ the right keywords in the right places, and get the right inbound links. Worth noting is the fact that an AdWords campaign already employs aspects of the first two of these three essential SEO components. The trick is to fold them into your organic search marketing strategy and then add the third component: Link building.

HOW TO GET STARTED WITH SEO

First of all, your web pages must be easy for search engines to find and process. Many site owners are completely unaware that their web pages are inadvertently configured to be difficult for search engines to index. And some sites are unknowingly blocking search engines from accessing them altogether—leaving their owners wondering why their site isn't doing better in the search results.

Whether it's *long and difficult to crawl dynamic URLs* or *poor use of page redirection* or *pages that use images when they should be using text* or *over-reliance on Flash and JavaScript*, the many ways to kill a site's ability to be indexed by search engines are relatively simple to avoid. And, even though the technical details for dealing with each of these maladies could fill a book, you'll be pleased to know that Google offers a service called Google Webmaster Tools (www.google.com/webmasters/tools) that features a Sitemap tool designed to make sure your pages get into Google's index no matter how search engine unfriendly those Web pages might be (within reason, of course).

For a more in-depth analysis of how to fix the technical glitches that scare off search engines, check out a good SEO manual like the Planet Ocean "UnFair Advantage" book (www.PlanetOceanNewsletter.com).

Keep in mind that making your site search engine-friendly, by itself, won't propel you to the top of the rankings. A search engine-friendly site is really more about avoiding the mistakes that will damage your search engine ranking than it is about reaching the top of the search results. To achieve that top rank, it's important that you take the next step and understand the interrelated role that keywords and inbound links play.

To put it simply . . .

Keywords tell search engines what your page is about.

Inbound links tell search engines that your page is important.

As you can see, because links identify your site as important, they are the key factor in determining exactly where your pages will rank in the search engines.

Although keywords are a critical part of search engine optimization, inbound links—and the keywords found within those links—actually have a far greater effect on ranking than the keywords found on the web page itself. In fact, we've seen cases where high ranking pages didn't even contain the keyword that they were ranking for.

Instead, in every such case, the page had inbound links that displayed the keyword in the visible text of the link (also known as the anchor text).

Of course, similar to AdWords, finding the right keywords plays a crucial role in letting a search engine know what search queries your pages should be displayed for, and you should be sure to place your best keywords into your web page's viewable content. But strictly from a ranking perspective, you'll find that *building quality incoming links to your site* is the single most effective approach you can take when it comes to ranking well over the long run. In fact, *a link to your page from an important site that uses your keywords in the anchor (or viewable) text of the link will likely produce a more positive ranking effect than all of your other ranking efforts combined!*

That's why link building is such an important component of getting your web pages ranked highly in the search engines.

BE REALISTIC IN YOUR TIME-FRAME EXPECTATIONS

Getting to the top of the search engine results for popular keywords is a gradual process. Chances are, some of your competitors may already have a fairly robust SEO program already up and running. It's possible they've been on the web for a long time and, these days, *time* is a search engine optimizer's greatest friend—or worst enemy, depending on your perspective. If a search engine has already determined that your competitor is the most relevant site for a particular keyword, then you should expect that it will take some time and effort to make that search engine change its mind.

Achieving top listings for a competitive keyword can often take six months to a year or more. Focus on gradually adding more and more relevant links while improving the overall quality of your site, and you will reach the top of the search results. If you're building a top-quality site with great inbound links, your hard work will pay off. For competitive keywords, that's the only way it can be done (a fact that can make life difficult for professional SEOs, since so many clients unrealistically expect immediate results).

Again, that's why so many professional online marketing specialists use pay-per-click (AdWords) to gain the immediate traffic they need to test their systems and juice their profits. This buys you time while your organic search strategies are allowed to grow, mature, and ultimately blossom into top rankings.

In the long run, top results in organic search can become a cost-effective money-making machine, provided your strategies are patiently built on a solid strategic foundation focused on creating valuable content and getting links from important, topically related sites.

KEYWORD SELECTION FOR ORGANIC SEARCH RANKING SUCCESS

If you have experience in keyword selection for an AdWords campaign, you'll find there are many similarities that transfer nicely to search engine optimization. For example, an AdWords campaign might focus on finding overlooked and underutilized keywords in order to get clicks for cheap.

In SEO, pages can be built around the concept that these overlooked keywords will also be easier to rank for in the organic search results, especially in the beginning stages of optimization. The Google Keyword Tool is a great way to find these bargain keywords, just as in pay-per-click keyword selection:

adwords.google.com/select/KeywordToolExternal

Planet Ocean's "UnFair Advantage Book on Winning the Search Engine Wars" devotes an entire section to Keyword Selection Strategies. There you can learn how to find the right keywords that allow you to get easy customer traffic from niches that your competition has overlooked.

Just be sure to bear in mind that, if you're competing only in popular keyword searches *where the majority of your competition is focusing their efforts*, you'll need lots of really good links to get to the top of the organic search results. By no means is that impossible—it just takes time.

KEYWORD PLACEMENT FOR ORGANIC SEARCH RANKING SUCCESS

To succeed in the organic search results over the long term, it's important to get your best keywords inserted into the appropriate places. Clearly there are on-page keyword placement locations, but there are also off-page locations that are extremely effective, ranking-wise.

On-page locations include:

- Title tag
- Meta Description Tag
- Headline tags (H1, H2, H3, . . .)
- Body copy

These are the most critical placements. In addition there is the element of *proximity* to consider. This is especially true when optimizing for two or more combined keywords that make up a keyphrase. It's better to place the keywords that make up a keyphrase *close* to each other. Also, it's better when the keywords appear early in the page's content. Usually, the earlier the better.

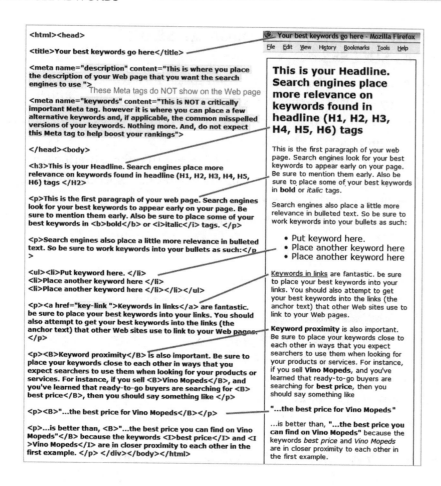

Off-page locations include:

· The anchor text of your incoming links
· The URL itself

Having your keywords in the actual link that points to your page is very, very important. And having the keyword in the URL itself tells both the search engine and the potential site visitor that the page is relevant to the keyword being searched for.

HOW TO GET NATURAL-LOOKING LINKS FROM IMPORTANT PAGES

One of the trickiest aspects of SEO is the process of building high-quality incoming links. It's also the single most important thing you can do to improve your rankings.

The challenge for most sites is to accumulate enough incoming links to appear relevant to the engines *without* tripping any one of the many spam filters and penalties that are applied to sites that (in the eyes of Google) cheat. The secret to getting it right is to take the search engine's point of view (SEPOV) when building your incoming link structure.

The key point to remember is that search engines like a natural link structure. They hate artificial link structure. Some of the qualities associated with an "artificial" link structure are:

- Most inbound anchor text is identical.
- Inbound link count increases suddenly.
- The site links out to link farms or web rings.
- A high percentage of links are reciprocal.

Here are some of the qualities associated with a "natural" link structure:

- Inbound anchor text varies.
- Inbound link count increases gradually.
- The site links out to only reputable pages.
- Links are rarely reciprocal.

From the search engine's point of view, natural links vary in anchor text, whereas artificial links tend to be identical. Natural links increase gradually over time as other sites add links one by one. Artificial links can sprout in great numbers all of a sudden. When they do, the search engine often suspects they are either purchased or artificially manipulated in some other way.

Sites designed around natural links don't usually swap links, so their outgoing links tend to point to pages that are already known by the engine to be in good standing. Oftentimes, these pages have been indexed for many years and may even be white-listed—a term that identifies trusted sites that are somewhat impervious to penalty.

Artificial links, however, often rely heavily on link exchange tactics, in which the sole purpose of the link is reciprocity—having little or nothing to do with adding value for the site visitor by way of linking to worthwhile content. Sites designed around artificial links will have outgoing links that point to pages that resemble link farms, web rings, or isolated nodes (i.e., groups of pages linking to each other but lacking inbound links from outside trusted sites).

Keeping these facts in mind, one should strive to build the most natural-looking incoming link structure possible. From the SEPOV, the best kinds of links are unsolicited links. The engines are looking to bestow high rankings on only those pages that people voluntarily link to due to great content—not because some webmaster has spent a lot of time swapping links.

CHOOSE YOUR LINKS WISELY

The best kinds of links are from authoritative pages—those pages considered by search engines to be among the most important on the web. One way to determine a page's authority is to use Google's PageRank scoring system, which you can access by downloading the Google Toolbar at:

toolbar.google.com

A simple rule of thumb is this: The higher the PageRank, the better the link. Of course, PageRank is not the only metric you should use in your site analysis, but it is an easy quick-and-dirty way to determine how important Google considers a web page.

As for examples of authoritative sites, directory examples include sites like Yahoo and DMOZ, while extremely well-known sites like PBS.org, NationalGeographic.com, CNN.com, and ZDNet.com would also be considered exceptionally authoritative.

GET LINKS FROM TRUSTED PAGES THAT MATCH YOUR TOPIC

Your next best option is to acquire links from sites that are trusted. Trusted sites are those that, while not necessarily top authorities themselves, are linked to from sites that are authorities. Trusted sites generally have been around for at least a few years, have lots of great content, and have established themselves as a credible online resource.

It helps even more if the pages linking to you from these trusted sites are on-topic—i.e., they match the topic of your page. Links from on-topic trusted pages can give you a significant boost in rankings.

COUNT THE NUMBER OF LINKS ON THE REFERRING PAGE

Another point to remember is the fewer the number of links on the referring page, the better. Ideally, the referring page would have only one link and it would be to your page. Of course, that's rarely the case. But having your link on a page with 100 other links is much less effective because the value of your link will be divided by the number of links on the page—a condition we call *link dilution*.

While easier said than done, try to get your incoming links from popular, on-topic, high-PageRank pages that have few outgoing links and are found on trusted sites. And if you can control how those links are formatted (in terms of your keywords appearing in the anchor text), you'll be in even better shape.

AVOID GETTING INVOLVED WITH RUN-OF-THE-SITE LINKS

Run-of-the-site links are those links where every page of a site links to you. When you have 1,000 incoming links all originating from the same site, it appears to search engines that your link count is artificially inflated. That's because when people buy links from other sites, those paid links are often run-of-site. Thus, search engines have come to view such links with suspicion.

MAINTAIN CONSISTENCY IN THE FORMAT OF YOUR INCOMING LINK URLS

You may not be aware of the fact that the following pages are technically four different URLs from the SEPOV, in spite of the fact that each of them will land the site visitor on the same page.

> http://your-site.com
> http://your-site.com/index.html
> http://www.your-site.com
> http://www.your-site.com/index.html

If those who link to you use four different URL formats to point visitors to your page, then your page's link popularity is being diluted by a factor of four. This is not good!

Therefore, you should do everything in your power to standardize your incoming link URLs in order to consolidate your page's link popularity (i.e., PageRank). Doing so will produce the maximum boost possible from your incoming links.

GET YOUR KEYWORDS INTO YOUR ANCHOR TEXT

It's very important that you get your keywords into the visible text of the link (anchor text) that other sites are using to point visitors your way. The boost in keyword relevancy is significant enough that it's worthwhile to contact everyone who is linking to you with a specific request regarding the text being used in your link.

For example: If you happen to be selling model airplanes, then anchor text such as *airplane models* or *model airplanes* will be infinitely more valuable to your relevance efforts than anchor text simply saying *click here*. From the SEPOV, the former states the topic of your page while the latter gives the engine no clue whatsoever what your page is about. This strategy can make a *huge* difference. Generally speaking, from the SEPOV, the anchor text is one of the largest influences in determining the topic of your web page.

A word of caution: it will look more natural from the SEPOV if the text links that are pointing to your site are not all identical. Strive to maintain slight variations, as would occur if the sites that are maintaining those links were generating the anchor text independent of your influence.

GO FOR DEEP LINKS

Make sure that some of your links are deep links—i.e., links to pages within your site other than your homepage. Again, this makes your inbound links look more natural, and it also indicates to search engines that you have valuable content on your site, since those other sites are linking directly to your content pages rather than pointing all their links just at your homepage.

BEWARE OF THE "NOFOLLOW" TAG

See to it that your incoming links do not include the rel="nofollow" attribute within the source code of the link. Nofollow renders the link useless to your ranking efforts because Google doesn't credit your page for that incoming link.

BE CAREFUL WHOM YOU LINK TO!

Avoid anything that looks like *an artificial effort to manipulate the engines*. That includes trading links with questionable or topically unrelated sites. Linking to these sort of unnatural linking structures can get you penalized, so always be very careful about who you link to.

Here are three cautionary steps you should take before linking to another site:

1. Search for their domain name on Google and Yahoo. If they're not listed on at least one of the engines, that's a bad sign. However, if they are listed, you can proceed to step two.

2. Determine who is already linking to them. The more incoming links they have, the better. And the more important the sites that are linking to them, the better. Their PageRank score is one indicator of how important Google thinks the site is.

   Planet Ocean's *Site Strength Indicator* (SSI) tool (available to SearchEngine-News.com members) can be used to determine who is linking to *you, your competition, or any other site*. This is a great tool to use when *analyzing the competitive ranking strength of sites or for prospecting for good link partners*. It's located at: http://www.SSITool.com.

   Beware of linking to sites or pages with a PageRank=0. This could mean that Google has penalized them. Granted, this test may not apply to very new sites, but if a site has been around for a while and lacks any PageRank, then you should be wary of linking to it.

3. Avoid linking to sites with controversial topics. Good examples of such sites would include gambling, adult, pharmacy, or loan/debt sites (unless you happen to be in one of these industries and the topic matches the content of your page).

Remember: You can definitely be hurt by whom you link to, so choose your link partners carefully.

TRAIN YOUR EYE ON THE PRIMARY GOAL—PROFITS!

Of course, our biggest assumption is that you're optimizing your site with profits in mind. That being the case, you'll want to always focus your efforts on strategies and relationships that will generate the most revenue relative to effort. Therefore, look first for link relationships that will produce traffic that fits the profile of your customer market.

While it's true that incoming links from just about any legitimate site provide a slight boost to your rankings, such links all too often fail to produce targeted traffic, which is what you really should be looking for. This is one of the many reasons a link from a topic-related site is immeasurably better than a link from an off-topic site.

THE BEST PLACE TO START GETTING LINKS

Rather than swapping links (which is arguably the most difficult and least productive link-building strategy), consider some of your alternative options for acquiring incoming links. Probably the best place to start is by submitting your site to web directories. Besides the two heavyweights—Yahoo Directory and DMOZ—there are others that come and go. Refer to Planet Ocean's "Ultimate Directory List" at searchenginenews.com/se-news/resource/directory-master-chart.

There you can see which ones are currently worth your time and effort to submit to.

Some of these directories are free, and some charge a fee which, when considering the value of your time, might be worth it to get a new site's foot in the link-popularity door. To add your site, look around on the directory's main page for a link that says something like "Add URL," "Suggest URL," "Add Your Site," or "Suggest a Site." Follow that link to get details about exactly how to add your site to their directory.

By the way, to avoid unnecessary delays in getting listed, be sure to submit your site to the proper category within each directory. Submitting your site to the wrong category can result in a ridiculously long delay or simply not getting listed at all. Remember that the directory editors receive an enormous number of site submissions, so save yourself some grief by carefully considering exactly which category your site belongs in *before* submitting.

Also, when getting listed in directories, be sure they provide a direct, static link to your site. Some directories will send your link through a script running on their own servers so they can track who clicked on the link and then send the link on to your site. This is called a redirected link, and is useless for boosting search rank. Although this may add to your traffic count, it does nothing to help your search engine ranking efforts. That's because engines fail to see the connection between the redirected link and your site's actual URL.

LINK OUTSIDE THE BOX

Deciding where to get your incoming links from is like solving a puzzle. It takes a little creativity coupled with various formulas and patterns. The following are several of our favorite strategies for building quality inbound links.

First, ask yourself: Who else has a site that might benefit from linking to me? Suppliers you do business with or professional organizations you're involved in might be willing to list you on their referrals page. Legal advisors, accountants, or financiers you do business with might also like to list you as a client or maybe showcase your business in their online portfolio. Your employees may have blogs or personal homepages that could link to you, and so forth.

Many online business owners write articles about topics related to their sites. Then they offer to let other sites use them as content in exchange for a link back to the author's site. You're probably an expert in the business you're in and therefore an authority on certain subjects that may lend themselves to interesting reading.

Look for compatible (but not competing) businesses, and then form a partnership where you link to each other actively through mutual promotion. The best partnerships come from websites that are useful to your own customers and whose customers will find your site useful as well. Not only can this bring in new traffic and boost your PageRank, but you may also develop important business relationships this way.

Press releases are also an excellent way to gain relevant links to your company's site. Again, be creative—chances are that there's a number of reasons (product launches, staff additions, promotions, partnerships, new services, etc.) you can find to release news about your company to the press. The engines quickly pick up press releases, and the links contained within them are typically trusted. They also tend to remain on the web for a good long time.

Another interesting way to promote your own site is to submit testimonials to other sites about products they offer that you are really enthusiastic about. If the testimonial is well written, the company will often post it on its site. Be sure to include a link back to your site with your testimonial.

Here's one of the most potentially productive tips: Find out who's linking to your competitors and convince them to link to you instead. To find out who's linking to your competition, enter their URL into Planet Ocean's *Site Strength Indicator* tool at www.SSITool.com.

Bear in mind that whenever you're successful in getting someone to switch their link to you, you gain twice: Once for gaining a new link, a second time for reducing the incoming link count of your competitor.

By using your imagination and dovetailing the nuances of your own business into the mix, you'll no doubt discover a plethora of opportunities for gaining legitimate incoming links.

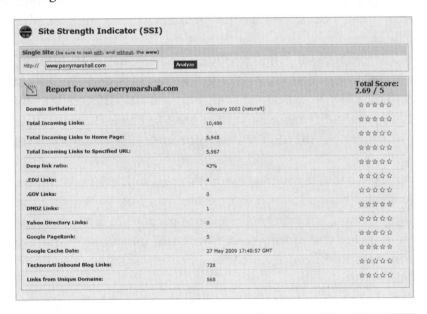

Understanding your Total Score

0 – 0.99 : This site has a very limited search engine presence and is getting far less search traffic than it could if it increased its optimization. Building quality links is often the quickest way to improve search engine rankings.

1 – 1.99 : This site has made some progress in achieving rankings, but is still far below achieving its potential. Targeting long-tail keywords is your best bet for traffic at this level.

2 – 2.99 : While there is still a lot of work to do, this site is on the verge of breaking into the arena of major search engine exposure. Creating some viral buzz could be enough to push it into the big leagues.

3 – 3.99 : This site is a powerful presence on the Internet. In a small to medium niche it's likely dominating, but can still be beat with the right optimization.

4 – 5.00 : This site is among the most powerful and authoritative on the Internet. If this is your site, then congratulations! If it's your competitor's site, they're going to be very tough to beat.

THE PROBLEM WITH RECIPROCAL LINKS

Your best strategy in terms of *reciprocal links* as a link-building tactic is to *be conservative* because, when done badly in the eyes of Google, it is viewed as an artificial linking pattern—something that search engines are getting increasingly sophisticated about detecting.

When you think about it, it makes sense that having a high percentage of reciprocal links would look like an artificial linking pattern because natural links are *not* typically reciprocal. If Yahoo lists a site in its directory, that site doesn't routinely link back to Yahoo; that's one of the reasons a link coming from Yahoo looks "natural" to Google.

Of course there are plenty of exceptions, but, regardless, the engines are looking for pages that rank well due to popularity based on content—and they want to avoid sites where it appears the site owners (or hired SEOs) have put a lot of effort into swapping links.

So, look at your incoming links from the search engine's point of view (SEPOV). If CNN runs an article about how great your company is, and your company's site links back to the CNN article, does that look normal from the SEPOV? Sure it does. Besides, CNN is an authoritative, important site. The link exchange looks like a natural link structure from the SEPOV. And, your site's page can expect a substantial boost in ranking.

On the other hand, if your site (with it's PageRank = 4 or 5) is linked by Joe Blow's homepage with a PR = 1, 2, or 3 and you link back to Joe's page, you shouldn't expect much, if any, boost in your rankings. In fact, it's entirely possible the two links are discounting each other based on an assumed link exchange arrangement that looks contrived because neither page is "authoritative" from the SEPOV.

Now, if you had, say, 50 similar link arrangements, and the links were all on-topic, and none of the pages involved had tripped the spam filters, then your page should get a reasonable boost in rankings. Still, you'd fare better simply by getting a single link from an authoritative site like CNN, Yahoo Directory, DMOZ, ZDNet, and so forth.

CREATE AND PROMOTE *BUZZ* TO TURBO-CHARGE YOUR WEBSITE RANKINGS!

One of the most powerful ways to *quickly* build inbound links is to create a useful tool, video, or comprehensive written resource designed to spread across the web via word of mouth—aka, *viral marketing*. SEO's often refer to such content as *linkbait*, since you're creating highly useful or entertaining content with the goal of compelling bloggers and other website owners to link to it (i.e., take the bait).

Often the easiest and most effective linkbait comes in the form of a detailed list with a catchy headline. We recommend making a list of topics your customers are interested in and then start cranking out articles that are loosely focused on your niche, featuring titles that begin like:

- 100 Tools and Resources for . . .
- 50 Tips to . . .
- 100+ Resources to Help You . . .
- 75 Online Resources for . . .
- 30+ Simple Things You Can Do to . . .
- 25 Ways to . . .

At its simplest, an article can be *"100 Resources for . . ."* followed by whatever your niche is, with a list of 100 sites, tools, and articles you've found online related to that topic and a short summary of each. You'll be pleasantly surprised to learn how many people will link to such articles and resource lists. By promoting this kind of content on social media sites like Digg.com, StumbleUpon.com, and Delicious.com, you can quickly reach a large audience of people who are very likely to link to your content.

DON'T SWEAT THE SMALL STUFF

You can't always control who links to you, so if you have a few low-quality or off-topic links pointing at your site, don't worry about it. This is actually not a big deal. Every site has a few off-topic links pointing to them. In fact, a small number of off-topic links makes your link-structure appear even more natural. But you should strive to make the bulk of your incoming links come from topically relevant sources.

CATCH THE LOCAL SEARCH TIDAL WAVE

We've discussed the details of keyword placement and link building, but businesses with a brick-and-mortar presence targeting a regional audience also should be aware of the increasing importance of local search. Perry and Bryan have discussed using local targeting in AdWords to reach prospects via pay-per-click. However, you may not know that Google does something very similar in the organic search results, too!

While the intricacies of *listing your business in Google's local search results* could fill a book by itself, you'll be pleased to know that Google has made the entire process very easy with the automated tools inside its *Local Business Center* at www.google.com /local/add.

If your business has a physical location that directly services customers (as opposed to being a strictly online endeavor that services a national or international market), then I can't stress enough the importance of creating a Local Business Center account and adding your business, or claiming it as your own if your business is already listed.

WHAT REALLY SMART ONLINE MARKETERS DO

Smart online marketing professionals are multi-dimensional in their strategies. They seldom put all of their eggs in a single basket. This is especially true in regards to pay-per-click and organic search marketing efforts. Because so many aspects of the two strategies run parallel to each other, it makes good sense to understand how both work and employ them in unison so your efforts work double-duty and your results are exponentially multiplied.

As you test your keywords, benefits, and features to learn what's working in your AdWords campaigns, it just makes sense to redeploy your successes along the parallel path of organic search as well. Failing to do so means you are probably leaving easy money on the table! Sometimes a LOT of money! We know of instances where successful AdWords campaigns have laid the groundwork for enormously successful and very long running organic search marketing campaigns—and at a fraction of the overall cost of maintaining the initial pay-per-click campaign.

As mentioned, success in the organic search results takes some time and patience. AdWords is quicker in the near term but arguably more expensive. However, by using AdWords to help you test and map out your organic strategies, it's possible to build a long-term cash cow with the potential for success that can run indefinitely and at a cost so low it's borderline free in the long run.

Bear in mind that this chapter is merely an organic SEO strategy primer. Therefore I will close by highly recommending the following resources since this is where we've obtained all of the info within this chapter—reprinted with permission, of course—as a sampling of Planet Ocean's in-depth research and useful resources:

Planet Ocean's Beginner's Guide to SEO—
http://Guide.PlanetOceanNewsletter.com

The UnFair Advantage Book on Winning The Search Engine Wars—
http://Advantage.PlanetOceanNewsletter.com.

Planet Ocean's Members-Only Monthly Publication—SearchEngineNews.com
http://www.PlanetOceanNewsletter.com.

Planet Ocean has been specializing in teaching people how to rank their sites at the top of the organic search results since 1997. It is a pioneer in the field and remains one of the foremost authorities on the subject—a trusted source for solid, long term SEO strategy. It is the resource we use when mapping out our own organic search marketing strategies.

CHAPTER 26

That Last Winner-Take-All Edge: Google's Tools for Smarter AdWords Results

In 1996 the Chicago Bulls won its fourth NBA title, and Michael Jordan, the star of the team, grossed $80 million.

Jordan's teammate Joe Kleine made $272,250 in 1996. Heard of Joe? Probably not.

Jordan takes the Bulls to the world championship and earns 294 times as much money as his teammate. Does that mean, therefore, that Michael Jordan is 294 times as good a basketball player as Joe Kleine? Not at all.

■ ■ ■

So why the difference in pay? Simply put, Michael Jordan drives sales of basketballs, tennis shoes, T-shirts, soft drinks, and toothpaste in Paris, Barcelona, Buenos Aires, Tokyo, Melbourne, Johannesburg, and Davenport, Iowa.

Joe Kleine doesn't.

In the words of Thomas Friedman, author of *The Lexus and the Olive Tree:* "The gap between first place and second place grows larger, and the gap between first place and last place becomes staggering. In many fields there is rarely one winner, but those near the top get a disproportionate share."

How would you like to be the winner who takes all? How would you like to have that disproportionate share?

> The process in this book gives you that last 1% of knowledge edge that makes you sharper than your competitors and smarter about your own market. That means you'll have better ability to grow faster by attracting more customers, and more long-term staying power in your business.

FOR BROAD- AND PHRASE-MATCHED KEYWORDS, KNOW PRECISELY WHAT YOUR VISITORS TYPED IN TO FIND YOU

This can go a long way toward cutting your spend and increasing both your click-through rate *and* your conversion rate.

There may be broad- or phrase-matched terms you're bidding on that have your ads showing on searches you don't really want to show for. How can you know?

Simple: Select one or several keywords in your list and click the "See search terms" button.

		Keyword	Status ? ↓	Selected / All		Impr.	CTR	Avg
		Total - all keywords			990	110,978	0.89%	
☐	●	cold calling for cowards			0	1	0.00%	
☑	●	cold calling			31	5,548	0.56%	
☐	●	cold calling tips			3	324	0.93%	
☐	●	cold calling tip			0	17	0.00%	
☐	●	cold call selling			0	23	0.00%	

+ Add keywords · Edit · Change status... ▼ · See search terms... ▼ · More actions... ▼

Google will then give you a listing of exact search terms people typed in to find you. If there are any on the list that you believe you shouldn't be showing for, now you can add them in as negative keywords.

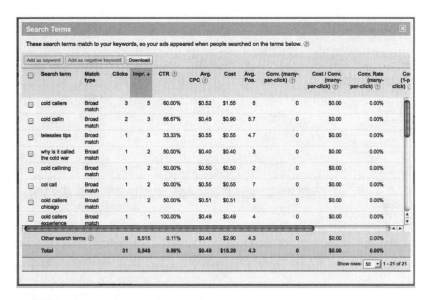

KNOW WHO YOUR VISITORS ARE, BETTER THAN ANYONE ELSE: GOOGLE ANALYTICS

The "conversion tracking" that's built into Google AdWords gives you a skeletal view of how well your keywords are producing individual actions like opt-ins and sales. Google Analytics goes far deeper to connect those keywords to very specific visitor activity everywhere on your site.

Google gives you graphics and reports that tell you that much more about who is finding you on the internet—and when, and where, and how, and how long. With Analytics you can know:

- How many visits your site gets, daily and hourly
- What websites your customers are coming from
- Where your visitors are finding you around the world
- How much time visitors spend on each of your pages
- Where your potential customers are bailing out
- What order they click from page to page
- What browsers, platforms, screen sizes, connection speeds your visitors are using
- And much more

We highly recommend the Analytics learning materials and tools available from our friends over at ROIRevolution.com.

WHY AREN'T MY ADS SHOWING?
THE ADS DIAGNOSTIC TOOL

Get a quick answer to why your ads aren't showing, see your quality score, or find out if you've unwittingly put the same keyword in multiple places and it's triggering the wrong ad. Just mouse over the tiny speech bubble icon next to your keyword and a box will pop up telling you whether everything's kosher or not:

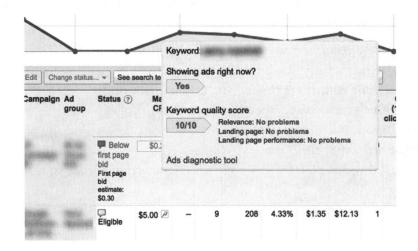

EDITING CPCS AND URLS FOR GROUPS OF KEYWORDS

You want to get the most value for the lowest expenditure from all of your keywords. But bid the same price on all of them and I virtually guarantee this won't happen. Send visitors from every keyword to the same landing page, and you've got the same problem.

To fix this, go into your ad group, find the "Keywords" tab, check off the keywords you want to edit, and click "Edit" at the top of the list:

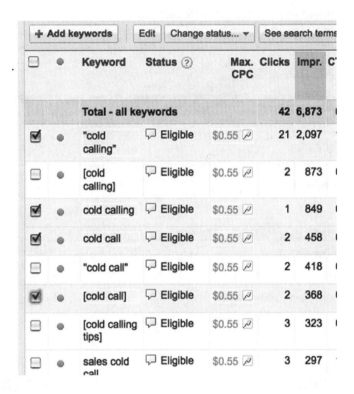

If I want better conversions and even a better quality score for a specific keyword, I can send all its traffic to a special landing page made just for it. Or I can use this feature to put in separate tracking code for individual keywords.

TWEAK YOUR MAJOR CAMPAIGN SETTINGS

The "Campaign Settings" are the most dollar-saving—or dollar-squandering—parameters you can adjust on your account, outside your cost per click. Set them for each of your campaigns and the ad groups in the campaign will follow suit:

· Plan for your ads to stop showing after a certain date.
· Adjust your daily budget.

ULTIMATE GUIDE TO GOOGLE ADWORDS

- Determine how evenly Google will "spend" your money during the day.
- Decide what times of day to show your ads.
- Set preferred positions on the page.
- Adjust whether you show better ads more, or rotate them evenly.
- Adjust whether you show on search, the content network, and mobile devices.
- Change your languages.
- Change your geographic settings.

To make these adjustments, open the campaign you want to tweak, and click the "Settings" tab in the middle of the page:

ACCOUNT MANAGERS LIVE AND DIE BY ADWORDS EDITOR

I know of no AdWords account manager who does not swear by AdWords Editor as the fastest and easiest way to keep track of large volumes of campaigns, ad groups, ads, and keywords.

It uses Google's API and allows you to download all necessary account information to your computer desktop, edit it there easily, and upload it back to your account.

254 · 26 / THAT LAST WINNER-TAKE-ALL EDGE: GOOGLE'S TOOLS FOR SMARTER ADWORDS RESULTS

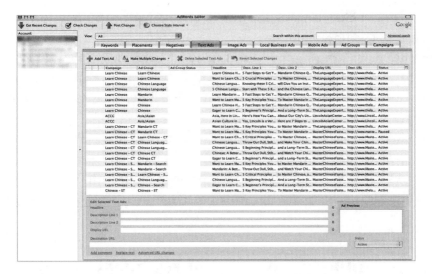

And it's free. Download it at google.com/intl/en/adwordseditor/.

AUTOMATIC BIDDING: SHOULD YOU USE IT?
BEWARE THE MYTH OF THE "MARKETING BUDGET"

You can set all your bids yourself, or have Google do it. This is also under your campaign's "Settings" tab.

Turn it on and you don't "bid" anything per se. You just tell Google what your daily budget is, and they'll automatically set your cost per click for you. That way you get the maximum number of clicks each day without going over your spending limit.

But do you want Google setting your cost-per-click for you?

Your goal isn't the maximum number of clicks. Your goal is to get the maximum value (VPV) from your clicks. Google doesn't figure that out for you here. They'll set your CPC based on how many possible clicks they believe they can get from you.

More importantly, if you know you're getting back $1.50 for every $1.00 you spend, why put a budget limit on it?

The idea of a marketing "budget" is flawed. Marketing is a form of investment. Its sole constraint is that every venue—e.g., a keyword on Google, an ad in a magazine—has its own sweet spot of maximum profitability, followed by a law of diminishing returns.

Of course you *will* set your budget within a certain reasonable limit to prevent losses in early testing. You also want to prevent anomalous spending, such as sudden changes in a market, click fraud, or unplanned errors with Google's system.

But don't let the fox guard the henhouse. Find the sweet spot yourself, and aim for it.

SCHEDULE YOUR ADS TO SHOW AT THE TIMES YOU GET THE BEST CONVERSIONS

Watch your conversion numbers and you may discover that your best clicks come in between 4 and 6 P.M. Or at breakfast time. Or early morning and late night.

You may also discover that your worst clicks always come in, for example, between 10 A.M. and noon.

So use Ad Schedule and turn off the traffic when it's bad and turn it on when it's good. This is a smart way to budget your dollars and pinpoint when and where you'll get the highest visitor value.

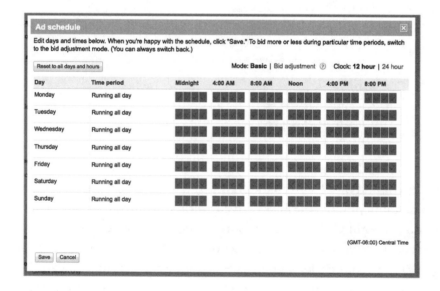

POSITION PREFERENCE

If you've done your homework and you know that for a particular keyword you can get the best ROI in, say, positions four through seven on the results page, then you can enable Position Preference to tell Google that you only want your ads showing there. Then set your bids accordingly.

To enable it, go into your campaign and under the "Settings" tab find the Position Preference option under "Bidding and Budget." This will simply turn the option on or off.

You choose your actual position by individual keyword. As with most price items in the interface, simply click on the appropriate row in the column to edit it:

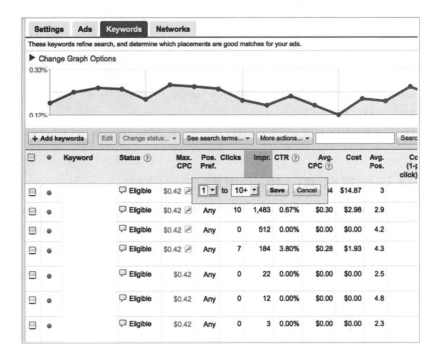

It's better to start broad than narrow. And be sure that your bids are high enough to merit the position you've selected, otherwise you won't show.

SHOW BETTER ADS MORE OFTEN, OR ROTATE THEM EVENLY?

If you're split-testing two or more ads in an ad group, Google will automatically show the better-performing one a higher percentage of the time, unless you tell them to "Rotate" them, or show them more evenly. They'll even give you a guilt trip for telling them so:

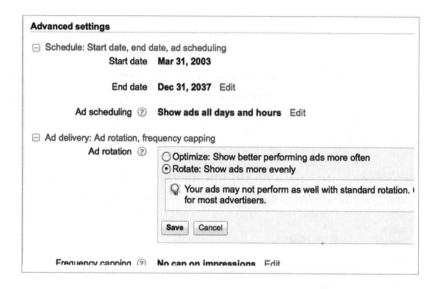

Google will tell you right under the CTR how much each ad is "served." It's virtually never an exact 50/50.

I prefer this setting, so that the results for each ad will come in at the same speed.

CUSTOM REPORTS TO MAKE YOU SMARTER

You can't fit every relevant detail about your campaigns on the summary pages. Sometimes you need specific data spelled out in a chart or customized list. So you can generate a report of your choice, which can include graphs and more.

You've got a ton of options:

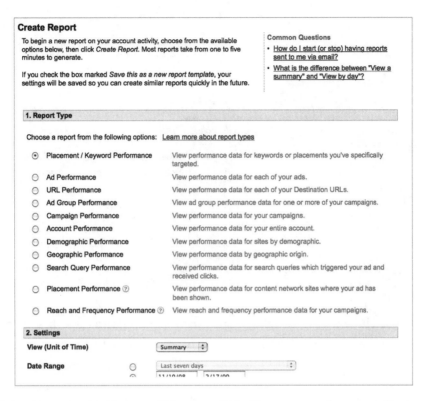

It's in these reports that you'll have an "Aha!" moment where you discover some hidden correlation among pieces of data, which can either save you money or earn you huge amounts more.

SITE AND CATEGORY EXCLUSION

This slices up content network traffic in totally different ways, so that you can block whole categories of websites from having your ads displayed.

We already dealt with automatic and managed placements, and individual site exclusion, in our chapters on the content network. This goes much further than that, so that your ads are kept away from whole swaths of online content if needed.

Site and Category Exclusion is accessed from the Tools page. Get there from the "Tools" or "Opportunities" tab in the dark green bar at the top of your campaign summary.

Site and Category Exclusion

Use this tool to prevent individual websites or categories of webpages in the Google Network from showing your ads. The e: selected campaign. Unless otherwise noted, exclusions will not apply to the search portion of your campaigns. Learn more

Campaign: [02 White Papers   ▼]
See which content sites have shown your ads

| Sites (4) | **Topics** | Media Types | Page Types |

Check one or more of the following topics to exclude related webpages. ⑦

Exclude	Impr.	Clicks	CTR	Cost	Avg. CPC	Avg. CPM
Conflict & tragedy ⑦						
☐ Crime, police & emergency	0	0	0.00%	$0.00	$0.00	$0.00
☐ Death & tragedy	0	0	0.00%	$0.00	$0.00	$0.00
☐ Military & international conflict	0	0	0.00%	$0.00	$0.00	$0.00
Edgy content ⑦						
☐ Juvenile, gross & bizarre content	155	0	0.00%	$0.00	$0.00	$0.00
☐ Profanity & rough language	0	0	0.00%	$0.00	$0.00	$0.00
☐ Sexually suggestive content	0	0	0.00%	$0.00	$0.00	$0.00

Data from the last 48 hours may not be available

[Save all changes] [Cancel]

You can exclude sites in the above categories. You can also exclude sites or pages with video. And under the "Page Types" tab you can choose to eliminate error pages and parked domains from displaying your ads. That's a big impression-waster right there.

You'll note also—though it's not clear from the above graphic—that Google shows your actual numbers and performance sliced up according to these different categories of sites and pages. Impressions, clicks, conversion rates, and more. That may signal site types that you clearly don't want to show on. You might also discover that you're doing better in some categories, and want to manually choose more places to appear.

CONVERSION OPTIMIZER

This is where you hand Google the controls to your clicks' prices and placement, so that you can target a specific Cost Per Action (CPA), or cost per conversion, that you want to pay.

You can read about Conversion Optimizer and get started with it by going to www.google.com/adwords/conversionoptimizer/.

It can be set up from your account, by going into the particular campaign you want to turn it on for, clicking on the "Settings" tab and choosing to edit your "Bidding option":

You can access it directly and turn it on in any campaign that's had at least 15 conversions in the last 30 days. History and track record are key here.

You're now paying a CPA instead of a CPC. Google manages your bids based on how you're performing in various geographic locations or times of day, on particular keywords, and so on.

Should you use it? For one thing, this is a question of risk. You're giving Google freer reign to choose where and when you show, and how your price breaks down for the impressions and clicks you get. Hate that kind of risk? Then don't use it.

Our customers' experiences with this vary. I recommend you try it in a small but productive corner of your account and watch it like a hawk for the first few days and weeks.

KNOW WHAT YOU *COULD* BE SPENDING, WITH BID SIMULATOR

This is already built in and functioning within your interface. Any keywords getting a decent amount of traffic where you're bidding by CPC, or cost per click (as opposed to CPM, cost per thousand impressions or CPA, cost per action), will show the Bid Simulator's prediction of what your traffic could be.

This answers the question, "How much traffic would I get if I bid higher or lower?"

To see it, click on the tiny icon next to your keyword's bid price:

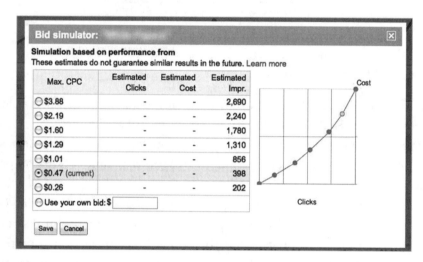

Max. CPC	Estimated Clicks	Estimated Cost	Estimated Impr.
◯ $3.88	-	-	2,690
◯ $2.19	-	-	2,240
◯ $1.60	-	-	1,780
◯ $1.29	-	-	1,310
◯ $1.01	-	-	856
◉ $0.47 (current)	-	-	398
◯ $0.26	-	-	202
◯ Use your own bid: $			

HAVING THE EDGE

In the Google world (and the rest of the world, for that matter) the winner takes all. That last 1% of edge that this level of leverage will give you can the mean the difference between you sitting at the top of a market, controlling it, or your competitor taking over. Which one will it be?

Uncle Claude Sez

Things done in one way may be twice as easy, half as costly, as when done another way. Advertising without this preparation is like a waterfall going to waste. The power may be there, but it is not made effective. We must center the force and direct it in a practical direction.

CHAPTER 27

FAQ: Answers to All Your Frequently-Asked Questions about Google AdWords

B ryan and I have personally consulted with hundreds of people about their marketing projects, and have been inside literally hundreds of Google AdWords accounts. The following questions are the most important and the most common ones we get.

■ ■ ■

ORGANIZING AND GETTING THE MOST FROM YOUR KEYWORDS AND ADS

· Why aren't my ads showing?

- How can I set up my new campaign in a way that will ensure that my keywords get the highest possible CTRs and convert traffic to sales?
- How do I find out in advance what it will cost to be in various positions on the page?
- Should I really have thousands of keywords in my ad groups?
- What do single keywords in quotes " " represent?
- What does "Bid is below first page bid estimate of $x.xx" mean?
- What can I do when Google says, "Bid is below first page bid estimate of $x.xx"?
- What is Quality Score, and what is it based on?
- Why does Google say I have to pay $10.00 per click? Should I pay it?
- Why does Google say my quality score is poor, or 1/10?
- Am I better off going after single keywords with a lot of searches like "Business," or combo-phrases like "Business Marketing"?
- What's the best way to find the right keywords for my product?
- What do I do when healthy, active keywords are still deathly expensive?
- Does Google disable ad groups or campaigns or keywords?

THE PEEL & STICK METHOD

- What is Peel & Stick and when do I use it?
- Google doesn't have a Peel & Stick feature. Do I have to do this manually?

GETTING A BETTER CLICKTHROUGH RATE

- What do you consider to be a good CTR?
- How do I split test ads?
- How many impressions or clicks do I need before I declare a winner?
- Do you recommend clicking on your own Google ad a few times when you first post it, in order to start it off with a high clickthrough rate?
- What's the best way to manage my daily, weekly, and monthly AdWords costs?

BETTER LANDING PAGES

- Should I have three different websites selling the same product, all bidding on the same keywords and advertising on Google?

TESTING AND CONVERTING YOUR TRAFFIC

- Do you recommend Google's Conversion Tracker?
- What tool do you recommend for split-testing landing pages?

- What do I do when I see that some of my keywords are converting to sales and some aren't?
- Do you recommend the Website Optimizer?

USING SPECIAL TOOLS

- How trustworthy is Google's Traffic Estimator?
- When is Ad Scheduling useful?
- Should I have Google fix my bids? Do you recommend the Budget Optimizer?

WHERE AND WHEN TO SHOW YOUR ADS

- How do I get my ads into the "preferred listings"—those ultra-high-visibility sponsored positions on the top left of Google's search results?
- I have two ads in my a, but Google doesn't show them evenly. Why is this?
- I've set it to show ads evenly, but my ads still don't get shown evenly. Sometimes it's 90%–10% or worse. What's wrong?
- If I delete an underperforming ad and write a new one, how can I compare the performance of the two together?
- With AdWords is there a "sweet spot" for my ad to be in—first, third, fourth, or sixth position on a page?
- I hear the content network is lousy traffic. Should I advertise on it?
- Should I advertise on Yahoo or MSN?

WORKING IN SPECIALIZED MARKETS

- Does network marketing or MLM work on Google?
- How do I do affiliate marketing on Google?
- How do I market a high-dollar item effectively on Google?
- My niche is specialized, and I have found very few keywords that draw more than a few thousand requests per month. Is this still a good avenue for me?

GOOGLE'S REGULAR SEARCH ENGINE

- What is your number-one Search Engine Optimization (SEO) strategy?
- Does using Google AdWords improve your ranking on Google's regular organic search engine listings?

Answers begin on the next page.

ORGANIZING AND GETTING THE MOST FROM YOUR KEYWORDS AND ADS

Q: Why aren't my ads showing?

First, did you trust Google's Traffic Estimator when you set up your campaign? Big mistake. It says you'll be in third position from the top on such-and-such a price, when in reality you'll be back on page 3. Set your bids conservatively, and check back after your ads have run to see what average positions your keywords have been in. Then adjust them accordingly.

Second, check what countries you're showing in. Your ads may be in position 1 in the United Kingdom but position 20 in the United States (or vice versa), while Google tells you your average position is 3 or 4.

Third, click the "search" button again, multiple times, to be sure.

Fourth, double-check the daily budget for the campaign you're in. Is it possible that you already hit the limit for the day and Google is done showing your ads?

Finally, understand that only a tiny percentage of advertisers in any market show up all the time, 100%, for all searches on a particular keyword. Those are the advertisers that get the most clicks and have the best quality score, and have been in the game the longest.

Q: How can I set up my new campaign in a way that will ensure that my keywords get the highest possible CTRs and convert traffic to sales?

First, wherever it's humanly possible, *only put keywords in an ad group that actually appears in the ad*—better still, in the ad's headline. If you've got keywords that don't match the ad, then take them out and stick them in a new ad group, and write a new ad that uses those specific keywords.

Create as many different ad groups as you need to, in order to make this work.

Second, only allow your ads at first to show on Google searches alone. Do this for the first few days or weeks until you've established that all your highest-traffic keywords are profitable. When that's settled, turn on the other sources. Google's traffic is a single, more predictable source. Content traffic, highly unpredictable.

When viewing one of your campaigns, click on the "Settings" tab and the Edit link next to "Networks, devices, and extensions." You'll see that the Networks option lets you choose:

```
Networks, devices, and extensions

Networks and devices  ?      ○ All available sites and devices
                             ◉ Let me choose...
                     Search   ☑ Google search
                                ☑ Search partners (requires Google search)
                    Content   ☑ Content network
                                ◉ Relevant pages across the entire network
                                ○ Relevant pages only on the placements I manage
                    Devices  ?  ☑ Desktop and laptop computers
                                ☑ iPhones and other mobile devices with full Internet browsers

                     [ Save ]  [ Cancel ]

Bidding and budget
```

By default all of these boxes are checked. *We suggest that you uncheck all of them except for Google.* At the very least, uncheck the content network. Why?

Because in all likelihood the traffic that comes from content network will be of much different quality than the traffic coming from just Google alone. Unpredictable; a very different mix. So start with the most predictable, homogeneous traffic that's most likely to turn into paying customers.

When you get that traffic profitable, turn on the other sources. In that case your total volume of traffic may double, or triple, or more, though it will be more of a challenge to turn into buyers. But why not start with traffic that's most likely to convert?

Q: How do I find out in advance what it will cost to be in various positions on the page?

Here are three sites you can check out. They will frequently be inaccurate, but no more so than Google's Traffic Estimator:

1. www.SpyFu.com
2. www.KeyCompete.com
3. www.iSpionage.com

Q: Should I really have thousands of keywords in my ad groups?

You want as many *relevant* keywords as humanly possible but not all in one group. The more good keywords the merrier—*if* they're turning out a good CTR.

And that only happens if they're in *small, tightly clustered groups* that match each ad's message well. Thousands of keywords in your whole account, yes. Thousands of keywords in individual ad groups, no.

Q: What do single keywords in quotes " " represent?

When used in the same list along with single keywords without delimiters, these represent correct spellings and normal usage of the term in a phrase or sentence. The term without delimiters then catches misspellings and any other odd, glitchy variation on the keyword. If you include these in your keyword list, you'll find they each get searches of their own.

Q: What does "Bid is below first page bid estimate of $x.xx" mean?

It means either 1) Google is showing you only on page 2 or 3 or lower of search results, and not the first page, or 2) they're showing you only a tiny percentage of the time.

Sometimes it means you're just not bidding enough. Most of the time it's because your quality score is low. If your ad group isn't already set to display quality score, just mouse over the magnifying glass next to the keyword in question and it will tell you what your quality score is.

If your quality score is low, your first priority is to repair that, before you try raising your bid.

Q: What all can I do when Google says, "Bid is below first page bid estimate of $x.xx"?

Two options: 1) Bid what Google asks, 2) tweak the copy of your Google ad and/or the content of your webpage, to convince Google's computers that your ad and website are relevant, thereby improving your quality score.

There are numerous ways to approach quality score. Among them: post more pages with keyword–rich content throughout your site and put links to those pages from your landing page, and then to provide more engaging/involving content on your landing page (surveys, audios, videos, etc.) to keep people there, and interested, longer.

Q: What is Quality Score, and what is it based on?

Google will never openly share the exact formula that they use to determine your Quality Score and minimum bid price. But here's what we've repeatedly found to matter most:

- Your CTR
- The match between your keyword and your ad
- How that keyword has always performed across Google, historically

· The amount and quality of keyword-relevant content on your landing page
· The amount and quality of keyword-relevant content on your whole website
· How quickly visitors hit the back button after visiting your site
· How quickly visitors leave and go elsewhere after visiting your site

And to further mystify things, Google grades you on the curve compared to your competitors.

As far as your specific rank on the page, the primary factors are 1) your bid price, and 2) your CTR.

Q: Why does Google say I have to bid $10.00 per click? Should I pay it?

No. See above. This is not a function of your somehow being in a hyper-competitive market; rather it's a function of your quality score.

Q: Why does Google say my quality score is poor, or 1/10?

A quality score of two or three out of ten is a sign that you just need to follow the fundamental advice we give in this book and match keywords to ads using peel & stick, and make your landing pages and website clearly and unmistakably relevant to the keywords you're bidding on.

However, if you're getting a quality score of 1/10, then something systemic is wrong. Among the possibilities:

A human editor at Google visited your site some time recently and asked the "Grandma" question, i.e., "Would I be comfortable sending my grandmother to this site?" The answer was "No," and your site was flagged internally, which then reflects itself in a poor quality score. The only way we know to reverse this is to have a customer service person or, more likely, a certified account rep inquire into it, and have it lifted if possible.

You clearly have hosts of affiliate links on your landing page, sending traffic to other merchant sites.

Too many affiliates are buying Google clicks and sending them to your site.

Your domain name is blacklisted because of spamming or similar reasons.

Your site is built on duplicate content, using copy and articles taken from other sites or used verbatim or nearly verbatim on other sites across the internet.

With the exception of the "human editor" problem above, the other issues can usually be fixed directly by adjusting or altering the content of your site.

Q: Am I better off going after single keywords with a lot of searches like "Business," or combo-phrases like "Business Marketing"?

Two issues here. First, "business" is a broad term that draws people looking for any number of things, and can be difficult to convert. Granted, bidding on the exact-match term [business] is more likely to be productive for you than bidding on the generic word.

Terms like this generally bring in low quality traffic. Test the conversion rate, and see if it's a worthwhile deal or not.

Q: What's the best way to find the right keywords for my product?

Do your free keyword research first using Google's keyword tool at google.com/key words, and freekeywords.wordtracker.com. Wordtracker (www.wordtracker.info) is a powerful paid tool that any serious AdWords marketer should have a subscription to.

Watch your competition:

- How many advertisers are there? The number could be anywhere from one or two to several hundred. If there are fewer than eight or ten bidders, you could get the bottom position on page one for as little as $0.01.
- Figure out which competitors are seriously response-oriented. Pay special attention to everything they do.
- Tip: Pay attention to Google advertisers who split-test their ads—when you do a search on a keyword that you're researching, click the "search" button multiple times and you'll see that some ads change while others stay the same. The advertisers who split test are almost always the sharpest pencils in the box.
- Go to Yahoo and MSN, and find out what advertisers are doing there.

Get keywords from dictionary/thesaurus sites such as www.LexFN.com and from printed sources on your topic, such as glossaries and indexes.

Q: What do I do when healthy, active keywords are still deathly expensive?

The top bidders in any established market on Google are going negative on the initial sale because they make it up later with a robust back end that includes cross-sells, upsells, and ongoing paid subscriptions. Can you provide this, too? The first baby step in this direction is to capture contact information and then market to those contacts aggressively, maximizing the value of every visitor you get.

Google artificially elevates prices for brand-new advertisers that they're unfamiliar with. Also, can you:

· Get the top bidders in your market to become affiliates of your site?
· Make a joint-venture offer to your competitors, playing like the little bank branch inside the giant supermarket?
· Offer your competitors who send traffic to you a pay-per-action deal (per-click or per download) to help them monetize some of their traffic and subsidize their $10.00 per click?
· Buy exit traffic from competitors' sites?

Q: Does Google disable ad groups or campaigns or keywords?

As of this writing, none of the above. It used to, though. Now Google just shows your keywords a paltry fraction of the time if the quality score is low.

Google does *disapprove* ads that don't meet its editorial guidelines. (And if you violate their policies repeatedly they'll shut down your whole account and ban you from Google entirely.)

But follow Google's policies and fully implement our advice, and these problems will take care of themselves.

THE PEEL & STICK METHOD

Q: What is Peel & Stick and when do I use it?

This can increase the CTR of your individual keywords. Very simply:

1. Move a keyword into a new ad group
2. Write an ad whose message matches it perfectly.

For Peel & Stick to improve a keyword's CTR, though, the keyword has to meet two conditions:

1. It gets a significant amount of searches.
2. It doesn't already match the ad perfectly, or it isn't used in the ad.

If the keyword doesn't meet both of these conditions, don't waste your time. *Tip: Don't delete the keyword from the old ad group. Just pause it.*

Q: Google doesn't have a Peel & Stick feature. Do I have to do this manually?

Sorry, it doesn't do it automatically. Pause the keyword and its closest variations in your old list, click on "Create a new ad group," and put in the new set of keywords with a new ad.

GETTING A BETTER CLICKTHROUGH RATE

Q: What do you consider to be a good CTR?

Broadly speaking, any time you're above 1.0% you're doing something right. Any time you're significantly below that, it means something needs attention.

However, this all depends on the market first, the keyword second. Keywords where people are looking for you by name will always have a high CTR. Keywords where you've got to introduce new ideas or educate people will have a much lower rate.

Regardless, *every tenth of a point of improvement you get by strengthening your copy brings you more visitors.*

Three percent is what I would consider to be a pretty respectable message-to-market match.

We've achieved CTRs of 10.0% or better when the text in the ad is a precise match to a question that the user types into a search engine. For example:

Ethernet Basics Guide
Simple Tutorial on Ethernet, TCP/IP
5 Page Paper, Free Instant Download
www.xyzcompany.com

. . . and note the phrase in the keyword list that got the highest CTR by far:

Keyword	Clicks	Impressions	CTR
what is ethernet	5,314	32,481	16.3%

16.3% is one dang high CTR! And it wasn't hard to achieve at all.

So this suggests a strategy: What ultra–specific questions can you answer for your audience? Using those questions as keyword phrases can earn you excellent CTRs.

Q: How exactly do I split test ads?

Write an ad. Stick it up in your ad group. Now look for "Create New Ad" down in your Ad Variations tab, and click "Text ad." Write a second one—still following the advice we give, but as different as possible from the first. Submit it, and you're set to go.

Google will automatically alternate the two and show you the impressions, clicks, and clickthrough rate for each one.

Split test as many ads at a time as you want. I personally prefer just two at a time, so each one can get results faster.

What should you test for? The best clickthrough rate, for starters. But if you can set up Google's conversion tracking in your account, then wait longer and find which ad has a lower cost per conversion.

Q: How many impressions or clicks do I need before I declare a winner?

Rule of thumb: get 30 *clicks* (not impressions) on each ad before declaring a winner and deleting the loser. But to be more sure, use the tool at www.SplitTester.com.

Q: Do you recommend clicking on your own Google ad a few times when you first post it, in order to start it off with a high clickthrough rate?

If you want to become a legitimate marketer, no. Google has their own built-in Click-Fraud-B.S.-Detector that tells the system when a person is trying to inflate their CTR with extra clicks.

The goal is to find out what works. Let the live market tell you what does and doesn't fly, and adjust your products and message to give people what they want.

Q: What's the best way to manage my daily, weekly, and monthly AdWords costs? Is there a difference between overall costs of advertising in the United Kingdom versus the United States or other countries?

There are two ways to control cost:

1. Adjust your daily budget, realizing that the daily amounts are very crude approximations.
2. Adjust your maximum bids.

There is a difference between each country you advertise in. In most cases the traffic is most expensive in the United States. *There are many keyword bargains to be found in other countries.*

With that in mind, if you sell all over the world, you might want to have United States/Canadian/Australian/United Kingdom campaigns separate from the rest of the world, because otherwise you'll likely pay more than you need to for non-U.S. Google ads.

BETTER LANDING PAGES

Q: Should I have three different websites selling the same product, all bidding on the same keywords and advertising on Google?

Sure . . . if you want to end up bidding against yourself. Google frowns on this.

Now if you have different versions of a product, designed for different markets, you can put bids for both on the same keywords and get different slices of the same traffic. For example, bid on "flowers" and have one site that sells fresh-cut roses and another site that sells gift baskets. The ads won't cannibalize each other.

TESTING AND CONVERTING YOUR TRAFFIC

Q: Do you recommend using Google's Conversion Tracker?

Yes, absolutely. It's far from flawless, but it lets you track conversion all the way down to individual keywords. I recommend it plus one or several other third-party conversion tools.

Q: What tool do you recommend for split testing landing pages?

Google's Website Optimizer is the simplest starting place for doing A/B split testing.

Hypertracker (www.hypertracker.net) is a powerful tool for doing split testing of multiple kinds—sales, opt-ins, landing page clickthroughs, and more. In fact, we've put together a free tutorial (http://video.hypertracker.net) that shows all the basics you need in order to set up and track landing pages, opt-ins, sales, and more.

You can also use integrated services such as 1Shopping Cart (www.1Shopping Cart.com). This is a full shopping cart service that lets you manage split tests, autoresponders, affiliates, and more.

Q: What do I do when I see that some of my keywords are converting to sales and some aren't?

Use Google's conversion tracker and you'll see this. Some keywords give you a cost per conversion of $1.00; others as much as $500.00.

There are always two directions you can go: grow their conversions and sales, or cut your spending on them. Both are valid. I recommend you do the former first. Do Peel & Stick on a keyword, send it to a landing page of its own; do what you can to get it to sell. If that doesn't work, cut its bid price or else pause it.

And remember, *high–bid positions get more low–quality traffic; low–bid positions get less traffic but it's higher quality*. Sometimes the solution is to just be at position eight instead of position two, or to be on page two instead of page one.

Q: Do you recommend Google's Website Optimizer?

Any tool that makes it easier for you to test and improve conversions, I'm a fan of. For an entire higher level of sophistication in testing and in growing conversions, read about David Bullock's expert approach at DavidBullock.com/whitepapers.shtml.

USING SPECIAL TOOLS

Q: How trustworthy is Google's Traffic Estimator? When I used this feature, Google predicted that the positions for my keywords would all be in the 1–6 range. However, the actual positions Google gave me, when my ads starting showing, were all over the place—from 1 to 45. Is there something wrong?

The "Traffic Estimator" can be wildly inaccurate. You'll have to base your bids on past traffic and actual recorded campaign statistics, not on Google's estimates.

Q: When is Ad Scheduling useful?

You may discover that your best clicks come in between 4 and 6 P.M. Or at breakfast time. Or early morning and late night. You may also discover, for example, that your worst clicks always come in between 10 A.M. and noon.

So use Ad Scheduling and turn off the traffic when it's bad and turn it on when it's good. This is a smart way to budget your dollars and pinpoint when and where you'll get the highest visitor value.

Turn this on and off from "Scheduling and serving" in your Campaign Settings.

Q: Should I have Google fix my bids? Do you recommend the Budget Optimizer?

I was looking just yesterday at an ad group where the top two keywords were both costing $0.37 a click. One had a cost per conversion of $13.00, the other nearly $68.00. Bidding the same for both wasn't working. To set this across the board with all the campaigns would be silly.

With Google's Budget Optimizer, you tell Google what your daily budget is, and they'll automatically set your cost-per-click for you. That way you get the maximum number of clicks each day without going over your spending limit.

Your goal isn't the maximum number of clicks. Your goal is to get the maximum value (VPV) from your clicks. Google can't figure that out for you. They'll set your CPC based on how many possible clicks they believe they can get out of you.

Don't let the Doberman guard the ham sandwiches. Be your own judge as to how much each click is worth to you, and control your spending yourself.

WHERE AND WHEN TO SHOW YOUR ADS

Q: How do I get my ads into the "preferred listings"—those ultra-high-visibility sponsored positions on the top left of Google's search results?

Google usually shows two or three:

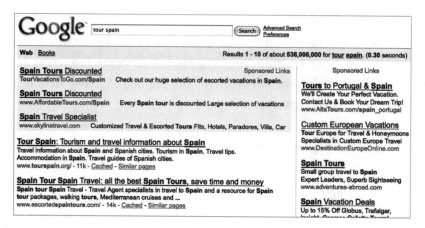

Our revered friends at Planet Ocean who specialize in search engine optimization (www.SearchEngineNews.com) offer these tips:

1. You have to be bidding in fairly competitive, commercially oriented keyword categories. Not all keywords can get ads to show this way.
2. Your ad has to already be ranking near the top of the AdWords list for that keyword.
3. Your ad has to be earning a high enough CTR for Google to justify giving you the preferred positioning. The exact CTR you need? That's part of Google's secret formula. Savor the mystery!

Q: I have two ads in my ad group, but Google doesn't show them evenly. One of them shows 85% of the time, and the other only about 15% Why is this?

Click on "Edit Campaign Settings" and under "Scheduling and serving" select "Rotate: Show ads more evenly." Google should now show your ads roughly equally. It's never exactly 50/50.

Your other option is "Optimize." With this, if you have more than one ad in each ad group, Google will automatically display the better-performing one more often. They want you (and them) to benefit from the ad that's getting the better CTR.

I prefer to disable this feature, since it will take longer to get complete data if the ads aren't showing evenly.

Q: I've set it to show ads evenly, but my ads still don't get shown evenly. Sometimes it's 90%–10% or worse. What's wrong?

Your ads will never be shown exactly 50/50; sometimes they'll be shown 55%–45% or thereabouts.

However, if you disable Optimized Ad Serving but your ads are still showing at wildly different percentages—e.g., one is showing at 60–65% or more—then your ads may be awaiting approval by a Google editor before they get put into syndication. All ads require editorial approval before going on Search Partners or the content network.

For any federally regulated subjects and markets—health and medicine, adult content, etc.—editors have to approve your ads before they'll show even on Google, not to mention Google's Search Partners or Content-Targeted sites.

So when you put up a new ad to run against your old one, it may take a week or more before your new ad starts to show on the Search Network and gets served as frequently as your older ad.

Also, be sure that both ads were active and showing for the time frame that you selected. Otherwise, change the time frame.

If none of this is true of your campaign but you're still getting uneven showing, you should call Google's customer support at 1–888–Google9.

Q: If I delete an underperforming ad and write a new one, how can I compare the performance of the two together? Do I have to reset or resubmit the old one so that it shows their performance for the same time period?

Keep a running log for your Google campaigns, such as in a Word document or text file, and record changes you make to your ads and the exact date that you made the change.

That way you can go back into your Google account, set the date to when you submitted the new ad, and compare your performance just for the time period that both ads have been running together.

Q: With Google AdWords is there a "sweet spot" for my ad to be in—first, third, fourth, or sixth position on a page?

This is something I talk about in more careful detail in my Ultra-Advanced Google AdWords Seminar. A quick summary:

> In the majority of markets people get the best ROI both away from the very top *and* away from the bottom of the page. That happens between positions 6 and 8.

> The higher you are on a page, the more likely you are to get clicked on. You also get tire kickers and looky-loos. Especially in position one. And the very last position on a page may get easily ignored as well.

It ultimately depends on your market. In some markets you'll want to be in top position as a means to become dominant. In other markets you'd just be throwing money away.

Our Ultra-Advanced Course (www.AdWordsBlackBelt.com) has more specific ROI charts and statistics on this question. Regardless, test it and go with what works best for you in your own market.

Q: I hear the content network is lousy traffic. Should I advertise on it?

The content network wouldn't be so massive if it were lousy for everyone. It depends on the market, what you're selling, and what sites your ads are showing on.

Set up a separate campaign that's content-only. Test and see with small dollar amounts and short keyword lists if you can make the clicks profitable. A powerful tool for getting the most out of the content network is Google's placement report, which you can run from the "Reports" section of your account. It helps you identify and filter out the sites that bring you crappy traffic.

Q: Should I advertise on Yahoo or MSN?

Short answer: Sure; try them both. They both now have intuitive and useful interfaces similar to Google's that allow for split testing and conversion tracking and more.

Only issue: There's a smaller volume of traffic, and these are different markets. MSN especially is more of a current-events, consumer, and lifestyle market. If you're selling beauty products, consumer items, weight loss, and such, that's a good venue for you. If you're selling 56G–HZ4200 valve controllers, probably not.

WORKING IN SPECIALIZED MARKETS

Q: Does network marketing or MLM work on Google?

Yes, absolutely, *if* you do in-depth keyword research, you use a noncookie-cutter site, and you don't bid against people in your own organization. The best examples of this operate like a sophisticated affiliate program.

The worst examples I see (and I see them often) are businesses that recruit people by telling them there's an infinite amount of traffic on Google. They tell their recruits to go bid on "make money online" and "homebased business," to send all the clicks to a prefab clone site, and then to go sign up more people to do the exact same thing.

Traffic on Google is not infinite. For each keyword there are 11 slots on page one, 11 on page two, and so on. Those keywords can be expensive. If you don't have a unique site with something unique and different to sell, then your new recruits simply become your direct competitors.

If you happen to be part of a network that provides a physical product, however, and there's little or no presence on Google yet, then you can simply sell the product and then get recruits later on, so long as they don't plan on competing with you directly.

Find ways to introduce your own product or information that you can give away or sell, thus differentiating you from people who sell for the same company as you. Create a report or guide that you can offer for $10 to $20 and make enough to offset your traffic costs, and you may find that you enjoy selling these books even more than selling the product itself.

Q: How do I do affiliate marketing on Google?

Odds are you won't be able to buy clicks and send them straight to someone else's site and get a commission. Google only lets one advertiser send traffic to any given site, and someone has probably already beaten you to it.

If you can create a site of your own with fresh, original content, bring people there via Google clicks and collect contact information before sending visitors on to the site you're promoting, you can make this work.

Q: We sell pricey machines that range from $35,000 to $250,000. How do I market a high-dollar item like this effectively on Google?

The core principles that apply to low-dollar, high-traffic B2C markets do also apply to high-dollar, low-traffic, suit-and-tie B2B markets. The important thing: 1) know whether Google is the right tool for finding your customer and 2) talk to your customers the same way they talk to each other and themselves.

Google is the ultimate quick-fix, get-it-now marketing machine. In this industry your ideal customer may not be as likely to search on Google for you, and you may need to go looking in other venues.

A website for capital equipment is going to be an information-driven lead generation and opt-in site, not an e-commerce site.

The objective is to trade your application and problem-solving information for prospects' contact information. Offer reports, white papers, and troubleshooting guides that help the customers solve problems. I have devoted an entire free course to this subject—www.perrymarshall.com/whitepapers.

After you have collected the person's contact information, you plug them into a highly targeted, content-rich autoresponder; use direct mail and telephone to contact them; and earn their trust by publishing quality information on a regular basis and "drip irrigating" them with follow-up mailings, your newsletter, opportunities to attend seminars, and more.

You can test and use all of the tools that are common to online marketers—autoresponders, multiple websites, search engine optimization, testing and tracking, streaming audio and video, Flash, live chat, and nearly every other tool used by mainstream marketers, even if you're in a highly specialized technical discipline. The only difference is how the copy is written.

Q: My niche is specialized, and I have found very few keywords that draw more than a few thousand requests per month. Is this still a good venue for me?

You *can* get worthwhile results on keywords that get just a few searches a month. I call them "nano-niches." Still, there are often a lot more customers in offline markets—trade shows, print media, direct mail, radio, TV, etc. Sometimes it's less expensive to mail out postcards than to buy clicks.

I know one very successful internet marketer and self-publisher, doing over $1 million per year, who generates most of his traffic by advertising in magazines.

For information products (i.e., books, e-books) as opposed to physical products, traffic that comes through search engines is often lower quality than traffic that comes from offline sources.

GOOGLE'S REGULAR SEARCH ENGINE

Q: What is your number-one Search Engine Optimization (SEO) strategy?

I recommend the following five steps:

1. Test a concept and tweak it using Google AdWords. Get it working smoothly and profitably there first.
2. Take it to Yahoo, MSN, and other paid search engines. Use the copy that worked on Google as a starting point.
3. Be certain about your conversion rate and profitability on Google, then use that data to attract affiliates and buy traffic from non-search-engine searches (banner ads, ezines, etc.).
4. After you've determined what keywords convert the best on Google, optimize (SEO) your website for those keywords.
5. Provide as much new, fresh, interactive content as you can, for the search engines to find and promote for you.

Once you've determined which keywords you want rankings on, pick your battles carefully. Some keywords will be *much* easier to win at than others.

Q: Does using Google AdWords improve your ranking on Google's regular organic search engine listings?

Google maintains an "editorial barrier" between paid listings and free ones. In fact, you can have a Google AdWords target page that *only* AdWords visitors are taken to, which is not accessible any other way, and it may not show up in Google's free listings—unless you submit it or link to it from other pages in your site. It is possible that AdWords advertisers get a small advantage in the organic rankings over non-advertisers.

CHAPTER 28

17 Things Yo' Momma Never Told You About Google

1. Ten Thousand Hours

Malcolm Gladwell in his book *Outliers* observes that the most talented boy wonders of the world (Bill Gates, Steve Jobs, the Beatles) were successful not merely because of innate talent—which they no doubt possessed—but because they were given the chance to invest 10,000 hours in their chosen profession. And they got that 10,000 hours in early.

I like the 10,000-hour theory, and lecture on it myself from time to time. Just the other day I was doing a phone consultation with a customer who asked, "If I were going to invest my 10,000 hours in pay–per–click, where would you suggest I focus my energy?"

I replied: "I'm not sure there exists 10,000 hours' worth of stuff to even *know* about pay–per–click. There's a keyword, there's an ad, there's a bid price. If you spent 10,000 hours studying that, I'm not sure what all you would study."

"However," I said, "You can *most definitely* invest 10,000 hours in understanding what came before that click, and what comes after that click. The story, the psychology, the progression of keywords from first inquiry to sale, the art of gently leading your customer where you want him to go."

And I can assure you, if you invest 10,000 hours (i.e., five years' worth of career time) aggressively honing your chops, you *will* be a master marketer and you *will* be in the driver's seat of one of the most lucrative careers in the world today.

2. The "Before" Circle and the "After" Circle

Like I said, that click is just one event. The click is a bridge between two circles: The story the person *is* in, before—and the story the person *wants* to be in, after.

Before and After. That's the game.

> Before the click she had a migraine headache. Not only that, she would experience mind-splitting, crushing headaches one or two times per week. Totally debilitating. She was short-tempered with her husband, yelled at her kids, and when those headaches came everyone knew to just get out the way.
>
> She felt so ashamed, so powerless, and . . . on some days, so lonely.
>
> She clicked on your ad and for the first time got a coherent explanation as to why she gets these headaches and why they refuse to go away. It wasn't just a doctor handing out pills; it was something she could sink her teeth into.
>
> She purchased your program—thinking to herself, "This had better work . . . because if it doesn't I'm going to lose my mind, or worse, my family"—and she began following it religiously, day by day.
>
> By week three she was down to one mild headache per week, and by the fourth week she was completely free . . .

She's in a story. She wants her story to have a different ending. Your job is to enter into her story and change it. That's what she wants. She's dying for it.

The way you do your job is: you find out what conversation is going on inside her head; you step into it; then you change it.

3. The Pie Chart of Desires

Name a keyword; name a market. What I'm about to describe applies to ALL keywords and markets. Let's say the keyword is "splitting headache." One hundred people search "splitting headache" and you ask them this question:

"What is the number-one thing you are looking for today?"

You ask this of 100 people, and you get 100 answers. You lump the similar responses together. They look like this:

· 36% have a headache right now, and are looking for something they can do *instantly* to make it go away. They're searching for good, immediate tips—some kind of direct, actionable information.
· 27% have a headache right now and are looking for a medication they can buy online that will make it go away. They're okay with waiting a day or two for a shipment.
· 19% suffer from migraines more than once a week.
· 12% have a friend, relative, or child who has a headache right now, and they're looking for a solution.
· 4% suffer from migraines more than once a month.
· 2% took a medication that made their headache worse, not better, and are looking for a completely different solution.

Total = 100%. The pie chart looks like this:

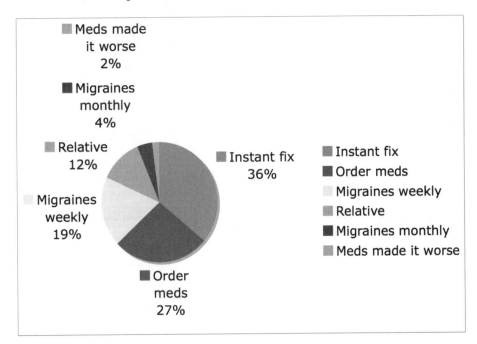

Now it would seem like the obvious thing to do is to write an ad that targets the biggest piece of the pie.

But that could be a costly mistake. Why?

Because the most frequently–asked question is usually already answered everywhere.

Don't miss this: The slice of pie you can make the most money with is the question or problem they're having the hardest time finding and answer for.

Which means if you're taking a survey, you need to ask a second question of your visitors:

"How hard has it been for you to find a solution to this problem?"

The problems for which they answer "very hard" are the ones you can most easily sell a solution for.

These are also, by definition, the problems your competitors aren't addressing.

4. The Tell–Tale Signs of Good and Bad Markets

Go search for [keyword]. Google returns a result.

FREEZE.

Don't touch that keyboard.

What do you see? What comes up and why? Hidden in this results page are countless clues that reveal powerful secrets about the market that you are trying to

compete in:

Let's say that fewer than eight ads appear, and only on the right: That means this keyword is not very competitive *and/or* its market does not generate enough money to support very many advertisers. It's like artic tundra where no large plants can grow.

Or let's say there are more than eight ads over several pages of search results, but no premium listings appear in yellow on the upper left. That means no advertiser is getting a high enough CTR/Quality Score to appear in the premium results. And it usually means people who search this keyword have a huge range of desires and the market is very fragmented.

Or there could be 9 to 11 ads on page one, including 1 to 3 ads across the top, but no new results on the second page. This means a few advertisers are getting high CTRs and good Quality Scores, but most of the other advertisers are doing poorly. There is often a marked difference between the two kinds of advertisers and if you study the difference you can tell what the market responds to.

Going even further, there could be 9 to 11 ads on page one, including 1 to 3 ads across the top, and many pages of results, i.e., a total of several dozen ads. This means the market is healthy and competitive. There's money in the market, and some advertisers are successfully nailing their customers' sweet spot.

A last scenario is where there are multiple pages of advertisers but they turn over from one month to the next. This means this market has a high churn rate. This is a *bad* sign because it means nobody is making lasting money. This is a very common occurrence in MLM and business opportunity keywords. It means those businesses are a revolving door and you should stay away unless you are a *very* experienced marketer with deep pockets and a better sales process than everyone else.

What about the ad copy that you find in these various markets?

If all the ads say fairly similar things, this means most people searching on this keyword are looking for the same kind of solution to the same kind of problem.

If the ads are all over the place in terms of their message, this means that there is no single desire that this keyword represents. There may be six to eight major distinct desires in the market.

And if the lowest-ranking ads advertise sites like eBay, SuperPages, and ReachLocal, this means you're in a market that is not very competitive and probably easy to win in. Often such markets don't have a great deal of traffic.

5. Impression Share

Most people don't realize this, but Google shows most advertisers' ads only part of the time. When you're brand new, they may only be showing your ads 10 to 20% of the time. While your reports may tell you that your ad got 2,236 impressions today, what they don't tell you is that your keyword got searched more than 10,000 times today.

Let's say you're bidding $1.00 per click and Google tells you "First page minimum bid is $1.50." This doesn't really mean your ad is never seen on the first page. Rather, it means that your ad is probably only seen on the first page 5 to 10% of the time.

If you increase your bid your impression share may grow to 25%, 50%, maybe even 100%. Google is serving up their inventory for maximum clicks. They know that people might search five, ten, fifteen times and they know that if they keep showing different advertisers they can get more clicks on advertisers' ads. This is good; Google is optimizing your CTR automatically.

But if you have a killer ad that gets a great CTR and if you have good quality scores (QS), your impression share *can* approach 100%.

Something to be aware of: If you have a competitor who has excellent CTR and high QS, Google may be showing their ad 100% of the time . . . and if your CTR and QS is lower than theirs, then increasing your bids in the hopes that you'll get 100% impression share may do little more than burn through your budget.

Bottom line is, high CTR and high QS get your ads shown more often.

6. Doing AdWords for Clients

All of the best AdWords practitioners I know developed most of their skills by managing campaigns for both themselves *and* clients—as well as masterminding with other AdWords experts. If you want to be an AdWords genius, these are my suggestions:

- You should always have some project that is exclusively your own. There is nothing like learning on your own dime. It teaches you more than anyone else. When there's money attached to it, the lessons are imprinted deep inside your mind.
- You should always have some project that is *not* your own. Other peoples' money. Other peoples' marketing results. I'll talk about how to get clients in a minute, but the reason this is so valuable is that it extends your knowledge into markets you would otherwise have no experience with. If one of your markets is CRM software and another market is natural health supplements and another client sells management consulting, you develop a wide perspective that you would otherwise never get. You will also find yourself transferring ideas directly from one market to another. Not just AdWords ideas, but ideas for website design, landing pages, offers, e-mail messages, and guarantees.
- Join our Mastermind Club. Yes, this is a shameless plug—but the world's

largest private AdWords discussion group online is my own group of paying members. Many of these sharp men and women have been using AdWords for literally years and know the system inside and out. When you get stuck on something, you can post a question to the forum and often get a qualified answer in less than an hour. We hold a monthly coaching call for our Mastermind members and do live Q&A. New members get a huge package of cool educational material. Details are at www.perrymarshall.com/mastermind.

How to get clients: Principle Numero Uno is to understand what you are selling when you are an AdWords consultant: You are selling *dollars at a discount*. What you are saying to your prospective client is:

> Right now you are buying new 1,000 new customers per month for $10.00 each and this is costing you $10,000 per month. If you pay me $2,500 per month I'll get you 1,200 new customers for $6.00 each. Your AdWords spend will go from $10,000 per month to $7,200 per month; you'll get 200 more customers than you were getting before, and after you've paid me my fee you'll still be spending $300 per month less than you're paying now.
>
> So you can leave things the way they are now, or you can hire me and save $300 per month and get 200 new customers every month that you're not getting now.
>
> Is that a good deal, or what?

Now in order to say this you have to do some research. You need to know how much it's costing them to get a new customer. You need to know what a customer is worth to them. You need to know what they're happy with, and unhappy with. Bottom line is, you need to earn your keep.

I offer a free report on building an AdWords consulting practice at www.perrymarshall.com/adwords–consultant

7. Hyper–Responsive Customers

There are three kinds of customers:

1. Customers who buy once and never come back again
2. Customers who buy from time to time, maybe for years
3. Customers who buy everything they possibly can from you

This last category is only about 5% of your customers but they may bring you as much as 50% of your profit.

These are the people that you design your business around: The raving fans.

Let me restate that: You want to design your business such that "raving fans" are not only possible, but inevitable.

Some businesses are so mediocre that they could not possibly earn raving fans of even the most desperate customers. You need to be outstanding at *something.* Which is to say you need a powerful USP, a unique selling proposition.

But even once you have that USP you want mechanisms (e-mail, snail mail, autoresponder follow-ups, and customer appreciation events) that stimulate customers to come back, and come back, and come back for more. You brainstorm things that will re-ignite your old customers' interest.

If you do the math on a typical website, about one Google click in 2,000 represents a hyper-responsive buyer. They buy compulsively from other companies, and they'll buy compulsively from you, provided you have an appealing offering.

We all know people like this. People who are Apple fanatics, who own five Apple computers and eight iPods. You know people who have dozens of pairs of shoes in their closet. You know people who constantly go to motivational seminars. You know people who buy and read every new Stephen King book.

Notice also that this kind of buying behavior is personality driven. People love buying from personalities and from companies who show a lot of personality. Don't be afraid to insert your personality every place in your business that you can.

8. Innovation and the Hyper-Responsive Buyer

Pinpoint a major keyword. Let's say it gets 50,000 searches a month.

Now picture all the people who are searching for that keyword.

And now a person so engrossed in this topic that he searches this *same* keyword repeatedly, month in and month out, year in and year out.

A rare bird, but not as rare as you think.

This person is a true *hyper-responsive buyer.*

So now I have a question:

What will get his attention?

I propose to you that a person like this is jaded. This person has seen everything before. He's hard to impress.

But if you succeed in impressing him—if you deliver something that's truly a breakthrough—he will tell all his friends. He'll give you a killer testimonial. All his friends are—or will become—hyper-responsive customers, too.

You can "flip" an entire market just by winning the affections of that rabid 5%.

9. Google Bottom–Rung Phone Support vs. Professional Account Reps

There are two kinds of Google reps:

1. *The rank and file AdWords person who answers the phone at 1–888–Google–9.* This person is typically an intelligent and friendly college grad who knows very little about AdWords and is trained to point you back to Google's online documentation. Unless there is a simple and screamingly obvious issue with your account (e.g., an ad disapproved for trademark infractions), they often won't know what the problem is.

2. If you are a medium- or large-sized business that spends upwards of $100,000 per year, you'll likely be assigned a *professional Google account rep*. Frequently these reps know the inside scoop about how Google's system works *and* the vagaries of quality scores, and can get access to the real reasons why your scores are low or your ads aren't showing.

There *are* people at Google who know how the system works, but you generally have to be spending money to talk to them. Fortunately Google doesn't give big companies a special discount—the clicks themselves are a level playing field—but it does give them more information.

If you want to be on the leading edge of that kind of information I have two suggestions for you: 1) our Mastermind Club, www.perrymarshall.com/mastermind—where members pool their experience and solve problems together; 2) www.AdGooRoo.com which collects data on hundreds of thousands of Google advertisers—as well as your own ads—and provides competitive data on your ad positions, impression share, and budgets.

10. "Would I Send Grandma to This Site?"

One of my colleagues was asked to help with a site that was severely "slapped"—had quality scores of 1 across the board—and because of his close relationship with Google, he was able to get a Google rep to give him the *real* answer to why the site was slapped.

The reason?

"I would not send my grandma to this site."

(So what does your grandma have to do with it?)

I looked at the site, and I would not send my grandma there either.

The person at Google didn't elaborate. Allow me to.

This particular site was selling a specific business opportunity. The hype factor was through the roof. It was a pure "squeeze page" with nowhere else you could go to learn about the vendor. All the bullets were tease, and the claims were extraordinary.

It had a smarmy feel.

Google didn't like it. So somewhere in the account, a Google reviewer punched in a low rating. This led to the quality scores of 1 . . . and all the keyword and SEO tweaks in the world couldn't change it.

Yes, this is totally subjective on Google's part. But it tells you a few interesting things:

- Google is *not* run by robots. They've got more than enough money to put real people on the assignment, and that's what they do.
- Grandma is a *great* standard to judge by. She don't know nuthin' about the internet. She trusts you to tell her who's okay to listen to. And in Google's opinion, if there's more than a 10% chance of her getting screwed by a biz–op or bad investment, then they're not going to let her see it. If grandma doesn't have a tech-savvy grandson like you, then she has to rely on Google, and Google knows it.
- The site had no proof to support its claims. If a business opportunity is completely legit, the site should be able to prove it. This means real names of real people in real places. Authentic testimonials. Numbers you can vet. Qualifications, requirements, caveats.
- The site must have contact information, including street address and phone number. If it has the feel of some guy hiding behind his computer, Google will nix it.

11. Every Market Has a Hole.

There is no such thing as a market where you can't "chisel your way in." Even if it has 100, 200, even 500 bidders, I can guarantee that a few of the top ten advertisers in that market still have a vulnerability.

That vulnerability can come in many forms, but all of them boil down to the inability to convert visitors to sales. Which means the market has an unmet need.

Want to crack into a new market? Ask: "What unmet need here are people willing to pay money for?"

The answer to that question is your "in."

12. Bootstrapping vs. Venture Capital

One time I was on the board of directors of an online startup company.

The president of this company had started four other companies. Two had failed, and two had gone public. A pretty impressive track record for startups.

His approach was "if you build it they will come." Raise venture capital or angel money from private investors faster than you "burn" the money, and eventually you get the attention of some big company who buys you out. Everyone makes millions of dollars, and you break out the champagne.

My approach was far less glamorous than that: *"Make $1.00."*

In other words, do whatever you have to do, build whatever you have to build, to get to a point where you can predictably spend $1.00 on Google clicks and get $2.00 from paying customers.

It's OK if you have overhead and investment far in excess of that $1.00. Maybe you've invested thousands, tens of thousands, hundreds of thousands of dollars.

The important thing is: in the marketing department you're making money on a small scale. Once you've accomplished that, just scale up.

That's my approach. I have personally coached more than 500 businesses through this process in over 200 industries. It's basic, it's humble, most of the time it's done from a spare bedroom or basement office, but it works. It's made me and countless others literally millions of dollars.

When I joined that online startup company, I was told that we were going to use a hybrid approach. That we were going to "make $1.00" but we were not in any way going to limit ourselves to the meager growth limits of a self-funded startup. We were going to raise money and scale this thing big and fast.

Gentlemen, start your engines.

So off we go. We built a Google campaign that acquired new members at an excellent, low cost–per–acquisition. We had tons of traffic coming to the site.

But for whatever confounded reason, I could not get the president of the company to make $1.00. That is, I could not get him to sell something to our online visitors.

Nothing you could realistically make money on, anyway.

Yet every quarter at board of directors meetings he would chide us for not bringing on enough investors.

I finally resigned and sent the board a nasty e-mail telling them that they were defrauding their shareholders. Two years into it they still had no business plan with any hope of turning $1.00 into $2.00.

This startup *could* have been a tremendous success. It served a rabid audience. There was nothing wrong with growing a company fast on the shoulders of investors. But the investors were so distracted by the dog–and–pony show about how big this market was and how much money was in this market and all the grandiose promises that they never bothered to nail down their own workable sales story.

The DNA of any sales machine is simple:

"What does it cost you to get a customer, and how much money do you make on that customer in one day, one month, one year, or one lifetime?"

If you do not have at least a partial answer to that question, you do not have a business; you have a pipedream. Doesn't matter if you've got a $10 million building and the Startup of the Year award from *Inc.* magazine.

On the other hand, if you've got a Google account, a teeny tiny little e-commerce store built on a free Blogspot site and a Paypal account, and you're putting $1.00 in and getting $2.00 out, *you have a real business.*

13. Just Buy the Stuff and Ship It

Notice that the DNA of a real sales machine is *not* having a manufacturing facility, ownership of the product, a flawless process for customer service, or anything other such thing.

With that in mind, consider a contrarian, renegade approach to building that business:

If your goal is to build the DNA of a real sales machine and doing so depends on your ability to put $1.00 in and get $2.00 out, then *you're off to a good start even if you put $1.00 in and can only get $0.80 out.*

Which means the first thing you must do is simply prove that you can *sell something.* That's it.

Doesn't matter where you get that something or how much it costs to obtain it. Let's say that you want to sell a slightly higher-end $1,500.00 bicycle and it's going to cost you $250,000.00 to put them into production. You know that after you put them into production it will cost $600.00 each to make them and you'll have a $900.00 gross margin.

Most people will put the bikes into production first, then try to sell them. Big mistake.

Let's say it cost you $5,000.00 to build them in your garage, by hand.

Then advertise the bikes at $1,500.00, take orders, and bite the bullet and build ten of them for $5,000.00 each—in your garage, by hand.

Yes, I know you're sending out $3,500.00 with each shipment. Doesn't matter. It's still the lowest risk way to enter the market. It'll cost you $35,000.00 to sell the first ten, but it's better than spending $250,000 to sell zero!

More importantly, you've proven that you build bicycles that sell.

Now it's just a matter of raising the capital needed to produce them at a lower cost.

Make sure there's water in the swimming pool before you jump off the diving board.

You can do this with something as simple as hand soap. Get the orders first. Then, if you have to, drive to Wal–Mart and buy a case of hand soap and sell it at a loss. But if you get the marketing and sales machine right before you hammer out the fulfillment issues, then you've got a sustainable model.

14. Artificially High Bids in a Ferociously Competitive Market

I have a student who's in a particular segment of the printing industry, which is a fiercely competitive niche. Typically he's battling against 90+ bidders in a price-sensitive commodity market.

He soundly established a presence on one keyword and after several months of fine-tuning he got his cost down to $2.00 per click.

He asked me what he should do next and I said, "Knock yourself off. Create another brand with a different USP in the same market." So he did.

For the first week, his cost per click was $11.00.

Ouch.

He was doubtful at first, but I told him to stay the course.

Sure enough, time went by and he "earned" Google's trust, and the cost per click dropped to $2.00.

What he had just encountered was Google's artificial barrier-to-entry for new advertisers.

It's daunting when you're new, but once you're established, it protects your territory from poachers.

Carefully follow the instructions in this book, and you'll be able to enter any market at will.

15. Personality vs. Transactional Marketing

There are two kinds of approaches that are most often used in selling products, even physical ones: Institutional "brand" advertising, and personality driven advertising.

Examples of the former: Nike shoes, Crest toothpaste, Chevy trucks, Harvard University.

Examples of the latter: George Foreman grilles, Donald Trump's real estate properties, Wendy's Dave Thomas, Video Professor training courses.

I submit to you that personality driven advertising is easier to "pull off," happens faster, and costs less money than traditional brand advertising.

Here's a way to think about it:

Think of authors and radio/TV personalities such as Oprah, Dr. Phil, Rush Limbaugh, and Dr. Laura. Think of Roger Ebert and the late Paul Harvey. Consider how these folks deliver news, entertainment, and opinions to people who are, literally, "fans." Their job is to communicate their version of reality to a clearly identified audience.

The way you do personality marketing is, you add a bit of Oprah or Rush Limbaugh to your product. You take a very specific position, you have strong opinions, and you talk about a far wider range of topics than merely what you sell.

People like that.

Thus your website is a platform for you being you, not just a machine that sells your product.

I've included a bonus chapter about personality marketing at www.perrymarshall .com/bookbonus.

16. What I Learned from Infomercials

Some people watch infomercials, and some buy from them. Some don't.

I for one have never bought a single thing from an infomercial. I'm not "an infomercial buyer."

In general I don't even care to watch them, though they're great education for sales people. (Tip: If you want to see a sales pitch that has been *proven* to work, just watch an infomercial that's been airing for three months or more. I can guarantee you it's making money. Take notes and look for ideas you can borrow.)

But in 2002, when I first began using Google AdWords, I almost instantly knew how the entire AdWords market was going to develop, even though it was undeveloped virgin territory and nobody understood it.

I knew that by 2010 it would be a fiercely competitive, dog–eat–dog marketplace and there would be certain things you *had* to do in order to win.

I knew that because I had *studied* infomercials.

What does Google AdWords have to do with infomercials?

If you were around and paying attention 30 years ago, you'll recall that most TV stations went off the air at 1:00 A.M. and came back on at 6:00. But in the '80s, broadcasting laws changed. It suddenly became possible for TV stations to sell late–night slots to advertisers.

So people started making 30–minute commercials, for cheap.

I remember as a teenager turning on the TV one night and seeing an infomercial shot at a Holiday Inn meeting room—a single camera pointed at an overhead projector and a guy pitching information on how to get rich in real estate.

Back then, airtime was incredibly cheap. You could shoot a cheap video at a seminar, air it for what seemed like pennies, and make money.

But then companies started discovering that this worked. So the airtime bid prices went up.

Today if you simply want to *test* an infomercial you're going to spend a minimum of $75,000.00 to $100,000.00 to produce the show and pilot it in a few narrow markets. And if it's not professionally produced and superbly scripted, it doesn't stand a chance.

Most of the players in the infomercial biz are companies who specialize in this and do hundreds of millions of dollars of business. The largest such company is Guthy-Renker, whose annual sales are about $2 billion.

The barrier to entry is now very, very high.

I knew instantly that AdWords would be a micro-business internet version of the same thing.

Here are some facts for you to think about:

- With infomercials the customer's hand is always on the remote control. She can change channels in an instant if she gets bored. The same is true online: People have 12 browser windows open and something more interesting and compelling on the internet is always a click away.
- Testing is crucial. You have to test ads, landing pages, and offers in order to maximize your sales. The most successful advertisers will be those who test more than everyone else. Fortunately it's not hard to do.
- Back end is everything. Real success is seldom achieved from a one-time sale. It has more to do with your ability to win a loyal customer who buys and buys again.

  Let's talk about that back end for a second.

  I frequently tell people to "pick the chicken clean." Find ways to satisfy all your customers' needs, not just one or two. Ask yourself these questions:

1. If you sell a $50 product, what might you offer that would cost $500? or $5,000? There is hardly a market where there is not an answer to this kind of question. There is always a small percentage of people who will spend lots of money to scratch an itch, and those people will contribute a large percentage of your profit.

2. What related things can your customers buy?

3. Can you get them to buy on a repeat basis—for example a membership or monthly shipment?

· Do your competitors offer something that you can sell to your customers and earn an affiliate commission for? At some point your customers will probably buy your competition anyway. Especially on the internet. Might as well get in on the action.

17. A Google Ad Has Infinite Possibility

Google gives you 130 characters to work with in an ad: 25 characters for the headline, and 35 characters for lines two and three and the display URL.

What can you do with a measly 130 characters?

Consider this:

If you take all the letters, numbers, characters, and spaces that are possible in a Google ad—just the ones on an English keyboard—there are 92 possible choices for 130 positions. That's 92^{130} combinations.

$$92^{130} \text{ is } 2 \times 10^{255}$$

The number "Googol" which is where the name "Google" came from, is 10^{100}. It's the biggest number anyone even has use for. There are, after all, only 10^{80} particles in the entire universe.

So there is an inconceivably large number of things you can say in that tiny little Google ad.

Now I realize that an ad that says

tgQwqBIg)JCmisLfhx
NC5AwUS oRxXghe VZ<d MoX
CUppEdJo,urXcOeol07J"[Sg
jP6paH$k&Fp Fae laVselog

is completely useless, and you can be sure that even a million monkeys typing for a million years could never fix it.

But even when you limit your choices to real words and sentences, there are *vastly* more things you can say than it seemed like you had room for when you first started.

Those tiny little Google ads aren't so tiny. They're a vast universe. The ultimate ad might be a needle in a haystack, but that needle is worth finding. Fortunes lie inside that ad.

CHAPTER 29

Epiphany in Nairobi, Kenya

I n September 2004 I returned, literally, from a trip around the world. A stop in Fiji, then to Coolum, Australia, where I spoke at the X10 Internet Marketing Seminar, then through Southeast Asia, the Middle East, and Africa. Seventeen days, 28,000 miles and a fresh set of insights on our vast yet very small planet earth.

■ ■ ■

Because my business runs on autopilot (thanks, in part, to the miracle of Google AdWords), I only spent about 30 minutes a day checking up on my business in cybercafés, and had more money in the bank when I came home than when I left.

That's a wonderful asset to have, but this chapter is about something bigger and more profound than that.

It's impossible to visit countries you've never been to before without having some kind of epiphany. Actually I had a lot of epiphanies on this trip. But what's the *big* lesson?

I'm somewhere southwest of Nairobi, Kenya, visiting George and Jane Karanga, two very special people who run a foster program for AIDS orphans. I'm meeting a woman whose husband is dying of AIDS, he's down to 66 pounds . . . all kinds of kids who've lost both parents to HIV and now live with aunts, uncles, or grandparents . . . people who are deathly sick for lack of $1.00 for a bus ticket to go to a medical clinic . . . a woman who's eight years a paraplegic, living under a tin roof in a dark mud hut, her sole entertainment her radio, her cat, and her kind neighbors who look after her.

Not a cheery scene.

But the epiphany occurs when I meet a fellow named Paul Mungai, who runs a cobbler shop. Paul, ironically, is crippled, but he knows how to make and fix shoes. And he knows how to run a business. He started with just $50.00 of seed money and now has, by Kenyan standards, a sound business. He's feeding his family, he's paying his rent, his kids have uniforms to wear to school, and everyone in his care has enough to live on.

We exchange a few words and share our mutual understanding: *There is one and only one path out of poverty. The one and only path out of poverty is entrepreneurship and business success.*

It ain't government. It's not social programs. It's not charity. It's not even jobs or technology.

It's **entrepreneurship**.

The message was loud and clear: *What you and I do may be daring, crazy, irrational and largely misunderstood. Condescending do-gooders may tell you you're greedy or too successful. Your brother-in-law may think you've got your head stuffed in a cloud. The government may think it has the right to confiscate your profits and give them to "education" or other well-intentioned social programs. You might cater to some strange market, doing something that most people consider frivolous.*

But the fact remains: What you and I do is profoundly important. You and I pave the road that leads from poverty to success. We create the ingenuity and jobs and wealth that makes good medical care possible. We *create* the world that has enough to eat, the world where even welfare kids in housing projects get three square meals a day.

So don't ever apologize to anyone for doing what you do. If it wasn't for you, me, and the rest of us entrepreneurs, "they" would still be sleeping on dirt floors.

That conversation with Paul in Kenya sparkled with the mutual awareness of what I just described to you. And as George took me to see other recipients of Micro-Enterprise seed funding—a lady selling sardines and tomatoes on a nailed-together stand on the side of the road, several women selling fruits and vegetables in the local markets, I thought of the entrepreneurs I meet in the United States, Canada, and Australia. I thought of those rah-rah Amway rallies I was going to years ago, and the easily-exploited naiveté that's so characteristic of "the Biz Op" market as it's sometimes called.

Like it or not, it's that raw enthusiasm and independent spirit that drives the prosperity of the West.

Where that drive, imagination, and ingenuity are lacking, people starve—literally.

So yes, some business people are too greedy. Some entrepreneurs *don't* care about their fellow man. Some people do make their money by dishonest means. But remember, the character quotient is no better on the poor side of the fence.

So if you're prospering by means of an honest enterprise—or if you're struggling to put one together—then I'm here to tell you that you are a hero. The bards and minstrels may not sing songs about you, and your handsome face may never appear on *The Apprentice,* but what you do every day when you get out of bed is a worthwhile and indeed necessary thing.

Don't ever forget it.

You can read the story of my entire 17-day trip, including strange tales of Oz, Singapore, Kuala Lumpur, and Dubai at www.perrymarshall.com/travelogue.

About the Authors

Perry Marshall

Perry Marshall is an author, speaker, and consultant in Chicago. He is known as "The Wizard of Google AdWords" and is the world's leading consultant on Google's advertising system. Google advertisers who use his methods generate well over a billion clicks per month (conservative estimate).

His company, Perry S. Marshall & Associates, consults both online and brick–and–mortar companies on generating sales leads, web traffic, and maximizing advertising results.

Prior to his consulting career, he helped grow a tech company in Chicago from $200,000 to $4 million sales in four years, and the firm was sold to a public company for $18 million.

Like direct marketing pioneer Claude Hopkins, Perry has both an engineering degree and a love for persuasive copywriting. He's published hundreds of articles on sales, marketing, and technology, and his works include *The Definitive Guide to Google AdWords* (ebook), *The Ultimate Guide to Google AdWords* (Entrepreneur Press, 2006, 2010), *Guerilla Marketing for Hi–Tech Sales People*, and a technical book, *Industrial Ethernet* (ISA, 2nd Edition).

He's spoken at conferences around the world and consulted in over 200 industries, from computer hardware and software to high-end consulting, from health and fitness to corporate finance.

Bryan Todd

Bryan Todd is a writer and web traffic specialist in Lincoln Nebraska. He's worked in both Europe and Asia and has spent most of his career teaching—from foreign language and world history to advanced testing methods for the internet. He has worked with clients in dozens of industries from health care and book publishing to manufacturing and computer software.

Index

305

Here's Where You Get Your $110 Worth of Tools and Bonus Information, Just for Purchasing This Book!

www.perrymarshall.com/bookbonus

Register now and you'll instantly get password access to a membership area with updates to the book. It also includes:

→ Google AdWords $25 coupon code for new advertisers

→ A "swipe file" of winning Google AdWords ads that generated hundreds of thousands to millions of clicks online—with copy ideas you can apply to your own ads

→ A special guide to "Personality Marketing"—why it sells better than the corporate approach, and how to pull it off with style

→ If you're new online, you need a handful of things to be in business:

- A domain name
- A website with web pages
- An e-mail broadcast/autoresponder service
- A shopping cart service
- A product to sell
- A Google AdWords account

The online supplement has links to dozens of resources for getting these things done, plus additional tutorials and MP3 files.

→ The entire book *Scientific Advertising* by Claude Hopkins in PDF—if you liked our "Uncle Claude Sez" sections at the end of the chapters, you'll find this 1918 classic extremely informative

→ MP3 seminars on marketing and publicity that you can load into your iPod and listen while you exercise, drive, or work around the house

→ The full contents of the interview with copywriting legend John Carlton (Chapter 20 only had room for one-third of the total conversation!)

→ An assortment of FREE keyword research tools with insightful discussion about how to use them for maximum effectiveness

→ A roundup of paid keyword research tools, with reviews of their pros and cons

→ And finally, you'll get timely e-mail updates from Perry Marshall about Google's ever-changing system

→ A special report on using your AdWords skills to get clients. I have students in a half dozen countries who make six figure incomes as marketing consultants—find out how!

Go to www.perrymarshall.com/bookbonus